AF328057

MATTHEW

MATTHEW

A Commentary for Bible Students

ROGER L. HAHN

WESLEYAN BIBLE COMMENTARY SERIES

GENERAL PUBLISHER
Donald D. Cady

EXECUTIVE EDITOR
David W. Holdren, D.D., S.T.D.

EDITORIAL ADVISORY COMMITTEE

Joseph D. Allison, M.Div.
Coordinator of Communications and
Publishing
Church of God Ministries

Ray E. Barnwell
Illinois District Superintendent
The Wesleyan Church

Barry L. Callen, M.Div., M.Th., D.Rel., Ed. D.
University Professor of Christian Studies
Emeritus, Anderson University
Special Assistant to General Director, Church
of God Ministries

Ray Easley, M.Div., Ed.D.
Vice President of Academic Affairs
Wesley Biblical Seminary

Maj. Dorothy Hitzka
National Consultant for Christian Education
The Salvation Army

Arthur Kelly
Coordinator of Christian Education and
Congregational Life
Church of God Ministries

Stephen J. Lennox, Ph.D.
Dean of the Chapel; Professor of Bible
Indiana Wesleyan University

Bonnie J. Perry
Director
Beacon Hill Press of Kansas City

Dan Tipton, D.Min.
General Superintendent (retired)
Churches of Christ in Christian Union

John Van Valin
Free Methodist Pastor
Indianapolis, Indiana

EDITORS
Lawrence W. Wilson, M.Div.
Managing Editor

Stephen J. Lennox, Ph.D.
Theological Editor

Darlene Teague, M.Div.
Senior Editor

In gratitude to God, I dedicate this volume to
my parents, Lee A. and Hattie L. Hahn.

CONTENTS

EXECUTIVE EDITOR'S PREFACE   **11**

AUTHOR'S PREFACE   **13**

Introduction   15

Outline   43

PART ONE—

THE BEGINNING OF JESUS AND HIS MINISTRY (1:1–4:25)   **49**

Chapter 1   The Origin of Jesus (1:1–25)   51

Chapter 2   The Beginning Days of Jesus' Life (2:1–23)   59

Chapter 3   John the Baptist and Jesus' Baptism (3:1–17)   67

Chapter 4   Temptation and the Beginning of Jesus' Ministry (4:1–25)   73

PART TWO—

THE AUTHORITY OF JESUS IN WORD AND DEED (5:1–9:38)   **81**

Chapter 5   The Beatitudes and Jesus' Teaching on the Old Testament (5:1–48)   83

Chapter 6   Devotion and Money in the Kingdom (6:1–34)   97

Chapter 7   Problems in the Life of the Kingdom (7:1–29)   107

Chapter 8   Miracles Teaching Jesus' Identity and Life in the Kingdom (8:1–34)   115

Chapter 9   Miracles Revealing Jesus' Authority (9:1–38)   123

PART THREE—

MISSION IN THE FACE OF REJECTION: PRECEPT AND EXAMPLE (10:1–12:50)   **133**

Chapter 10   Jesus' Teaching on Mission (10:1–11:1)   135

Chapter 11   Questions and Uncertainty about Jesus (11:2–30)   145

Chapter 12   Conflict with Judaism (12:1–50)   153

PART FOUR—

**THE VARIETY OF RESPONSES TO JESUS: TEACHINGS
AND EXAMPLES (13:1–17:27)** **165**

Chapter 13   Jesus' Parables Teaching the Kingdom (13:1–53)   167

Chapter 14   Jesus Provides Light in the Darkness (13:54–14:36)   181

Chapter 15   Jesus Provides Bread for All (15:1–39)   191

Chapter 16   The Meaning of Following Jesus (16:1–28)   201

Chapter 17   The Promise of Glory and Frustration in
Discipleship (17:1–27)   209

PART FIVE—

**GRACE AND JUDGMENT IN THE KINGDOM: TEACHINGS AND
EXAMPLES (18:1–23:39)** **217**

Chapter 18   Jesus' Teaching About Life Together in the
Kingdom (18:1–19:1)   219

Chapter 19   The Demands of the Kingdom (19.2–30)   229

Chapter 20   Grace for the Journey (20:1–34)   237

Chapter 21   Jesus' Prophetic Authority in Jerusalem (21:1–46)   245

Chapter 22   Conflict with Jewish Religious Leaders in
Jerusalem (22:1–46)   259

Chapter 23   Jesus' Denunciation of the Pharisees (23:1–39)   269

PART SIX—

**THE END OF THE AGE AND THE END OF JESUS' EARTHLY
MINISTRY (24:1–28:20)** **279**

Chapter 24   Teachings on the End of the Age (24:1–51)   281

Chapter 25   Parables Teaching Readiness for the End of
the Age (25:1–26:1)   293

Chapter 26   The Unfolding Plot to Kill Jesus (26:2–75)   305

Chapter 27   Jesus' Trial before Pilate and the Crucifixion
(27:1–66)   323

Chapter 28   Jesus' Resurrection and Missionary Commission
(28:1–20)   341

Select Bibliography   349

EXECUTIVE EDITOR'S PREFACE

Life change. That, we believe, is the goal of God's written revelation. God has given His written Word so that we might know Him and become like Him—holy, as He is holy.

Life change is also the goal of this book, a volume in the Wesleyan Bible Commentary Series. This series has been created with the primary aim of promoting life change in believers by applying God's authoritative truth in relevant, practical ways. This commentary will impact Bible students with fresh insight into God's unchanging Word. Read it with your Bible in hand.

A second purpose of this series is to assist laypersons and pastors in their teaching ministries. Anyone called to assist others in Christian growth and service will appreciate the practical nature of these commentaries. Writers were selected based on their ability to soundly interpret God's Word and apply that unchanging truth in fresh, practical ways. Each biblical book is explained paragraph by paragraph, giving the reader both the big picture and sufficient detail to understand the meaning of significant words and phrases. Their results of scholarly research are presented in enough detail to clarify, for example, the meaning of important Greek or Hebrew words, but not in such a way that readers are overwhelmed. This series will be an invaluable tool for preaching, lesson preparation, and personal or group Bible study.

The third aim of this series is to present a Wesleyan-Arminian interpretation of Scripture in a clear and compelling fashion. Toward that end, the series has been developed with the cooperative effort of scholars, pastors, and church leaders in the Wesleyan, Nazarene, Free Methodist, Salvation Army, Church of God (Anderson), Churches of Christ in Christian Union, Brethren in Christ, and United Methodist denominations. These volumes present reliable interpretation of biblical texts in the tradition of John Wesley, Adam Clarke, and other renowned interpreters.

Throughout the production of this series, authors and editors have approached each Bible passage with this question in mind: How will my life change when I fully understand and apply this scripture?

Let that question be foremost in your mind also, as God speaks again through His Word.

DAVID W. HOLDREN

AUTHOR'S PREFACE

The gospel of Matthew has been one of my favorite New Testament books at least since W. D. Davies' doctoral seminar on Matthew at Duke University over thirty years ago. For every other year, for more than twenty-five years, I have taught either the English or the Greek text of this gospel. So when the invitation came to write this commentary, I was delighted.

The joys of working with the gospel of Matthew are many. The question of Matthew's structure is intellectually intriguing and never fails to challenge me. The alternating patterns of narrative and teaching blocks model a most effective method of communicating both the life and the message of Jesus. Matthew's clear dependence on the Old Testament and the ways in which he links Jesus and the Old Testament are extremely helpful, especially in an era when resurgent gnosticism threatens the Church. Working with the Sermon on the Mount, the Lord's Prayer, and the Great Commission puts one in touch with some of the most influential texts of the New Testament. Matthew's treatment of discipleship is readily applicable to life in the church today.

The debts of gratitude I owe to the many who have resourced me in some way for the writing of this commentary are too many to mention. However, I would be remiss if I failed to express appreciation to those most directly influencing me as I wrote. Out of the rich heritage of Matthean scholarship, partially represented in the select bibliography, the commentaries of Davies and Allison, France, Garland, Hagner, and Keener have been my most constant companions. The "Times Square" Sunday school class that I teach at Kansas City First Church of the Nazarene has provided field testing for the application of Matthew to life in the twenty-first century. They have interacted with me at the rate of no more than a paragraph of Matthew per Sunday morning for several years now, and we are not yet halfway through the first Gospel. My administrative assistants in the dean's office at Nazarene Theological Seminary, Pam Rider and Pam Asher, have worked hard to create time in my schedule to write. I am especially grateful to Don Cady and Darlene Teague of the Wesleyan Publishing House for their grace and patience in guiding me through the process of writing and preparing the commentary. Without their encouragement I would have, no doubt, given up.

I owe a special debt of gratitude to my wife, Dorothy, and three sons, Jonathan, Matthew, and Timothy, who have surrendered time they deserved to the commentary. One can never describe the debt owed one's parents, but mine have been profoundly influential in my vocation of teaching the Bible. At the turning points of my life, my father would simply offer me a Scripture text that he thought best fit my situation. I regret that he did not live to know of the writing of this commentary. My mother modeled the teaching of the Bible to me in my childhood and teen years. The first scripture she taught me to memorize was 2 Timothy 2:15 from the King James Version: "Study to shew thyself approved unto God, a workman that needeth not to be ashamed, rightly dividing the word of truth." Looking back, the journey from memorizing that text at five years of age to this commentary has been remarkably direct. So in gratitude to God, I dedicate this volume to my parents, Lee A. and Hattie L. Hahn.

ROGER L. HAHN

INTRODUCTION TO MATTHEW

The Gospel of Matthew has been read and loved by the Church for almost two thousand years. In the early centuries of church history, it was the most quoted of all four Gospels. Its influence among New Testament scholarship has waned in the modern era for several reasons, but it continues its profound influence in the life of the Church. From Matthew's gospel come the Sermon on the Mount, the Lord's Prayer, and the Great Commission. Thus the mission, the worship, and the educational ministry of the Church are all in profound debt to the first Gospel.

Matthew is the supreme teaching Gospel of the Church. From the structure the author employed in composing the Gospel to the profound content contained in it, Matthew was designed to teach the Church the mission and message of Jesus. It was also intended to convince a group of Jewish believers of the abiding value of what Jesus taught and who He claimed to be. In so doing, Matthew created a bridge from Jesus to a late-first-century community of Jewish Christians. But that bridge does not stop at the intersection of Matthew's community and the late first century. It connects Jesus with any community of faith that will submit to the discipline of studying it. Such study inevitably leads to the conclusion that Jesus' yoke is easy and the burden of following Him in discipleship is light. The student also discovers that the traditional questions of modern New Testament study provide fascinating possibilities for the interpreter.

AUTHORSHIP

As far as can be known, the original text of Matthew gave no indication of authorship, though some find it hard to imagine a Gospel written in the first century without indication of authorship. If, as most scholars assume, the ascription, "According to Matthew," was not original, it began to appear at the beginning of manuscripts during the second Christian century. However, nothing in the body of the Gospel text reveals the identity of the author.

Modern discussion of the authorship of Matthew's gospel yields three perspectives. The traditional view that Matthew, the tax collector who became a disciple of Jesus, wrote this Gospel still has supporters. The most common view among Matthean scholars is that an unknown Jewish Christian wrote the Gospel. A minority view is that this book was the product of a community or school that came into being under the influence of Matthew the disciple.

MATTHEW THE DISCIPLE AS AUTHOR

The view that Matthew, the disciple of Jesus, wrote the first Gospel is based almost entirely on external evidence. The only clue within the text for traditional Matthean authorship is that the tax collector summoned to be a disciple is called Levi in Mark's gospel (Mark 2:14) but Matthew in Matthew 9:9. However, there are many possible reasons other than authorship for this change of name.

The foundational evidence for Matthean authorship of the first Gospel is a quotation of Papias found in Eusebius. The statement of Papias is usually thought to have come from about A.D. 135, perhaps no more than a single generation after it was written. Actual copies of Papias's statement no longer exist, so it is only available to the modern world through a quotation from Eusebius, who was writing a history of the church in the early fourth century A.D. Papias's statement may be translated, "Therefore, Matthew compiled the oracles in the Hebrew dialect and each translated them as he was able."

The primary problems with Papias's statement are that his word *oracles* does not seem to describe the form of the present book of Matthew and that he describes Matthew as written first in Hebrew. Papias's word *oracles* (*logia* in Greek) indicates sayings or teachings of Jesus rather than a Gospel with a narrative framework like Matthew's. It is possible that Papias did not use the word "oracles" with the precision expected by modern scholarship. Another second-century writer called the Gospels the "memoirs" of the apostles indicating that the Church had not settled in on the literary term to describe these books.

Papias also declared that Matthew wrote in Hebrew and others translated his work into Greek. Most scholars, however, are confident that the first Gospel was originally written in Greek. There is little doubt that the author was Jewish and that he appears capable of thinking in Hebrew categories and structures. However, Papias's assertion that Matthew first wrote in Hebrew is the most difficult part of his statement to reconcile with the evidences we find in the first Gospel. Matthew is far more at home in Greek. His quotes come from the Septuagint, a Greek translation from the Hebrew Old Testament.

Papias is not the only second-century Christian author to attribute the first Gospel to Matthew the former tax collector. Writing about A.D. 180, Irenaeus declared that Matthew had written a Gospel in the Hebrew dialect among the Hebrews at the time Peter and Paul were preaching in Rome and founding the church there. A number of other church fathers are often mentioned in support of the traditional ascription of the authorship of the first Gospel to Matthew the former tax collector. However, all of them appear to be dependent either on Papias or a similar source, so they do not provide independent testimony.

Two assertions against the traditional ascription of authorship to Matthew are often made but should not be given the weight they often assume. The most common conclusions regarding the date of the first Gospel place its writing between A.D. 70 and 90. Many scholars then dismiss traditional Matthean authorship on the grounds that the former tax collector could not have lived long enough to write the Gospel that late. Many scholars, however, still affirm John the apostle as author of the fourth Gospel and that it was written between A.D. 90 and 100. The date of A.D. 70–90 should not be taken as prohibitive of Matthean authorship.

A second objection to the traditional view builds on the assumption, widely accepted in Gospel scholarship, that the author of the first Gospel used the second Gospel, Mark, as a source in composing the first one. The objection is that an apostle, who had lived, traveled, and studied with Jesus, would not need to—nor be willing to—use a Gospel written by a non-eyewitness such as Mark as the primary source. This argument owes its persuasiveness to the assumptions of modern academic life with its emphasis on publishing, independent research, and copyright issues.

Writing in the ancient world was a much more communal process, and what moderns would call plagiarism was seen as a compliment rather than a theft. Thoughtful consideration of the writing patterns of antiquity will find no problem with an apostle using the work of a non-apostle as the primary guiding document for his Gospel. The significant use of Mark by the first Gospel is not a persuasive argument against traditional Matthean authorship.

The difficulty with the traditional view is not the objections; there are not many persuasive reasons that Matthew the former tax collector could not have written the first Gospel. The problem is that there is no internal evidence supporting the traditional view, and the external evidence of Papias is problematic. To say that the apostle Matthew *could* have written the first Gospel is easily defended. To say *positively* that he did is much more difficult to support. For this reason, most scholars conclude that all we can say about the author of the first Gospel is that he was a Jewish Christian.

AN UNKNOWN JEWISH CHRISTIAN AS AUTHOR

If one is not confident in asserting Matthew the former tax collector as author, there are no other candidates whose names are known in church history to suggest as the author. However, the inability to name the author does not mean that nothing is known about the author. Though there are a few noteworthy scholars who argue that the author was a Gentile believer, the vast majority of Matthean scholars believe the author was a Jewish Christian. Several arguments can be amassed to support such a view. The most common are the author's knowledge and love of the Old Testament, his interest in the Law, and a number of linguistic considerations.

One of the most noteworthy features of the first Gospel is the powerful influence of the Old Testament: the opening genealogy fashioned after the Old Testament genealogies, the numerous Old Testament quotations said to be fulfilled by Jesus, the themes of a new Moses and new exodus, and the very language of many passages. No other Gospel quotes the Old Testament as frequently or as pointedly as does this Gospel. The author quotes across a broad spectrum of Old Testament texts and uses the texts in a characteristically Jewish manner. The common pattern by which the author introduces Old Testament quotes is, "All this took place in order that what was spoken by the prophet might be fulfilled." This pattern reflects the *pesher* method of biblical interpretation that was widely practiced in the Judaism of that day. It is certainly possible that a Gentile could amass the vast knowledge of the Old Testament demonstrated by the author of the first Gospel, but in the first Christian century it is far more likely to have been a Jewish believer.

In a similar fashion, the first Gospel demonstrates significant interest in the Jewish Law. Only here does Jesus say, "Do not think that I have come to abolish the Law or the Prophets; I have not come to abolish them but to fulfill them" (5:17). In the very next verse, He affirms that neither the smallest letter nor even the least stroke of a pen will disappear from the Law until it has all been accomplished. This Gospel is interested in how to sum up the Law and the Prophets. The Great Antitheses of 5:21–48 are often taken as rejecting the Law, but the pattern of quoting the Law and then saying, "but I say to you . . . ," reflects the practice of Jewish argumentation over the interpretation of the Law that was common in the first century. The expression "Go and learn . . ." (9:13) was used in Jewish interpretive debates as a put down of the opponent's understanding of the Law. It is possible that a Gentile could demonstrate the concern for the Law found in this Gospel, but it is far more likely that such interest in the Law is the result of a Jewish author.

There are also a variety of linguistic considerations that suggest Jewish authorship of the first Gospel. The use of Aramaic terms like *raca* for fool in 5:22 and *korbanas* for treasury in 27:6 are more easily explained by Jewish authorship than by Gentile. This author assumes the meaning of Jewish hand-washing rituals and the use of phylacteries and sees no need to explain them to his audience. His explanation of the meaning of Jesus' name in 1:21 and his preference for the phrase "kingdom of heaven" instead of "kingdom of God" reflect the assumed knowledge and patterns of a Jewish writer rather than a Gentile. The structure of Jesus' genealogy, and the choice of Abraham and David as its pivot points, is further evidence of the Jewishness of the author. To be sure, there are linguistic considerations that are not as easily explained by the Jewishness of this author. His pattern of not repeating the Aramaic words found in his source document, Mark, such as *Abba, talitha koum, rabboni,* and *Bartimaeus,* is occasionally mentioned as evidence that the author was a Gentile.

A more serious linguistic problem is the "anti-Jewish" bias that seems to pervade this Gospel. The author often describes Jewish places of worship as "their synagogues" and frequently characterizes the Pharisees or other Jewish leaders as hypocrites. Chapter 23 seems an unrelieved diatribe aimed particularly against the Pharisees. The Jewish religious leaders are presented in almost constant conflict with Jesus. Of all the Gospels, only John is considered more anti-Semitic than Matthew by modern Jews. How can this pattern of attacking the Jewish religious leaders be explained with Jewish authorship? The answer does not lie in modern Western sensibilities about proper procedures and protocols in debate, but in the Jewish practices of argument in Jesus' and Matthew's time. If one reads the Dead Sea Scrolls and documents from the collection—often called the Old Testament Pseudepigrapha— the so-called anti-Jewish language in the first Gospel sounds very Jewish. Many members of the various Jewish sects in the two centuries each side of Jesus' birth were convinced that the sinfulness of Israel was the reason the Messiah had not come and delivered them from foreign oppression. They did not see the sinners as members of their own sect but of one or more of the other sects. The language with which they charged their fellow Jews with sin sounds very similar to the language of this Gospel. In some ways, the most Jewish characteristic of the first book is the "anti-Jewish" language hurled at the Pharisees and other religious leaders.

Though arguments can and have been made for the Gentile authorship of the first Gospel, the evidence clearly supports the idea that the author was a Jewish Christian. As will be indicated below, his audience consisted of Jewish Christians who were also under pressure, presumably from non-believing Jews, for their faith in Jesus. Our author marshals the resources of Jewish Scripture, Jewish Law, Jewish interpretation of the Law, Jewish words, and Jewish practices of religious debate to make his case that faith in Jesus is not anti-Jewish, but the most Jewish response possible.

THE AUTHOR AS A JEWISH COMMUNITY

A few scholars seek the solution to the problem of the authorship in a Jewish community of believers. The theory first arose in the mid-twentieth century after the discovery of the Dead Sea Scrolls. The commonly accepted view is that those scrolls were written by an Essene community devoted to communal life governed by their particular interpretation of Scripture. This approach to authorship argues that a Jewish Christian community devoted to following Jesus' pattern of interpreting Scripture produced the first Gospel.

This approach allows, though does not require, for Matthew the former tax collector to have been an influential member of the community. This would explain the tradition of Papias that Matthew composed the sayings of Jesus. The community authorship approach also addresses the concern with the date of this book. If students of Matthew did the actual writing under his influence, then the final form of the Gospel could have easily been written after the apostle's death. Though the community authorship approach has been very influential in discussion of the authorship of John's gospel, it has never gained widespread support as an explanation of Matthew's gospel.

The question of the authorship of biblical books is an established subject of study in the modern era. However, beyond the fairly obvious conclusion that the author of the first Gospel was a Jewish Christian, there is little benefit for interpretation in the discussion of the authorship of this Gospel. In fact, naming the author as Matthew—or considering the author an anonymous Jewish Christian—has very little impact on how one interprets the text. That is one reason that, since about 1980, authorship questions are receiving less attention in the world of biblical scholarship than in the century prior. It is common to use the traditional name—in this case Matthew—even when one assumes that the author was anonymous. The unknown Jewish Christian could have been named Matthew and could even have been the apostle Matthew. There isn't evidence to prove it. However, using the name Matthew without prejudice as to whether he was the apostle or not will be the custom observed in this commentary.

DATE

When one surveys the dates for the writing of Matthew's gospel proposed by various modern authors, one can find support for virtually every year from A.D. 45 to at least A.D. 125. However, the majority of scholars suggest a date within the decade of A.D. 55–65 or the two decades of A.D. 70–90.

The case for Matthew being written between A.D. 55 and 65 usually rests on an appeal to the apostle Matthew as author, the importance of preserving "predictive prophecy," and a sense that the Jerusalem Temple was still standing when the Gospel was written. A few scholars who support this "early" date also mention the deteriorating relations between believing and unbelieving Jews in Jerusalem in this decade. The appeal to the traditional view of authorship does not require a date in the fifties or sixties. Assuming that Matthew was no older than Jesus, it would be quite possible to defend the traditional view of authorship and a date as late as A.D. 90. The question regarding predictive prophecy has to do with Jesus' prediction in 24:2 of the destruction of the Temple which occurred in A.D. 70. The concern of many conservatives of a previous generation was that a date later than A.D. 70 undermined the prophetic nature of Jesus' prediction. The assumption was that the author must have made up the prediction since he already knew the Temple had been destroyed. Lost in that argument is the possibility that Jesus could have authentically predicted the Temple's destruction and that the author could have described that predicted destruction with language influenced by the reality of the events.

The question of whether the Temple was still standing when Matthew's gospel was written tends to be answered subjectively. The mention of the Temple tax in 17:24 does presuppose the Temple still standing, but Matthew narrates that conversation as part of Jesus' life and ministry. There is no doubt about the Temple still standing throughout Jesus' lifetime. It is quite imaginable that Matthew wrote of Jesus' prediction of the destruction of the Temple knowing that it had happened before he published this Gospel. The impact of Jesus' prediction and the reader's knowledge would be sufficient support for Jesus. The author did not have to insert an, "I told you so," in the text. The primary arguments for the decade of A.D. 55–65 suggest possibilities but no necessity of that decade.

The case for a date between A.D. 70 and 90 is built entirely on the perceived purpose of this Gospel. First, Matthew reads as a defense of the Jewishness of Jesus from the opening genealogy to the story of the Jewish leaders bribing the guards at Jesus' tomb to say Jesus' disciples had stolen His body. No alternative purpose fits the content and logic of Matthew's gospel as much as the purpose of reassuring Jewish believers that believing in Him does not compromise their Jewishness. It, in fact, supports it. A secondary and related purpose attempts to affirm the Gentile mission for the post-resurrection church. The question of the date of Matthew then becomes a question of what part of the first century most fits these two purposes.

Prior to the First Jewish War that began in A.D. 66 and ended with the destruction of Masada in A.D. 73, the evidence suggests that the leading Jewish religious groups were the Sadducees, the Pharisees, the Essenes, some unaffiliated apocalyptic fanatics, and the "Nazarenes," the most common first-century Jewish title for Jews who believed in Jesus as the Messiah. The Zealots might be included, though they were more of a political than a religious party. These religious groups vied with each other for influence over the larger unaffiliated Jewish population. They argued over Scripture, theology, worship patterns, politics, and devotional practices. The Sadducees and Pharisees were the most influential of the parties and had negotiated a certain balance of power in the first half of the first century. The destruction of Jerusalem in A.D. 70 changed all these circumstances.

The defeat of the Jews in the First Jewish War and the destruction of Jerusalem, including the Temple in A.D. 70, effectively destroyed the Sadducees and the Essenes, as well as discredited the Zealots and apocalyptic fanatics as viable voices for Judaism. That left the Pharisees and the Jewish Christians vying for the leadership of Judaism after A.D. 70. Because of the destruction of Jerusalem, the Pharisees moved the center of their operations to Galilee after A.D. 70 and began a systematic effort to define all of Judaism in their own terms. By A.D. 90, they were finalizing the shape of the canon of the Hebrew Scriptures and expelling Jews who believed in Jesus from *their* synagogues. They edited the Eighteen Benedictions used in the synagogue liturgy so that the Twelfth Benediction became a curse on the "heretics" who continued to confess Jesus as the Messiah.

The position that Matthew was written in A.D. 70–90 argues that the two primary purposes of Matthew best fit in these two decades. As the Pharisees began to pressure Jewish believers out of the synagogues, one of their arguments must have been that believing in Jesus was an anti-Jewish activity. As Matthew records the trials of Jesus on the last day of His life, the charge that He spoke against the Temple figured largely in the Jewish case against Him. It would have been a short step from that accusation of Jesus to the conclusion that He and His followers opposed the very institutions upon which Judaism was built. In that context of struggling to define Jewish identity, the Gentile mission that Jesus commanded in the final verses of the Gospel would have been unacceptable. Jewish believers, struggling to prove their Jewishness, might have been tempted to abandon the Gentile mission.

With this in mind, Matthew affirmed the Jewishness of Jesus and the rightness of Jewish belief in Him, but Matthew also refused to allow Christ's followers to reject the Gentile mission. The activities of the Pharisees in the period of A.D. 70–90 create the historical context in which Matthew's gospel seems to fit perfectly, particularly between about A.D. 80 and A.D. 90.

One can argue—and some have—that these purposes of Matthew's gospel also fit well in the decade of A.D. 55–65. Early Christian tradition suggests that James the brother of Jesus had become head of the church in Jerusalem by the mid-forties. He appeared to have enjoyed the respect of Jewish leaders in Jerusalem for a while. However, those leaders placed increasing pressure on him in the late fifties and early sixties because he would not support the rising talk of rebellion against Rome. This led to his martyrdom in A.D. 62. One can make the case for A.D. 55–65, but the evidence makes a better case for A.D. 70–90. That will be the assumption of this commentary.

PLACE

The discussion of where Matthew was written has been more subdued than the debates over authorship and date. Perhaps the reason is that there is simply no evidence that allows a certain—let alone a dogmatic—position on the place of writing. It is generally assumed that Matthew wrote for people who lived near where he wrote. The Jewish believers who fled Jerusalem and Judea at the outbreak of the First Jewish War moved northward to Galilee and Syria. These two locations are the most common suggestions for the place of writing. The emphasis on Jesus' meeting His disciples in Galilee after the resurrection would be consistent with this Gospel being written in Galilee. However, this emphasis does not require that conclusion for the place of writing. A location in Galilee would also place Matthew in closest proximity to the Pharisees who were engaged in defining Jewish Christians out of Judaism.

Because Antioch in Syria was an early center of Jewish Christian faith, Syria is perhaps the most commonly suggested place of writing for the first Gospel. Some scholars argue for Antioch specifically, but most believe "somewhere" in Syria is as precise a location as can be determined. A few scholars have argued that Matthew was written in Alexandria in Egypt, but this view has never been widely accepted.

There is no internal evidence in Matthew that clearly identifies a place of writing. There is no external evidence in the church fathers that makes a clear case for the place of writing. The interpretation of this Gospel is not materially affected by one's position on the place of its writing. Thus, this commentary will not consider the place of writing in its interpretation of Matthew's gospel.

AUDIENCE

The audience of Matthew's gospel has already been indicated in the earlier discussion of date and place. Matthew wrote to Jewish believers who were under pressure to choose between faith in Jesus and their Jewish heritage. It is possible, though not necessary, that these Jewish believers lived in Galilee or somewhere in Syria. It is most likely that they were living through the efforts of the Pharisees in A.D. 70–90 to force them to abandon faith in Jesus or abandon their claim to Jewish identity. It is likely that those who clung to their faith in Jesus, and to their Jewish identity, were tempted to abandon or downplay the Gentile mission.

REASONS FOR MATTHEW'S GOSPEL

The earlier discussion regarding the date of Matthew's gospel has indicated the two primary reasons for the writing of the Gospel: to affirm the Jewishness of Jesus and to support the Gentile mission of the church. Within these reasons, Matthew had several goals that are important to understand the contribution of his Gospel to the Christian faith.

The first evidence for Matthew's purpose of demonstrating the Jewishness of Jesus appears in the structure and content of the genealogy. One of Matthew's goals was to clarify the identity of Jesus for his readers. The centrality of David in the genealogy was the first piece of Matthew's argument that Jesus was the Messiah long awaited by the Jews. The other important piece of Jesus' identity Matthew wanted to present was Jesus as the Son of God. The birth narrative began that argument, and the voice from heaven at Jesus' baptism provided significant validation of that truth. Another Matthean goal was to show Jesus as the fulfillment of the Old Testament. Not only did Jesus fulfill the prophecies, He also fulfilled the Law. This leads to two conclusions Matthew wanted his readers to understand. First, since the Jews of Matthew's time regarded the Scriptures as self-revelation of God, then—as the fulfillment of Scripture—Jesus is also revelation of God. Indeed, He is the completed revelation of God. Second, to the degree that Scripture reveals the development of God's purposes through time, Jesus—as the fulfillment of Scripture—represented the goal of God's work in human history. Thus Matthew wanted to show that Jesus was the culmination of salvation history.

Another evidence of Matthew's argument for the Jewishness of Jesus was His interpretation of Scripture. Matthew makes it clear that Jesus interpreted Scripture very differently than the Pharisees did. Though the Pharisees are not directly mentioned in the Great Antitheses of Matthew 5:21–48, they were clearly in view. However, Jesus' interpretation of

Scripture was in line with Jewish tradition. Matthew makes it clear that Jesus provided a way of interpreting the Old Testament that differed from the interpretive methods of the Sadducees, the Pharisees, and the Essenes. It is equally clear that Jesus' method of interpreting Scripture takes one back to the purposes of God in the Old Testament rather than to the agendas of a contemporary Jewish religious party. Thus, one of Matthew's goals was to demonstrate the unique characteristics of Jesus' method of interpreting Scripture. For Matthew, Jesus' interpretation was the right interpretation, and Jesus' method of interpreting Scripture models for Matthew's readers the right method of interpreting Scripture.

Another goal of Matthew was to organize Jesus' ministry and message in a form that could be easily used to instruct his community in the meaning of discipleship. This goal is sometimes expressed as Matthew's desire to provide a teaching manual for the church. The way Matthew accomplished this goal is instructive. He alone among the Gospel writers collected the teachings of Jesus into blocks of related subject matter. He did not create five books of Jesus' life and ministry analogous to the five books of the Pentateuch and the five sections of the Psalms, but he did create five blocks of Jesus' teachings. Even within most of the narrative sections—which alternate with the teaching materials—Matthew collected his material around a basic theme. All this appears to reflect the patterns of oral teaching he learned within Judaism. This Gospel was designed to be learned—indeed, memorized and remembered—as an instructional manual on discipleship.

The content of the five teaching blocks also suggests two other goals that arise from Matthew's purpose of showing Jesus' context within the Old Testament and salvation history. The odd-numbered teaching blocks deal with the nature of the kingdom of heaven: The Sermon on the Mount in Matthew 5–7 paints a picture of how Jesus envisions life in the Kingdom; the third teaching block, the collection of parables in Matthew 13:1–52, describes the nature of the Kingdom as it is present in the ministry of Jesus; the final teaching block, found in Matthew 24–25, opens up the end of time and how the Kingdom will finally come to consummation. The even-numbered teaching blocks focus on the life of the church. In the narrative flow of Matthew's gospel these teaching blocks simply describe expectations of Jesus' disciples. But it is quite clear from the subject matter that Matthew saw this material in its application to the church of his and all time. The second teaching block, found in Matthew 10, addresses the mission of the church. Matthew 18 comprises the fourth teaching block and addresses the nature of relationships within the church. Interwoven in the narrative material are further moments of teaching by Jesus that instruct the reader in the nature of the Kingdom and the expectations Jesus has for the church.

One of those expectations for the church is clearly the missionary outreach to the Gentiles. The final and climactic paragraph presents Jesus' last words as commissioning the Church to the Gentile mission. Matthew had been prepared for that commission from the beginning of his Gospel by working with the centrality of Jesus' Jewishness and his focus on the Jewish people while always mentioning the Gentile connections and positive contributions to His ministry.

Matthew never explicitly mentioned the purposes of his Gospel as Luke (1:1–4) and John (20:30–31) did. However, his careful organization of both the large structure of the Gospel and the development of individual paragraphs makes it clear that he wrote strategically to accomplish his purposes. Careful attention to the structure of the book and the focus on the specific paragraphs reveals the goals he sought to accomplish as a means to his two primary purposes.

MAJOR THEMES

The reasons for writing suggest the major themes Matthew developed. Perhaps the most important themes are the nature of the Kingdom, Christology, and discipleship. Almost everything Matthew wrote in this Gospel fits within these three themes.

THE NATURE OF THE KINGDOM

The first words found on Jesus' lips in Matthew's gospel sound a call to repentance because the Kingdom is arriving (4:17). The beginning of Jesus' ministry corresponds to the arrival of the Kingdom. The meaning of Jesus' ministry and the meaning of the Kingdom become indistinguishable in Matthew. Not only is Jesus—and virtually everything He did and taught—the fulfillment of Old Testament Scripture, the Kingdom that Jesus brought is the fulfillment of God's purposes in salvation history. Through the emphasis on the fulfillment of Scripture, Matthew demonstrates the continuity of Jesus and the Kingdom with what God had been doing in Israel's history. Through the radical nature of Jesus' teaching and the miracles that function as Kingdom signs, Matthew demonstrates the discontinuity of the radically new Realm with the old structures and patterns of Judaism. The discontinuity means that the first response to the Kingdom is repentance. The coming of Jesus meant that it was time to turn from the old structures and patterns to the new realities of the Kingdom as taught by Jesus.

However, despite the fact that the Kingdom was arriving in the ministry of Jesus, the present and evil age would not end with His ministry. Matthew clearly envisioned a future consummation of the Kingdom that was arriving with Jesus. The final teaching block portrays the coming of divine judgment on Jerusalem and the Temple, the end of the present and evil age, as well as the coming of Jesus to establish the Kingdom in its fullness. Matthew does not make clear how those coming events are related to each other in time. The parables that conclude that teaching block make it clear that Jesus' followers are to live in readiness for each of these events. (If the date suggested earlier for the writing of Matthew is correct, the judgment of Jerusalem and the Temple had already come.) The final consummation of the Kingdom will come with the devastating consequences of divine judgment for those who are not prepared, but authentic disciples need not fear it. When the final form of the Kingdom has arrived, oppression and injustice will come to an end, and the promises of all Scripture will reach complete fulfillment.

CHRISTOLOGY

Matthew attempted to reveal the identity, mission, and significance of Jesus by using a variety of literary devices. He addressed the identity of Jesus through three main titles as well as through the various connections of Jesus and the Old Testament. Certainly Jesus' identity as Messiah is a major theme for Matthew. This identity is affirmed by the genealogy, the question of the Magi, the message of the voice from heaven at both Jesus' baptism and Transfiguration, the Kingdom teachings, the miracles, Peter's confession, and Jesus' own confession before Caiaphas and Pilate. There can be no doubt to the answer to John the Baptist's question from prison of whether Jesus was the Messiah or if they should expect someone else. Matthew did not engage the question of what kind of messiah the Jews were expecting. As one who lived in the first century, he was aware of the wide variety of messianic understandings that existed in Judaism at that time. But there is no doubt that Matthew believed Jesus to be the Messiah and that His teachings about the Kingdom and His miracles were designed to shape the messianic expectations of His followers. Jesus was the Messiah who fulfilled both the Scriptures and God's plan. So, His followers should live within that plan, rather than imposing their own political or religious agendas on the Messiah.

There is no clear evidence that the Judaism of Jesus' or Matthew's day used the title Son of God as a messianic title. Matthew views Jesus as the Son of God in contexts that are distinguishable from, but often intertwined with, His messianic role. Jesus' role as God's Son first appears in the birth narrative, is affirmed most powerfully in the baptism account, is challenged in the temptation, and is reaffirmed in the Transfiguration and in His trial and crucifixion. Though the phrase "son of" was a Hebrew idiom functioning as an adjective, Matthew envisioned Jesus as more than simply a godly man. His regular address of God as His Heavenly Father revealed the unique relationship between Jesus and God. Matthew 11:27 expresses an equality of function or role between Jesus and the Father. This familial relationship also finds expression in Matthew's gospel as the context in which Jesus and the Father communicate on intimate terms with each other. When Caiaphas described Jesus' confession that He is the Son of God as blasphemy, he must have meant that claiming such a title was another way of claiming equality with God. Neither Jesus nor Matthew deny the implication of Caiaphas' charge.

The title Son of Man is the most common phrase used by Jesus in the four Gospels to describe himself. The title is not as prominent in Matthew as in the other synoptic Gospels, but it appears at significant points in the narrative. The background of the term was much argued in twentieth-century New Testament scholarship, but the most likely point of reference for Matthew is Daniel 7 with specific attention to verse 13. There the son of man is an almost angelic being who is coming on the clouds of heaven with great power and glory. In Daniel, He is authorized to usher in the Kingdom of the Ancient of Days and is given great authority and power to accomplish that goal. With the possible exception of the author of the noncanonical Similitudes of Enoch—the date of which is greatly debated—Jesus is the first known person to use this title after Daniel. The unfamiliarity of the title allows Jesus to develop His own identity through it and, from the Daniel background, associate himself closely with God and the coming of God's kingdom.

DISCIPLESHIP

The first action taken by Jesus at the beginning of His ministry was to call disciples. From the abrupt, "Come, follow me," spoken to Peter and Andrew in 4:19 to the end of His teaching ministry, Jesus was about the calling and formation of disciples. The very Greek word translated "disciples" means "learners." This assumes the ancient pattern of teaching-learning, in which the disciple lived with the master teacher and learned both by hearing and by observing the teacher's life. The disciples left everything to follow Jesus. The disciples trusted the Master even in the storms of persecution or affliction according to 8:23–27. The disciples denied themselves and took up the cross to follow Jesus according to 16:24. The disciples left father, mother, and children, as well as houses and fields, to make the journey with Jesus to the cross according to 19:28–29.

Discipleship is also described in the teaching sections that deal with the Church in Matthew 10 and 18. Jesus sent the disciples to replicate His own ministry (10:6–8). He asked them to engage in mission without regard to reimbursement or financial security (10:9–10). He asked them to become dependent on others for their daily shelter and food (10:11–16). The disciples would risk persecution and death for the opportunity to proclaim the Kingdom (10:17–23). The disciples would leave the comfort of fellowship with other disciples to seek the one disciple who wandered away (18:10–14). Jesus required His disciples to submit to a rigorous discipline of mutual accountability according to 18:15–18. Jesus expected His disciples to forgive others beyond their most extravagant vision of forgiveness (18:21–35).

In the final analysis, the life of discipleship is a life of the imitation of Jesus. Rather than shrinking from such a challenge, disciples commit themselves to loyalty to Jesus exceeding their ability.

WESLEYAN THEMES

Obviously, as one writing in the first century, Matthew did not concern himself with the issues or vocabulary of Wesleyan theology. However, his vision of discipleship is thoroughly consistent with the Wesleyan vision of the Christian life. Further, Matthew's use of "perfection" language—and the centrality of love in his presentation of Jesus' teachings—contribute significantly to the Holiness theological vocabulary.

For Matthew, the life of discipleship requires one to deny self and to take up the cross in the imitation of Christ (16:24). Family ties and relationships, political allegiances, and even religious commitments cannot stand above the call to follow Jesus and to conform one's life to His pattern. Religious language, participation in the community of faith, and even miracle-working abilities are no substitute for obedience to Jesus (7:21–23). Evangelistic efforts, pious testimonies, and even rigorous religious disciplines are no substitute for heart purity (23:15–26). External religious practices matter little to Matthew; it is what comes from the heart that determines whether one is clean or unclean (15:10–20). Though Matthew does not use the word "holiness," holiness of heart is a clear theme in his understanding of discipleship.

Regarding Wesleyan vocabulary, there are two places where Matthew records the word "perfect" on Jesus' lips. Both provide significant understanding for the Wesleyan understanding of Christian perfection. In Matthew 5:48, Jesus commands both His disciples and the crowd to be "perfect, . . . as your heavenly Father is perfect." The Greek word here is *teleios*, which speaks of completeness or fullness of function rather than a static and absolute perfection. The context clearly indicates that the perfection Jesus desires is perfection in love. The follower of Jesus is to love like God loves. The paragraph that concludes with the command to be perfect is the final paragraph of the Great Antitheses. Jesus rejected a legalistic religiosity that obeys the scriptural command to love one's neighbor but limits the scope of who constitutes the neighbor so as to not require love beyond what any pagan would give. Rather, the disciple is to love even one's enemies, just as God loves both the righteous and unrighteous. As the final antithesis, Jesus' command to perfection sums up the whole approach He took toward the interpretation of Scripture as being a matter of the heart rather than a legalistic rule.

The second occurrence of the word "perfect" comes in Matthew 19:21. To the rich young man who wanted to enter eternal life and had kept all the commandments, Jesus commanded, "If you want to be perfect, go, sell your possessions and give to the poor, and you will have treasure in heaven." Here the counsel of perfection is still the application of the command from Leviticus 19:18 to love one's neighbor as oneself. The young man had claimed obedience to that command. Jesus then applied the command to the poor and asked the rich seeker to give up all the human resources upon which he depended, give the benefits to the poor, and then to join the poor as one who lived in total dependence on God. This pattern of moving from the verbal claim of total obedience to the application of obedience in ministry to the poor was foundational for John Wesley and his understanding of holiness.

Finally, Jesus' response to the Pharisee's question about the greatest commandment in the Law began the essence of John Wesley's understanding of Christian perfection. Jesus responded to the Pharisee by quoting as the first and greatest commandment the command from the *Shema* in Deuteronomy 6:5 that every Israelite is to love the Lord God with all one's heart, soul, and mind. He then identified the second as Leviticus 19:18, the command to love one's neighbor as oneself. This text clearly resources Wesley in his frequent assertions that by Christian perfection he meant nothing more nor less than loving God with one's whole heart, soul, mind, and strength, and loving one's neighbor as oneself. The close association of Christian perfection and love that supported the Wesleyan theological vision is clearly based in Matthew's gospel.

MATTHEW'S PLACE IN THE CANON AND SIGNIFICANCE FOR CHRISTIAN THEOLOGY

Before there was a New Testament, the collection of Gospels was Matthew, Mark, Luke, and John with Matthew always being listed first. The common assumption of the early church was that Matthew was first because it was written first. That assumption is no longer held by scholars, but Matthew's place as the first book in the New Testament canon is not threatened in the least by a later date for its composition. Matthew belongs first in the New Testament canon because it provides a bridge from the Old Testament to the New.

Many of the unique "Jewish" features of Matthew's gospel admirably equip it to be the transitional book from Old Testament to New. The genealogy, which seems so strange to modern readers as the first words of this Gospel, forms a natural transition between the testaments. Jesus is introduced in terms of Abraham and David, two of the most significant Old Testament personages. The form and content of the genealogy, as well as the language Matthew employs in the birth narratives, are so much at home in the Old Testament that a reader might hardly recognize the transition that was taking place from one testament to another. The concern for the role of the Law and the Prophets, as well as the numerous Old Testament quotations, demonstrate the numerous links between Old and New Testaments.

Further, though these questions are no longer at the forefront of Christian theology, the question of Jesus and the Law, Jesus and the Old Testament, how followers of Christ relate to Judaism, and the status of Jewish traditions were some of the most critical topics for first- and second-century Christianity. Matthew fits best as the first book of the New Testament canon because this Gospel addresses these very questions and sets them in the context of the teaching of Jesus and of His commitment to the Gentile mission. As the church became increasingly Gentile in its makeup in the late first and the second centuries, Matthew's gospel provided a stable connection to the Old Testament roots of the faith as Christians struggled with Gnosticism and other syncretizing religious movements. When Marcion began teaching around A.D. 140 that the Old

Testament was contrary to Christian faith and that the Creator God revealed in the Old Testament was not the father of Jesus Christ, the Church found its answers already articulated in Matthew. So when the Church began the process of finalizing its canon, apparently in response to Marcion, Matthew was the natural choice of all apostolic writings to place at the head of the New Testament canon.

For several reasons Matthew is rarely mentioned in modern times as the favorite Gospel of the four. The conclusion that Mark was written first and that Matthew used Mark as a source contributed to the decline of interest in Matthew during the twentieth century. The modern interest in all things new and postmodernity's passion for spontaneity find unappealing Matthew's habit of grounding all of Jesus' ministry and message in the Old Testament and his carefully organized structuring of Jesus' life and teaching. However, the clear value of Matthew continues to offer important resources to Christian life and faith. Matthew's understanding of the kingdom, of Christology, and of discipleship is as relevant in the twenty-first century as it was in the first century. The theological grounding of the Kingdom in the heart of God revealed first in the Old Testament continues to resource Christian theology in significant ways.

CONTEMPORARY ISSUES IN THE STUDY OF MATTHEW

In addition to the issues discussed thus far in this introduction, three issues relating to Matthew as literature are also at the forefront of scholarly debate in Matthean studies. The literary genre of Matthew, the appropriate method of reading Matthew, and the structure of this Gospel have generated significant discussion and debate among Gospel scholars in the later part of the twentieth century.

THE LITERARY GENRE OF MATTHEW

The question of what kind of literature the Gospels represent has percolated through most of the twentieth century. Early in the twentieth century, scholars began to suggest that the Gospels were a form of ancient biography that chronicled the stories of various famous persons in antiquity. With the rise of Neo-orthodoxy in the 1920s, the Gospels were not affirmed as a unique genre in themselves. Neo-orthodoxy emphasized the centrality of the Word of God in theology, and the Canonical Gospels came to be regarded as a narrative proclamation of the Gospel itself. Their uniqueness from every other kind of literature was proclaimed.

About the same time a new method of Gospel studies emerged that focused on the oral transmission of Jesus' words and on the oral forms of the records of Jesus' teachings and ministry. With the spread of this method called *form criticism* in the 1940s and 1950s, other genres featuring collections of miracle stories and ethical examples were suggested for the Gospels. By the 1970s an investigation of the ancient biography genre resumed, and in the final decades of the twentieth century, many scholars would claim the genre of the Gospels was the ancient laudatory biography.

The question of the genre of Matthew has followed this trajectory of scholarly debate. However, Matthew presents some unique challenges to the general discussion of gospel genre. Matthew, alone of the four Gospels, collects the teachings of Jesus by subject matter into large blocks of teaching material. These teaching blocks "interrupt" the narrative flow of Matthew's story of Jesus' life and ministry. Further, Matthew appears to collect incidents in the narrative sections by subject matter also. For example, chapters 8–9 form a narrative section consisting almost completely of miracle stories. This very content structuring of material leads some scholars to argue that Matthew's gospel was a teaching manual for the teachers or a catechism for the new converts of the early church. A weakness of this view is that it often envisions a Gentile audience rather than Matthew's Jewish context.

A mid-twentieth-century suggestion that Matthew wrote his Gospel to be a lectionary for readings during Christian worship has failed to gain support. Even ingenious variations that tie the Gospel to the Jewish calendar of religious festivals have not proven persuasive. A more common suggestion is that Matthew is an example of a Jewish form of commentary on Scripture called *midrash*. In Jewish *midrash*, the biblical accounts of selected events are embellished and enlarged homiletically to provide moral instruction or inspirational edification for life. The frequent appeal to Old Testament passages has fueled the ongoing discussion of Matthew as *midrash*. However, careful comparison of Matthew with Jewish *midrash* shows Matthew would have been a dull *midrashic* writer. His accounts are direct and, when compared to Mark as his source, he tends to reduce rather than enhance elements that might be considered embellishments.

Though there are elements in Matthew that correspond to ancient biography, the emergent interest in the so-called Gnostic Gospels should alert students of Matthew to the value of considering his book as a Gospel, a narrative proclamation of the death and resurrection of Jesus. From 16:21 on, the shadow of the cross looms ever larger over Jesus as Matthew recounts the events and teachings that marked His final journey to Jerusalem. Certainly the narrative sections of Matthew from the beginning of the Gospel engage the question of Jesus' identity. But Matthew is unique in the way he combined narrative and teaching materials. That combination continues to challenge scholars attempting to describe the literary genre of the first Gospel.

THE BEST METHOD OF ANALYZING MATTHEW AS LITERATURE

One of the results of the nineteenth-century historical-critical method of studying the Gospels was the rediscovery of the priority of Mark's gospel. From the second century, Christian teachers had confidently declared that Matthew was the first Gospel to be written and that Mark was an abbreviation of Matthew. By the end of the nineteenth century, the study of sources used for composing the Gospels had convinced most students that Mark was written first and that Matthew used Mark as a source. The source critical question debated in the first half of the twentieth century was whether Matthew also used a collection of sayings, usually called the Q Document, and another document, called M, that contained material from Jesus unique to Matthew's gospel. The weight of opinion through most of the twentieth century was that Matthew used two sources, Mark and Q, though the content, structure, and extent of Q continued to be debated. It is interesting to observe that Matthew was much more free in his use of Mark in the first eleven and a half chapters. Starting with 12:22, he follows Mark's gospel much more closely.

The rise of form criticism after World War I placed greater emphasis on Mark than on Matthew. Form criticism sought to return to the oral forms of the teachings and stories of Jesus found in the Gospels. Because Mark was considered the first Gospel, his form of Jesus' teachings was preferred to Matthew's because it was closer to the oral—and thus the original—words of Jesus. The neglect of Matthew during the period of the ascendancy of form criticism was reflected even in the quality of the commentaries written on this Gospel.

In the 1950s, the method of study called redaction criticism developed. This approach analyzed the way Matthew and Luke used the sources of Mark and Q. Redaction critics suggested that the ways Matthew altered or edited Mark revealed the theological purposes the author wished to communicate regarding Jesus and the Kingdom. This form of criticism brought a revival of interest in Matthew that has continued to the present. In the 1980s, another form of literary analysis of the Gospel emerged called narrative criticism. These critics were not interested in analyzing Matthew's editorial work on Mark, but insisted on reading Matthew as a whole. The way in which he developed characters and plot and portrayed settings was seen as the key to understanding his purposes in writing this Gospel. The structure of this book also played an important role in narrative studies of the Gospel, for it revealed themes and points of emphasis. Narrative criticism furthered the revival of interest in the first Gospel. Thus, the final decades of the twentieth century and the early years of the twenty-first century have produced the finest scholarly works on Matthew to be published since the Reformation. Though there is considerable value in the study of Matthew's editorial work on Mark, the primary method adopted in this commentary is to pursue the narrative logic of Matthew's unfolding of the message and ministry of Jesus.

THE STRUCTURE OF MATTHEW'S GOSPEL

Discussion of the structure of Matthew's gospel has been lively and creative through much of the twentieth century, though no firm consensus has been reached. The lack of agreement is not because there is no evidence of structure as is the case with Mark. Rather, there are so many structural markers that scholars are not able to take account of all of them.

Three major approaches to the structure of Matthew have found sustained support through several decades of study. The first is the Pentateuchal proposal of Benjamin Bacon, the second proposes a three-part structure for Matthew, and the third sees some form of a centered structure.

Bacon suggested, early in the twentieth century, that Matthew had intentionally structured his Gospel with five books containing both narrative and teaching material. The structural key for Bacon was the expression, "When Jesus had finished saying . . . ," which appeared at the end of the five blocks of teaching material Matthew had assembled (7:28; 11:1; 13:53; 19:1; 26:1). Bacon's proposal looked like this:

Prologue	Matthew 1–2	The birth narrative	
Book 1	Matthew 3–4	Narrative	
	Matthew 5–7	Teaching	The Sermon on the Mount
Book 2	Matthew 8–9	Narrative	
	Matthew 10:1–11:1	Teaching	The Mission of the Church
Book 3	Matthew 11:2–12:50	Narrative	
	Matthew 13:1–53	Teaching	Parables of the Kingdom
Book 4	Matthew 13:54–17:27	Narrative	
	Matthew 18:1–19:1	Teaching	Relationships in the Church
Book 5	Matthew 19:2–22:46	Narrative	
	Matthew 23:1–26:1	Teaching	Readiness for the future Kingdom
Epilogue	Matthew 26:2–28:20	The arrest, trial, crucifixion, and resurrection narrative [1]	

The strength of Bacon's proposal is the way it incorporates the teaching blocks and the "When Jesus had finished . . ." formula. The weakness of Bacon's proposal is the way it dismisses the birth narrative as prologue and Jesus' death and resurrection as an epilogue. The birth narrative is far more than a prologue to Matthew's gospel. There Matthew establishes some of the most important themes about Jesus that he will develop throughout the remainder of the Gospel. Just as labeling the birth narrative as a prologue is problematic, the description of the final three chapters of Matthew as epilogue is completely inaccurate. These chapters form the climax of the book. Matthew had been anticipating the death and resurrection of Jesus from the first passion prediction of Jesus in 16:21. The final chapters must be integrated into the flow of the whole book. Bacon's proposal is also problematic in its assignment of chapter 23. Though it contains no narrative at all, only the final verses of the chapter fit well with the teaching material found in chapters 24–25.

In response to the weaknesses of Bacon's proposed structure, a three-part structure emerged in the last quarter of the twentieth century as a widely accepted description of Matthew's structure. This view is often associated with Jack Dean Kingsbury of Union Theological Seminary, but it was proposed earlier by several scholars and has gained wide acceptance since Kingsbury's work. The key structural element to the three-part structure is the expression, "From that time on . . . ," which appears twice in Matthew (4:17; 16:21). Using Kingsbury's focus on the title Son of God as key to Matthew's theology, the three-part outline is as follows:

Part 1	Matthew 1:1–4:16	The person of Jesus, Son of God
Part 2	Matthew 4:17–16:20	The preaching of Jesus, Son of God
Part 3	Matthew 16:21–28:20	The passion of Jesus, Son of God[2]

The strength of the three-part structure is its simplicity and that it avoids the weaknesses of Bacon's approach. The weakness of this analysis of the structure is its failure to account for the five-fold formula, "When Jesus had finished . . . ." It also divides 16:13–20 from 16:21–28. These two paragraphs appear closely related to each other in the flow of Matthew's narrative logic. It is difficult to imagine a structural outline could be valid that places these two paragraphs in such disparate sections as the three-part structure does.

As the 1980s unfolded, the three-part structure of Matthew—endorsed by Kingsbury—surged in influence in Matthean scholarship. It would have been easy to assume near the end of the 1980s that this view would soon become the consensus view on Matthean structure. However, in the final decade of the twentieth century and in the beginning years of the twenty-first century, the weaknesses of the three-part structure were recognized, and alternative explanations of Matthew's structure began to appear.

CHIASTIC PROPOSALS FOR MATTHEW'S STRUCTURE

The most common structural proposals that responded to the weaknesses of the three-part structure were described as *chiastic* or center proposals. These return to the strengths of the Bacon proposal and build on the five blocks of teaching materials and the alternating pattern of narrative and teaching. The center proposals note that in the odd number of teaching blocks there is a central portion, and the blocks before and after roughly correspond with each other. To the degree the material before and after the center correspond with each other, the structure forms a *chiasm*, so named after the Greek letter *chi*. A sample chiastic structure is as follows:

Narrative	A	Matthew 1–4: Birth and beginnings
Teachings	B	Matthew 5–7: Blessings, entering the Kingdom
Narrative	C	Matthew 8–9: Authority and invitation
Teaching	D	Matthew 10: Mission discourse
Narrative	E	Matthew 11–12: Rejection by this generation
Teaching	F	Matthew 13: Parables of the Kingdom
Narrative	E`	Matthew 14–17: Acknowledgement by disciples
Teaching	D`	Matthew 18: Community discourse
Narrative	C`	Matthew 19–22: Authority and invitation
Teaching	B`	Matthew 23–25: Woes, coming of the Kingdom
Narrative	A`	Matthew 26–28: Death and rebirth[3]

The strength of such a chiastic or centered proposal for Matthew's structure is that it takes into account the alternating narrative and teaching material and recognizes the significant role of the blocks of teaching material. It also avoids the most serious weaknesses of the Bacon proposal, while taking advantage of its strengths. The weakness of this and other chiastic proposals is the occasional artificial nature of the section descriptions that seem forced into correspondence. For example, to describe Matthew 11–12 as "Rejection by this generation" fits the material in these chapters fairly well. However, to describe Matthew 14–17 as "Acknowledgment by disciples," extends the content of one paragraph—Peter's confession at Caesarea Philippi in 16:13–20—as the title for a section with a wide variety of content. The description *Acknowledgement by disciples* seems more governed by the desire to make the chiastic structure work than by the content of the chapters in question.

It seems clear that Matthew intentionally alternated narrative and teaching material. The alternation is clearer in the first half of the Gospel than in the last half. It may be that he began with a chiastic structure in mind and simply was not able to sustain the precision that modern scholars expect. Presumably Matthew constructed the outline of his Gospel in his mind and then began writing and published his first draft. If this book was produced in that way, perhaps he can be forgiven for failing to sustain the initial pattern all the way through his Gospel. The following outline that will provide the basis of this commentary works with the alternating narrative and teaching blocks. Rather than seeking a chiastic structure, this outline begins with a narrative introduction to Matthew's gospel in chapters 1–4. Five sections follow, each beginning with a block of teaching material followed by a narrative section that illustrates through Jesus' life the truth of and His commitment to what He taught.

ENDNOTES

1.   W. D. Davies and Dale C. Allison, *A Critical and Exegetical Commentary on the Gospel According to Saint Matthew*, vol. 1, The International Critical Commentary (Edinburgh: T. & T. Clark, 1988), 59.

2.   David R. Bauer, *The Structure of Matthew's Gospel: A Study in Literary Design* (Sheffield, England: Almond Press, 1989), 40–45.

3.   C. H. Lohr, "Oral Techniques in the Gospel of Matthew," *Catholic Biblical Quarterly* 23 (1961): 403–435

OUTLINE OF MATTHEW

I. The Beginning of Jesus and His Ministry (1:1–4:25)
  A. The Origin of Jesus (1:1–25)
    1. The Genealogy of Jesus (1:1–17)
    2. The Birth of Jesus (1:18–25)
  B. The Beginning Days of Jesus' Life (2:1–23)
    1. The Visit of the Magi (2:1–12)
    2. Jesus' Retracing Israel's Journey Home (2:13–23)
  C. John the Baptist and the Baptism of Jesus (3:1–17)
    1. The Ministry and Message of John the Baptist (3:1–12)
    2. The Baptism of Jesus (3:13–17)
  D. Temptation and the Beginning of Jesus' Ministry (4:1–25)
    1. The Temptation of Jesus (4:1–11)
    2. The Beginning of Jesus' Ministry (4:12–25)

II. The Authority of Jesus in Word and Deed (5:1–9:38)
  A. Jesus' Authoritative Teaching in the Sermon on the Mount (5:1–7:29)
    1. The Beatitudes and Jesus' Teaching on the Old Testament (5:1–48)
      a. The Narrative Introduction to the Sermon on the Mount (5:1–2)
      b. The Beatitudes: The Grace of the Kingdom (5:3–12)
      c. Disciples as Salt and Light in the Kingdom (5:13–16)
      d. The Old Testament in the Kingdom (5:17–48)
    2. Devotion and Money in the Kingdom (6:1–34)
      a. Devotion in the Life of a Disciple (6:1–18)
      b. Money in the Kingdom (6:19–34)
    3. Problems in the Life of the Kingdom (7:1–29)
      a. Problems in Relationship with Others (7:1–6)
      b. Problems in Relationship with God (7:7–12)
      c. Problems in the Life of the Kingdom (7:13–27)
      d. The Narrative Conclusion to the Sermon on the Mount (7:28–29)

B. Jesus' Authoritative Actions in Ushering in the Kingdom (8:1–9:38)

   1. Miracles Teaching Jesus' Identity and Life in the Kingdom (8:1–34)

      a. Miracles Revealing Jesus' Identity (8:1–17)

      b. Miracles Teaching Life in the Kingdom (8:18–34)

   2. Miracles Revealing Jesus' Authority (9:1–38)

      a. The Authority of Jesus (9:1–17)

      b. The Faith that Brings Healing (9:18–34)

      c. Conclusion and Transition (9:35–38)

III. Mission in the Face of Rejection: Precept and Example (10:1–12:50)

A. Jesus' Teaching on Mission (10:1–11:1)

   1. Authorizing and Introducing the Twelve Apostles (10:1–4)

   2. The Mission to Israel (10:5–15)

   3. Mission in the Face of Persecution (10:16–39)

      a. Readiness for Persecution (10:16–23)

      b. Persecution as Imitation of Christ (10:24–25)

      c. Courage in the Face of Persecution (10:26–31)

      d. Confessing and Denying Christ (10:32–33)

      e. The Divisiveness of Following Jesus (10:34–39)

   4. The Rewards of the Mission (10:40–11:1)

B. From Questions about Jesus to Conflict with Jewish Leaders (11:2–12:50)

   1. Questions and Uncertainty About Jesus (11:2–30)

      a. Questions from and about John the Baptist (11:2–19)

      b. Judgment on Three Unrepentant Cities (11:20–24)

      c. The Mystery of Response to Jesus (11:25–30)

   2. Conflict with Judaism (12:1–50)

      a. Sabbath Controversies (12:1–21)

      b. Accusations by the Pharisees (12:22–45)

      c. The True Family of Jesus (12:46–50)

VI. The Variety of Responses to Jesus: Teachings and Examples (13:1–17:27)

A. Jesus' Parables Teaching the Kingdom (13:1–53)

   1. The Variety of Responses to the Kingdom (13:1–30)

      a. The Parable of the Sower (13:1–9)

      b. Jesus' Purpose in Teaching with Parables (13:10–17)
      c. The Interpretation of the Parable of the Sower (13:18–23)
      d. The Parable of the Wheat and the Weeds (13:24–30)
   2. The Powerful Effect of the Kingdom (13:31–35)
   3. The Judgment of Wrong Choices in the Kingdom (13:36–50)
      a. The Interpretation of the Parable of the Wheat and the Weeds (13:36–43)
      b. The Parables of the Hidden Treasure and the Pearl (13:44–46)
      c. The Parable of the Net (13:47–50)
   4. The Conclusion of Jesus' Teaching with Parables (13:51–53)
  B. The Variety of Responses to the Kingdom (13:54–17:27)
   1. Jesus Provides Light in the Darkness (13:54–14:36)
      a. Jesus Rejected in His Hometown (13:54–58)
      b. The Death of John the Baptist (14:1–12)
      c. Feeding the Multitude (14:13–21)
      d. Jesus (and Peter) Walking on the Water (14:22–33)
      e. A Summary of Jesus' Ministry (14:34–36)
   2. Jesus Provides Bread for All (15:1–39)
      a. Debate over Eating with Unwashed Hands (15:1–20)
      b. Table Scraps for a Canaanite Woman (15:21–28)
      c. Feeding the Gentile Multitude (15:29–39)
   3. The Meaning of Following Jesus (16:1–28)
      a. The Rejection of the Pharisees and Sadducees (16:1–12)
      b. The Identity and Mission of Jesus (16:13–20)
      c. The Cost of Following Jesus (16:21–28)
   4. The Promise of Glory and the Frustration of Discipleship (17:1–27)
      a. The Transfiguration of Jesus (17:1–13)
      b. The Frustrations and Joys of Discipleship (17:14–27)

V. Grace and Judgment in the Kingdom: Teachings and Examples (18:1–23:39)
  A. Jesus' teaching about Life Together in the Kingdom (18:1–19:1)
   1. Greatness in the Kingdom (18:1–4)
   2. Care for the Little Ones in the Kingdom (18:5–9)
   3. Restoring the Lost Sheep (18:10–14)

4. Restoring the Sinning Church Member (18:15–20)
5. The Extent of Forgiveness (18:21–19:1)
B. Examples of Grace and Judgment in the Kingdom (19:2–23:39)
1. The Demands of the Kingdom (19:2–30)
  a. Jesus' Teaching on Divorce (19:2–12)
  b. Jesus' Blessing of the Children (19:13–15)
  c. The Cost of Perfection in the Kingdom (19:16–30)
2. Grace for the Journey (20:1–34)
  a. The Parable of the Workers in the Vineyard (20:1–16)
  b. Jesus' Coming Death and Resurrection (20:17–28)
  c. Two Blind Men Receive Their Sight (20:29–34)
3. Jesus' Prophetic Authority in Jerusalem (21:1–46)
  a. Jesus' Royal Entry into Jerusalem (21:1–11)
  b. The Cleansing of the Temple (21:12–17)
  c. The Withering Fig Tree (21:18–22)
  d. The Authority of John the Baptist and Jesus (21:23–27)
  e. The Parable of the Two Sons (21:28–32)
  f. The Parable of the Tenants (21:33–46)
4. Conflict with Jewish Religious Leaders in Jerusalem (22:1–46)
  a. The Parable of a Wedding Feast (22:1–14)
  b. Paying Taxes to Caesar (22:15–22)
  c. A Question about Resurrection and Marriage (22:23–33)
  d. The Greatest Commandment (22:34–40)
  e. Jesus' Question About David's Son (22:41–46)
5. Jesus' Denunciation of the Pharisees (23:1–39)
  a. A Warning about the Pharisees' Harmful Practices (23:1–12)
  b. Seven Condemnations of the Pharisees (23:13–32)
  c. A Final Warning to Jerusalem (23:33–39)

VI. The End of the Age and the End of Jesus' Earthly Ministry (24:1–28:20)
A. Jesus' Teachings on the End of the Age (24:1–26:1)
1. Teachings on the End of the Age (24:1–51)
  a. The Setting of Jesus' Final Teachings (24:1–3)
  b. Indications Anticipating the End (24:4–14)

     c. Signs of the Impending Crisis (24:15–35)

     d. The Unexpectedness of the Messiah's Coming (24:36–51)

  2. Parables Teaching Readiness for the End of the Age (25:1–26:1)

     a. The Parable of the Ten Virgins (25:1–13)

     b. The Parable of the Talents (25:14–30)

     c. The Parable of the Sheep and the Goats (25:31–26:1)

B. The End of Jesus' Ministry and Life (26:2–28:20)

  1. The Unfolding Plot to Kill Jesus (26:2–75)

     a. The Plot to Kill Jesus (26:2–16)

     b. Jesus' Final Passover (26:17–35)

     c. Jesus Arrested (26:36–56)

     d. Jesus' Jewish Trial and Peter's Denial (26:57–75)

  2. Jesus' Trial Before Pilate and the Crucifixion (27:1–66)

     a. The Death of Judas (27:1–10)

     b. The Trial Before Pilate (27:11–26)

     c. The Crucifixion of Jesus (27:27–56)

     d. The Burial of Jesus (27:57–66)

  3. Jesus' Resurrection and Missionary Commission (28:1–20)

     a. The Resurrection of Jesus (28:1–15)

     b. Jesus' Commission to His Disciples (28:16–20)

Part One

The Beginning of Jesus and His Ministry

MATTHEW 1:1–4:25

The Gospel of Matthew begins with a long narrative introduction. Chapters 1–4 describe important events that introduce the person of Jesus. Before the first section of teaching material appears in Matthew 5–7, we learn of Jesus' origin and birth in Matthew 1, of His earliest days in Matthew 2, and of the events surrounding the beginning of His ministry in Matthew 3 and 4. All of this sets the stage for the rest of the story.

1

THE ORIGIN OF JESUS

Matthew 1:1–25

Matthew's intention to show the relationship between Jesus and the Old Testament is clear from the opening words of his Gospel. The very first words evoking memories of Genesis, the genealogy providing a roll call of Old Testament heroes, and the first of Matthew's many quotations from the Old Testament all appear in chapter 1. The chapter consists of two sections: verses 1–17 contain the genealogy of Jesus, and verses 18–25 describe Jesus' conception by the Holy Spirit and His acceptance by Joseph.

1. THE GENEALOGY OF JESUS 1:1–17

The first words in Matthew, **A record of the genealogy**, translate two well-known words in the Greek text. Those words are *book* (*biblos*) and *origin* (*genesis*). The expression, "The book of the genesis," comes directly from Genesis 2:4 and 5:1 in the Greek translation of the Old Testament—called the Septuagint—used in Matthew's time. While we might accurately translate these words as the **record**, history, or book of the **genealogy of Jesus Christ**, we miss the concept Matthew intended. Clearly he wanted his readers to see the coming of Jesus as related to the creation of the universe and of the first Adam.

Both the opening verse and the structure of the genealogy highlight **David** and **Abraham**. Jews of Jesus' time considered Abraham to be the father of their nation and David the greatest king in Israelite memory. However, there is a more important reason to emphasize these two Old Testament heroes. Both were recipients of significant promises that shaped Jewish identity. God had promised to Abraham the land named

Canaan, later called Israel and Palestine; innumerable descendants; and descendants that would become a blessing to all nations (Gen. 12:2–3; 13:14–17). God had promised David that his descendants would rule forever over the people of Israel (2 Sam. 7:12–16).

The **exile to Babylon** (Matt. 1:12) raised serious questions about these promises. The Davidic dynasty no longer ruled. The land was lost. Though Jews regained occupancy of the land, they could not win back consistent ownership in the generations between the exile and the birth of Jesus. This contrast between the promises made to Abraham and David—and the loss of the land and sovereignty—fueled Jewish hopes for a Messiah. The common thread of the differing expressions of Jewish messianic hope was the faith that the Messiah would fulfill the promises once made to Abraham and David.

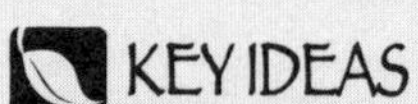

CHRIST

The word *Christ* is the English form of a Greek word meaning *anointed one*. Messiah is the English form of the Hebrew word meaning *anointed one*. Eventually the word *Christ* became simply another name for Jesus. However, in many passages of the New Testament, the word *Christ* can be translated as *Messiah* and should be in passages where the Jewish background of the term is clear. When Matthew introduces his gospel by describing it as the book of the genesis of Jesus Christ, we should understand him to mean Jesus the Messiah. Thus verse 1 in miniature, and the genealogy as whole, portrays Jesus as the Messiah who will restore the promises made to David and to Abraham.

Matthew's **genealogy of Jesus** is constructed like the Old Testament records found in Ruth 4:18–22 and 1 Chronicles 2–3. There are four points at which Matthew's genealogy breaks away from the normal pattern of these Old Testament genealogies.

First, when a genealogy is constructed forward in history (X was the father of Y), as Matthew's genealogy is, the ancestral father is mentioned first and the person whose genealogy is being presented is mentioned last. This is the pattern beginning in verse 2 with the statement **Abraham was the father of Isaac.** However, verse 1 reverses the order as the **genealogy of Jesus Christ the son of David, the son of Abraham.** This reversal of order shows that Matthew considered Jesus superior to Abraham and David.

Second, the mention of **Judah and his brothers** in verse 2 and **Jeconiah and his brothers** in verse 11 is unusual. This appears to be Matthew's way of indicating the corporate nature of Israel at key points in the genealogy. Further, **Judah and his brothers** are part of the genealogy between **Abraham** and **David. Jeconiah and his brothers** (1:11) appear between **David** and the **exile to Babylon** (1:12). There is no corresponding corporate reference in the final segment of the genealogy.

The third unusual feature of Matthew's genealogy is the mention of four women: **Tamar** in verse 3, **Rahab** and **Ruth** in verse 5, and **Uriah's wife** in verse 6. Not only is it unusual to mention women in a Jewish genealogy, these women were either Gentiles or married to a Gentile. Perhaps Matthew includes these Gentile women to show the universal nature of the gospel. Also, these women were examples of tenacious faith, the kind of faith that will be necessary to follow Christ. As such they serve to prepare the reader for the introduction of the fifth woman in the genealogy, **Mary.**

The fourth unusual feature in this genealogy is the introduction of **Joseph** as **the husband of Mary** (1:16). We would have expected Mary to be introduced as the wife of Joseph. Further, Matthew shifts from the active voice of the verb **was the father of** that he had used from verse 2 to verse 16a to a passive voice of the verb, **was born,** to describe the birth of Jesus to Mary. Clearly Jesus' birth was something very unusual. Matthew cannot say that Joseph was the father of Jesus. He will carefully explain this unusual feature of the genealogy in the following section. However, the way God used Tamar, Rahab, Ruth, and Uriah's wife should remind the reader to not immediately reject Mary and what God would do through her.

Matthew concludes his genealogy by noting in verse 17 that there were **fourteen generations** in each of the three segments of the genealogy: Abraham to David, David to the exile to Babylon, and the exile to Babylon to Jesus. Clearly the three sets of fourteen were important to Matthew. Why that is so is not clear. It is true that the Hebrew word for David has three letters and a numerical value of fourteen. Perhaps Matthew emphasized the three sets of fourteen to highlight the centrality of David in understanding the story of Jesus.

2. THE BIRTH OF JESUS 1:18–25

Matthew 1:18–25 is usually titled, "The **Birth of Jesus Christ**," and that birth is described in verse 25. However, the majority of the paragraph is about Jesus' conception, the survival of His parents' marriage, and His being named. The word usually translated **birth** in verse 18 is the same Greek word *genesis* that Matthew used in verse 1, where it is translated *genealogy*. By repeating this word, Matthew connects this new paragraph with the genealogy and reemphasizes the new creation theme by which he understands Jesus. The contemporary debate about when life begins should sensitize us to the importance of the fact that Jesus' beginning or origin preceded his birth.

The unexpected shift from the active to the passive voice in the verbs of the genealogy that appears in verse 16 and the unusual description of Joseph as the husband of Mary has alerted the reader that there is something very unusual about Jesus' birth. Beginning in verse 18, Matthew proceeds to describe how this unusual **birth came about**. The strange course of events began when **his mother Mary was pledged to be married to Joseph**.

The process of engagement and marriage was quite different in Jesus' time than it is today. Parents arranged marriages for their children. In the bride's early teen years, a formal betrothal occurred a year to a year and a half before the marriage ceremony itself. This betrothal involved a contract with payment of a bride price, and thus it constituted a binding legal procedure. This contract could only be broken by a legal reversal, which was considered a divorce. This betrothal was a pre-marriage marriage. The death of one of the partners caused the other to be labeled a widow or widower. Sexual infidelity was considered adultery and subject to the legal penalties of adultery in that society. At the end of the betrothal period, a wedding ceremony and feast took place, after which the couple began to live together as husband and wife.

During the betrothal, **Mary . . . was found to be with child** (1:18). Joseph's response makes it clear that he was not the father of the child. It is often claimed that Joseph could have had Mary stoned to death for adultery. While the Old Testament provided the death penalty for adultery

(Deut. 22:22), it was no longer used by Jesus' time for what we call pre-marital infidelity. Rather, the divorce laws of the Old Testament (Deut. 24:1–4) were applied. The question Joseph faced was whether to proceed with a public trial to determine whether Mary had been seduced, raped, or had prostituted herself (Deut. 22:13–25). This would establish Joseph's innocence in the pregnancy and force Mary's parents to repay the bridal price. Unfortunately such a procedure would have subjected **her to public disgrace**. Joseph's only other choice would be to seek a private **divorce**.

In verse 19, Matthew describes **Joseph** as a **righteous man**. The most natural meaning of this term is that he was a law-abiding person. Even a private divorce would have required two witnesses. His conflict was with how much public disgrace he would force Mary to suffer. It is likely that Matthew's use of the word **righteous** to describe Joseph also reflected this concern for Mary's well-being.

Though Matthew had named **the Holy Spirit** as the agent of conception in verse 18, this fact was not revealed to Joseph until verse 20. Joseph's thinking about divorce was interrupted by the appearance of **an angel of the Lord**. Both the Hebrew and Greek words for **angel** had the basic meaning of *messenger*. The function of the angel was to deliver a message from God to Joseph.

The divine message had five elements.

First, **Joseph** was to **not be afraid** to proceed with his marriage to **Mary** (1:20). To do so would require that he drop the consideration of divorce and accept her child as his own.

Second, the **angel** informed **Joseph** that Mary's pregnancy was the result of **the Holy Spirit** rather than of her infidelity (1:20). Though we may imagine that this information would have been helpful for a righteous man, we should not imagine that it was easily understood or believed. God required a great deal of faith on Joseph's part to act on the divine message.

A third point of that message was that the unborn child would be a **son** (1:21).

Fourth, **Joseph** was to **name** the child **Jesus**. In Joseph's culture, naming the child would be an act of acknowledging the child to be his own. This would provide the child a lineage and a place of honor in the society. For Joseph to obey the command to name the child would be somewhat equivalent to adopting Him. In this way, the reader grasps how to understand the strange passive voice of the verb back in Matthew 1:16 and Joseph's description as being the husband of Mary. These are to be held together with the fact that it is Joseph's genealogy that Matthew provides.

The fifth element of the angelic message is that the child would **save his people from their sins**. This provides the reason for naming the child **Jesus** (1:21). This name comes from the Hebrew name *Yeshua*, which means *Yahweh will save*. Thus the very naming of Jesus anticipates the salvation He will provide.

Verse 22 states a common concept in Matthew's gospel: the fulfillment of prophecy. The verb Matthew uses, **fulfill**, means more than just prediction. There was meaning to the text of the Old Testament in its original time and setting. But the coming of Jesus fills the meaning of the Old Testament full of all the purposes of God in salvation history. The text Matthew quotes in verse 23 is Isaiah 7:14. The reference to the **virgin** being **with child** gives a scriptural context for the description of Jesus' virginal conception that Matthew has described in the preceding verses. Though the Hebrew text of Isaiah 7:14 refers to a young woman being pregnant and giving birth, the Greek translation of the Old Testament used in Matthew's time translated the word as *virgin*. By quoting from the Septuagint, Matthew is able to give scriptural support for Mary's pregnancy and point to the unique nature of Jesus as **Immanuel**. He is **God with us**. This is Matthew's testimony to the Incarnation and, thus, both the deity and humanity of Christ.

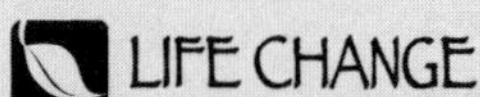

The names Immanuel and Jesus point to an important truth about the Christian life. The very purpose of Jesus coming to earth was to save us from our sins as that very name implies. However, being saved is not something mechanical or separate from our daily lives. The name Immanuel tells us that the purpose of our being saved is so that we live in personal relationship with God. Salvation is stripped of its essential meaning and purpose if we do not live day by day experiencing God with us.

The angel's message was effective. Joseph obeyed each of the instructions given. Verses 24–25 repeat the verbs and phrases from the preceding verses to show Joseph's obedience was complete.

2

THE BEGINNING DAYS OF JESUS' LIFE

Matthew 2:1–23

Following the birth of Jesus, Matthew narrates several key events in the earliest days of Jesus' life. These events are not found elsewhere in the New Testament and portray important truths Matthew wished to communicate about the meaning of Jesus. The first of these events is the Magi's visiting Jesus in Bethlehem, described in Matthew 2:1–12. Then verses 13–23 tell of Jesus' journey to Egypt and back, as well as the decision to make Nazareth the home of His childhood. Throughout chapter 2, Matthew points out the way in which God's purposes from the Old Testament find fulfillment in these events.

1. THE VISIT OF THE MAGI 2:1–12

The first link between Jesus and ancient history appears in Matthew 2:1 in that Jesus' birth was **during the time of King Herod**. Reliable historical evidence places the death of **Herod** in 4 B.C. How much earlier **Jesus was born** is not clear. The text simply does not say.

The word **Magi** is the Greek word used by Matthew put into English letters. Its use in ancient Greek suggests magicians and astrologers. It is possible the word came into Greek from Persia, where it referred to the priests of Persian society. Their knowledge of the stars suggests that these first visitors to Jesus were astrologers. In the ancient world astrologers were the scientists. Since they assumed a unity between the divine control of history and the movements of the stars, they tried to understand human history through the movements of the stars.

Some try to provide natural explanations of the **star** (2:1) seen by the **Magi,** suggesting that it was perhaps Halley's comet or the explosion of a nova or supernova. A common suggestion is that the star was a conjunction of the planets Jupiter and Saturn. Astronomers have been able to determine that these two planets appeared to overlap each other in the constellation Pisces in 7 B.C. Since Jupiter was the planet of royalty, Saturn the planet of Palestine, and Pisces the sign of the last days, ancient astrologers might easily have concluded that an end-time king of the Jews had been born. Interesting as these explanations may be, they do not explain the way in which the star led the Magi directly to the house where Jesus was in Bethlehem as mentioned in Matthew 2:9.

That **King Herod** would be **disturbed** (2:3) is a natural response to the news that another king who would replace him had been born. Historical sources reveal Herod to have been extremely paranoid. He had three of his own sons and one of his wives killed because he feared they were plotting to overthrow him. That **all Jerusalem** would have been upset **with him** is less understandable. One might have expected rejoicing at the news that Herod's days were numbered. However, when a tyrant is upset, even his subjects who hate him have reason to be worried.

That **Herod** consulted with the **chief priests and teachers of the law** is also surprising, but the wily king was cunning, as verse 4 makes clear. The reply of the priests and teachers is that **the Christ**—the Messiah— would be born **in Bethlehem in Judea** (2:5). **Bethlehem** was a small town five to six miles south of Jerusalem. It was most noted in the Old Testament as the village from which King David came. Judea was the name assigned in Roman times to the province surrounding Jerusalem. It is the New Testament form of the word *Judah.*

Matthew's focus on the Old Testament finds further support from the **priests and teachers**, who quote Micah 5:2 as evidence for the Messiah's birth in **Bethlehem** (2:6). The form of the quotation is a free paraphrase. While the Hebrew text of Micah 5:2 portrays Bethlehem in a poor light as **insignificant, poverty-stricken**, Matthew's paraphrase heightens our respect for the significance of the town. He also enlarges the reference to a **ruler** by adding a word from 2 Samuel 5:2, which describes King David as both **shepherd** and **ruler** of God's **people Israel.** In combining Micah 5:2 and 2 Samuel 5:2, Matthew demonstrates a common technique of Jewish interpretation of Scripture in the first century. It is interesting that both nature—the stars—and Scripture combined to direct the Magi to Jesus.

In his paranoia about the birth of a rival king, Herod had not sent the Magi to the priests and teachers. Rather, he served as broker for the information they would provide. When that information came to him, he summoned the **Magi secretly**; inquired about the **exact time the star appeared** (Matt. 2:7); and instructed them to **make a careful search for the child**. His secrecy is evidence of the insincerity of his promise to join the Magi in **worship** of the child (2:8).

The Magi did not need the instruction of Herod because **the star went ahead of them** and led them directly to Jesus. Upon encountering Jesus, they **worshiped**. In fact, worship is the central theme of verses 9–12. This is evidenced by the joy of the Magi, by their bowing down, and by their offering of **gifts** to Him. In the gospel most often labeled *Jewish*, it is significant that the first worshippers of Jesus were the Gentile Magi.

Psalm 72:15 identifies **gold** as the gift that honors a king. Isaiah 60:6 mentions **gold and . . . incense** as expressions of praise offered to God. Psalm 45:8 and Song of Songs 3:6 portray **myrrh** as a fragrance associated with kings. Modern Christians connect the myrrh with the crucifixion (Mark 15:23) and burial (John 19:39) of Jesus and so associate it with His sufferings and death. However, the Old Testament saw myrrh as a symbol of joy and celebration. Thus Matthew's readers, who were attentive to Old Testament

LIFE CHANGE

WORSHIP

The appropriate response to Jesus is always worship. Information about the historical background of Jesus, investigation of the literary devices of the Gospels, and even interest in the theological truth of Jesus' divine and human nature are valuable and important. But until that knowledge turns one's heart to worship, it is only more information in an age in which we are saturated with information. The purpose of Christ is transformation, and that only comes through worship.

themes, realized that the **gifts** from the **treasures** of the Magi affirmed both Jesus' kingly and divine roles.

The significant role Jesus will play is also indicated by Matthew's subtle reference to the magi **having been warned in a dream** to return **to their** own **country** (2:12). The reference to the **dream**, as well as the passive voice of the verb **having been warned**, point to God as the actor in this sentence. Thus we are told that God intervened to spare Jesus' life at the point of Herod's threat to kill Him. This can only mean that God had significant purposes for Jesus' life. These purposes will unfold as Matthew's gospel progresses.

2. JESUS' RETRACING ISRAEL'S JOURNEY HOME 2:13–23

The Magi returning home without revealing Jesus' location did not end the danger to His life. Matthew's theme of divine intervention continues in verse 13 as an **angel of the Lord** used a **dream** to warn **Joseph** to flee **to Egypt.** Flight to Egypt was a common theme in the Old Testament. Abraham, Jacob and his sons, Jeroboam, and Jeremiah all traveled to Egypt in search of safety whether escaping famine or political threats.

The instructions of the **angel of the Lord** appear in a series of commands: **get up, take the child, escape to Egypt**, and **stay there**. The theme of Joseph's obedience can be seen in the way this sequence of verbs is repeated in verse 14: Joseph **got up, took the child, left for Egypt**, and **stayed** there until God gave further instructions following the **death of Herod**. The completeness of Joseph's obedience described here and in Matthew 1:25 confirms his description as a righteous man in Matthew 1:19.

It is not surprising that in verse 15 Matthew will interpret these actions of God and Joseph as fulfilling Old Testament prophecy. The quotation in verse 15 derives from Hosea 11:1: **Out of Egypt I called my son**. The context of Hosea 11:1 clearly portrays Israel as God's **son** who is **called out of Egypt** through the Exodus. This quotation reveals profound theological understanding of Jesus and His role.

Through the quotation, Matthew identifies Jesus and Israel. The early church commonly taught that Jesus represented all Israel and accomplished through His obedience what Israel failed to do through her disobedience.

For this reason several New Testament writers, including Matthew, saw promises made originally to Israel as finding their fullest meaning in view of Jesus. The quotation also introduces the idea of the Exodus and of Jesus as a "new Moses" who will lead God's people out of bondage. This Moses motif will reappear in several places in Matthew's gospel.

In verses 16–18 the scene changes back to Bethlehem and Judea. These verses confirm the wisdom of the flight to Egypt. They describe the rage of **Herod** when he discovered that the **Magi** had **outwitted** him when they returned to their own country without informing him of Jesus' location. In a response all too typical of him, Herod ordered the slaughter of **all the boys in Bethlehem and its vicinity who were two years old and under**.

That this fact is not mentioned in secular history is no reason to doubt the accuracy of Matthew's account. Such savagery was only too typical of Herod. Second, it reinforces the Moses motif already noted. Exodus 1–2 describes the rescue of Moses when Pharaoh ordered the death of all the male children born to the Hebrews in Egypt. Matthew 2 describes the rescue of Jesus when Herod ordered the death of all the boys in the vicinity of Bethlehem. Third, tragic as these deaths were, scholars are correct in noting that Bethlehem did not have a large population, and it is likely that less than twenty babies were victimized by this slaughter. Many parts of the world experience the death of far more babies through genocide, starvation, disease, abortion, and other tragedies that are hardly noted and rarely lamented outside the families affected.

Matthew sadly notes in verse 18 that the slaughter of the innocents fulfilled a Scripture text. Careful observation shows that Matthew

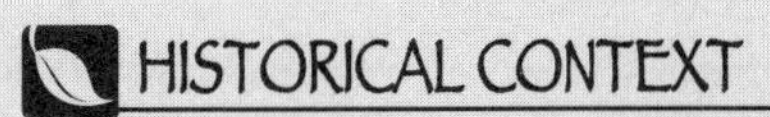

HISTORICAL CONTEXT

HEROD

Herod's violence was well known in the ancient world. In addition to all the members of his own family that he assassinated, *The Assumption of Moses* reported that Herod killed the old and the young indiscriminately. That non-canonical book compared Herod to Pharaoh as a killer of children. Josephus, the first-century Jewish historian, reported that Herod had a number of Jewish noblemen arrested as the time of his death drew near. Herod ordered these Jewish leaders to be executed as soon as he died, hoping to ensure a wave of grief across the country at his death. However, when Herod died, the noblemen were released, and a double celebration took place.

does not say this killing took place *in order* that Scripture be fulfilled. He did not see the death of the boys as an expression of the will of God. However, once Herod accomplished the terrible deed, the lament of Jeremiah 31:15 was filled with fuller meaning. The citation from Jeremiah speaks of Rachel weeping. Genesis 35:19 describes Rachel has having died near Bethlehem. In the context of Jeremiah, Rachel weeps for her children—the Israelites—who were being killed or carried away into captivity by the Babylonians. But, Jeremiah 31:15 is a single verse of lament. The verses before and after speak of joy and hope. The promise that God will bring His—and Rachel's—children back to their own land appears in Jeremiah 31:17. A reader of Matthew who knew the Old Testament well would have heard both the despair and the hope in the quotation from Jeremiah 31:15.

The final paragraph of Matthew 2 narrates Jesus' return to Judea and the holy family settling in Nazareth. Verse 19 once again describes this journey as initiated by **an angel of the Lord** appearing **in a dream to Joseph**. Thus the return and home in Nazareth is not the result of Joseph's wisdom or insight; it is the result of God's clear direction. Again, verse 21 repeats the verbs of instruction given in verse 20, highlighting the theme of Joseph's obedience.

Upon arriving in Israel, Joseph discovered that **Archelaus was reigning in Judea in place of . . . Herod** (Matt. 2:22). After Herod's death in 4 B.C., his kingdom was divided among his three sons who managed to survive him. Archelaus was named ethnarch, or ruler of an ethnic group, in Judea and ruled that province surrounding Jerusalem. He was more cruel and violent than his father, but lacked his administrative skills. It is no wonder that Joseph **was afraid** to settle in Judea. The Jewish leaders sent several delegations to Rome, begging for a Roman military ruler to be installed instead of Archelaus. Their wish was finally granted in A.D. 6.

Before that point, Joseph had once again been **warned in a dream**, and he took his family from Judea to **Galilee** and settled there in a **Nazareth** (2:23). Matthew will describe Galilee as Gentile territory in Matthew 4:15, and Nazareth apparently had no or a negative reputation (John 1:46). Thus the escape from Herod and his son took Jesus to Egypt and then to the Gentile territory of Galilee. The one whom Magi worshipped will grow up unknown in a place unrecognized by the movers and shakers of that time. But the clear demonstrations of God's protection over Jesus through His earliest years made it clear to Matthew's readers that the story of Jesus would not end in Nazareth.

Matthew also explains the destination of **Nazareth** as the fulfillment of Scripture in verse 23. The obscurity of Nazareth is matched by the uncertainty of the quotation **He will be called a Nazarene.** There is no text from the Old Testament that contains these words. Matthew attributes the quotation to **the prophets**. The use of the plural suggests that Matthew didn't know a precise text or that he was drawing on concepts—rather than exact words—found in several prophetic texts. Some scholars suggest a connection between **Nazarene** and Nazirite. It is more likely that Matthew was almost remembering a word play between the words **Nazarene** and branch (*nezer* in Hebrew) found in Isaiah 11:1 and 60:21. Regardless of the explanation, Matthew is sure that Jesus fulfills all the hopes of Scripture. And he is right.

3

JOHN THE BAPTIST AND THE BAPTISM OF JESUS

Matthew 3:1–17

Matthew 3 begins almost thirty years after Matthew 2 ends. The scene shifts from Nazareth in Galilee to the wilderness of Judea as John the Baptist moves to center stage. Matthew 3:1–4:11 describe the preparation for Jesus' ministry and are set in Judea. In 4:12–25, the scene moves back to Galilee and Matthew presents the beginning of Jesus' ministry.

1. THE MINISTRY AND MESSAGE OF JOHN THE BAPTIST 3:1–12

Matthew introduces John the Baptist with a very general phrase: **In those days** (3:1). This does not mean Matthew was unaware that almost thirty years had passed since Jesus arrived in Nazareth. Rather, the phrase shows that the birth of Jesus and the beginning of John the Baptist's ministry are part of the same period of salvation history. The phrase **in those days** appears in the prophets to describe the time of God's coming intervention, the so-called last days, the days of the Messiah (see Joel 3:1 in context). With these words, Matthew tells us the long-hoped-for Messiah is on the doorstep.

John the Baptist came, preaching. The Greek word for **preaching** referred to public proclamation. The content will be given in the following verses, but it is important to recognize that John's message was not a private matter nor limited to a small circle of insiders. It was public proclamation taking place **in the Desert of Judea**, east of Jerusalem and west of the lower Jordan Valley and the Dead Sea. Though hot, dry, and sparsely populated, there was considerable travel around the edges of the desert. John's ministry would likely have been near Jericho along the banks of the Jordan River, where there would have been plenty of traffic.

Verse 2 states that John's message was, **Repent, for the kingdom of heaven is near.** The word **repent** had an important history in the Old Testament. In Hebrew it means *to turn around.* The prophets used the word to describe the radical change of life that total obedience to God demanded.

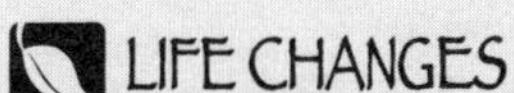

LIFE CHANGES

REPENTANCE

The biblical concept of repentance is sometimes confused with confession in the modern, evangelical church. However, the New Testament was under no such delusion. Repentance is not just saying you are sorry for your sins. It is the hard work of changing the direction and patterns of your life. Repentance is not feeling better because you got something off your chest; it is embarking on a new direction in life.

In the centuries between the Old and New Testaments, Jewish religious leaders emphasized the importance of repentance as a condition for the coming of the Messiah.

John also announced that **the kingdom of heaven is near.** Almost all New Testament scholars believe that Matthew's expression of **the kingdom of heaven** is equivalent in meaning to the phrase *the kingdom of God* found in the other Gospels. It is probable that Matthew's Jewish background contributed to his choice of the phrase kingdom of heaven in place of kingdom of God. Many Jews were reluctant to pronounce the name of God, and heaven was one of the substitutes they used (see Matt. 5:34).

The word **Kingdom** described a relationship rather than a territory in Jewish usage. That is, the kingdom of God or heaven is the sovereign rule of God in the world. The Kingdom is where God's will is done completely (see Matt. 6:9–10). The kingdom of God or heaven was one of several synonyms for the age of the Messiah or the coming age of the Spirit eagerly anticipated by Jews of Jesus' time. John's pronouncement would have been heard as a call to prepare for the arrival of the Messiah.

In Matthew's gospel, it is not surprising that verse 3 describes John the Baptist's ministry as the fulfillment of Scripture. In fact, all four of the Gospels quote from Isaiah 40:3 to explain the significance of John the Baptist. Matthew quotes from the Greek Old Testament, which spoke of the **voice** of a person crying out in the **desert** for a **way** to be prepared for the Lord. That translation fits Matthew's description of John's ministry being in the desert. Though Matthew does not mention it here, clearly he saw John the Baptist as one who prepared **the way** for Jesus **the Lord.**

Verse 4 describes John the Baptist's **clothes** as **made of camel's hair** and his diet as consisting of **locusts and wild honey**. These details show the similarity of John the Baptist to Elijah, whose clothing is described in a very similar way in 2 Kings 1:8. From Malachi 4:5, Judaism had developed an expectation that Elijah would return as a forerunner of the Messiah. This picture of John the Baptist would present him as Elijah the forerunner. Matthew will affirm this in Matthew 11:14.

John's ministry had a large response. Verse 5 notes that **Jerusalem and all Judea and the whole region of the Jordan** went out to hear the message. Verse 6 indicates this large group confessed **their sins** and **were baptized by** John. According to verse 7, among the visitors were **Pharisees and Sadducees**, representatives of the two most powerful religious groups in Judaism at that time. Matthew does not say that they came to be baptized, which would indicate repentance on their part. Rather, they came to see what John the Baptist was doing. Their suspicion of him was matched by his suspicion of them.

John's message to the Pharisees and Sadducees was one of judgment. To call the most influential religious leaders of the time a **brood of vipers**—the offspring of snakes—was a direct attack. He challenged them to demonstrate actions **in keeping with repentance**. This was a call for them to turn from their regular religious activities to a genuine relationship of complete obedience to God. The call to **produce fruit** is a summons to right actions rather than just saying the right words. The lack of integrity between right words and right actions is a theme throughout Matthew's gospel.

His demand that they not presume to claim **Abraham as** their **father** was a direct challenge to their reliance on their spiritual and national heritage (3:9). Obviously, the **Pharisees and Sadducees** had said, "We don't need to repent and be baptized. We are the chosen people of God." John replied that God could **raise up children for Abraham** from the stones (3:10).

Both verses 10 and 12 speak of judgment using the metaphor of **fire**. John announced that God was ready to unleash a purging process that would rid His people of everything worthless and evil. Though the Pharisees and Sadducees may have refused to repent, John's message was still one of good news for the people. The coming judgment would end with a purified people fit for the coming of the Messiah.

2. THE BAPTISM OF JESUS 3:13–17

In contrast to the **Pharisees and Sadducees**, who needed to be baptized but refused to repent, **Jesus came . . . to the Jordan to be baptized by John** (3:13). The baptism of **Jesus** quickly became a theological problem for early Christianity. John's baptism was a baptism of repentance and confession of sins. From some of the earliest documents written by Christians, we find the affirmation of the sinlessness of Jesus (2 Cor. 5:21; Heb. 4:15). A sinless Jesus being baptized seem contradictory. If He was sinless, there would have been no need for Him to submit to a baptism of repentance.

Though Mark's gospel does not seem concerned with this issue, the other Gospels are; and Matthew confronts it most directly. In verse 14 **John tried** to avoid baptizing Jesus by suggesting that he needed to **be baptized by** Jesus. Jesus' reply in verse 15 is Matthew's answer to the question of why Jesus was baptized: **it is proper for us to do this to fulfill all righteousness.**

In Jewish thought, righteousness was conduct that pleased God or expressed God's will. Most simply, Jesus' answer is that John should baptize Him because it was God's will. Matthew does not answer the question of why that was God's will. Perhaps more important is the contrast between Jesus' willingness to be baptized when He did not need to be and the refusal of the Pharisees and Sadducees to be baptized when they needed to repent.

When **Jesus was baptized, he** came **up out of the water, . . . heaven was opened, and . . . the Spirit of God** descended **like a dove on him** (3:16). The descent of the Spirit is important for several reasons.

First, in Jesus' ministry—and for Matthew's Jewish audience—an outpouring of the Holy Spirit was one of the events that would accompany the arrival of the Messiah. Matthew relates this part of Jesus' baptism to confirm His role as Messiah.

Second, in Jewish thought, a major role of the Spirit was to inspire prophecy. The descent of the Spirit on Jesus marked Him as a prophet. Though this is not a sufficient title, it is a true title for Jesus.

Third, the descent of the Spirit on Jesus marked the empowerment of Jesus for ministry. It was an important part of His preparation for the ministry that lay ahead.

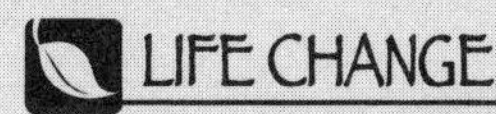

LIFE CHANGE

SUBMISSION TO GOD'S WILL

Jesus' humility in obeying God and identifying with sinful people who needed to be baptized is an important lesson for us. Personal status or religious standing never provides sufficient reason to disobey God or to distance ourselves from the people He loves. Neither should we be surprised that God's will for us might call on us to be with sinful people and to participate in the processes that bring healing and salvation to them. That was God's will for Jesus when He asked His Son to be baptized.

Further, by means of the descent of the Spirit, Jesus became a bearer of the Spirit, which would allow Him to impart the Holy Spirit on His followers, as Luke and John will point out.

The **voice from heaven** joins together two brief lines of Old Testament Scripture (3:17). **This is my Son** paraphrases Psalm 2:7, which reads, "You are my Son." The themes of messiahship, sonship, and kingship permeate the second psalm. These words **from heaven** would have communicated to Matthew's audience that Jesus was Messiah, Son of God, and the true King of Israel.

The final words of the **voice from heaven** are **whom I love; with him I am well pleased.** These words echo Isaiah 42:1, the verse that begins the Servant Songs of Isaiah. These words would have communicated to Jesus the servant role that ministry would require. The voice from heaven prepared Jesus for ministry by identifying key roles that He would fulfill through His ministry.

4

TEMPTATION AND THE BEGINNING OF JESUS' MINISTRY

Matthew 4:1–25

M atthew's account of the preparation of Jesus for ministry—that began with John the Baptist and Jesus' baptism, then continues with the temptation of Jesus—continues with a description of the actual beginning of Jesus' ministry.

1. THE TEMPTATION OF JESUS 4:1–11

One might think that the commissioning words from heaven, the descent of the Holy Spirit upon Jesus, and His obedient submission to God's will in baptism would have sufficiently prepared Him for the beginning of His ministry. However, Matthew records a significant experience of temptation following the baptism of Jesus. Though we may not like it, testing is an important part of preparation for service.

The identity of Jesus has been a major concern of Matthew. Jesus as Messiah and as Son of God have been prominent themes. The baptism affirmed that Jesus was God's Son. The temptation will test both His awareness that He is God's Son and His understanding of being the Messiah.

Jesus was led by the Spirit into the temptation experience (4:1). The experience of the Spirit descending upon Jesus was prominent in His baptism. Being led by the Spirit results in complete submission to God's will. Thus the temptation offers the opportunity for obedience as much as Jesus' baptism had. The Spirit's leading Jesus **into the desert** would have suggested the Exodus and the new Moses motif. Jewish discussion about the Exodus in Jesus' time emphasized the work of the Holy Spirit. The reference in verse 2 to **fasting forty days and forty nights** echoes the wording of Exodus 34:28 and Deuteronomy 9:9, describing Moses' stay on Mount Sinai while receiving the Law. Matthew is presenting Jesus as a new Moses.

The word **tempted** could also be translated *tested*. Some try to distinguish between the concepts of temptation, in which one is incited to do evil, and testing, in which one has the opportunity to obey. However, even when the **devil** incites us to do evil, we still face the choice of obedience or disobedience. While one can distinguish between the purposes of temptation and of testing, the difference in human experience is not significant.

The first temptation challenged Jesus to change **stones** into loaves of **bread if** He was **the Son of God** (Matt. 4:3). The temptation questions Jesus' divine sonship. It also offers a comparison between Jesus as Son and the people of Israel as God's son. This connection was first made in Matthew 2:15, which applied Hosea 11:1—"Out of Egypt I called my son,"—to Jesus. Like Israel, Jesus was in the desert facing hunger. Israel complained and rebelled against God (Ex. 16:2–3). Jesus, as God's Son and the new Israel, trusted God and refused to demand a miracle. In fact, Jesus' response to the devil in verse 4 quotes from Deuteronomy 8:3: **Man does not live on bread alone, but on every word that comes from the mouth of God.** Rather than demanding **bread**, Jesus was willing to wait for a creative word from God His Father. The genuineness of His sonship passed the first test.

The first temptation also tested Jesus' understanding of His messiahship. Some Jewish teachers believed that when the Messiah came, He would repeat the miracle of the manna. Had Jesus turned thousands of small stones in the Judean desert into bread, the result would have been a new miracle of the manna. People would have flocked to follow Him, but the servant understanding of messiahship revealed at His baptism would have been denied.

In the second temptation, the **devil took** Jesus to Jerusalem to **stand on the highest point of the temple** (Matt. 4:5) and tempted him to **throw** himself **down**. Jumping from the highest point of the Temple would have won instant Messianic acclaim for Jesus. However, this also tested Jesus' sense of divine sonship. Yielding would have challenged God to rescue Jesus. According to verse 6, the **devil** quoted Psalm 91:11–12, suggesting that all Jesus needed to do was to claim the biblical promise that **angels** would keep God's Son from striking His **foot against a stone**. Surely, a faithful Father would fulfill His promise.

But such a challenge to God is the very opposite of an authentic father-son relationship. The mutual trust that comes from knowing each other's heart and mind was completely lacking in the scenario proposed by the devil. Jesus responded in verse 7 by quoting Deuteronomy 6:16, where God himself told Israel they were **not** to **put** him **to the test**. Such challenges are the opposite of trust.

The third temptation also tested Jesus' commitment to being a servant-Messiah. The goal of the Messiah was to become king of **all the kingdoms of the world** (Matt. 4:8). The **devil** offered Jesus the ultimate goal of the Messiah without having to pay the price of being a suffering servant. The price demanded by the **devil** for **all the kingdoms of the world** was to **bow down and worship** him (4:9). The temptation also tested Jesus' sense of divine sonship. Israel, as God's children, had failed to protect the rich gift of monotheism God had given them. However, Jesus, as the New Israel, God's Son, resisted the lure of idolatry and chose to **worship the Lord**, His Father, **only**. His reply (4:10) to the devil quotes Deuteronomy 6:18.

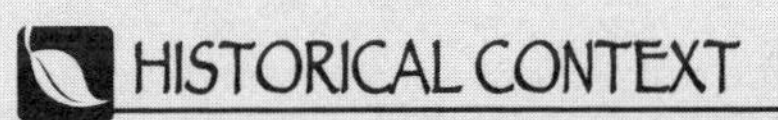

The **highest point of the temple** refers to the southeast corner of the great retaining wall that supported the whole Temple complex on top of ancient Mount Moriah. It towered almost two hundred feet above the Kidron Valley below. The Spring of Gihon would have been almost directly below this point. Because the Spring of Gihon was the major water supply in ancient Jerusalem, there would have been a number of people there at almost any time of the day. They would have provided a natural audience for the leap the devil was trying to entice Jesus to take.

The temptation account ends with the comment in Matthew 4:11 that **angels came and attended him.** Because Jesus did not demand anything from God, His Father was gracious to give Him everything He needed. The ministry of the angels demonstrates this grace.

Several conclusions stand out in Matthew's account of Jesus' temptation. He triumphed over the devil and demonstrated the true nature of His divine sonship. In every case, He faced a temptation parallel to a test experienced by Israel in the desert. Israel failed. Jesus trusted, obeyed, and succeeded. In every case, He responded to temptation through the support of Scripture. This enabled Him to understand and embrace a servant understanding of His messiahship.

Jesus' two resources in His temptation are instructive for us. He was led by the Spirit and He answered every temptation with a quotation from Scripture. Often we are tempted to think that the fiery trial of temptation is evidence that we are no longer being led by the Holy Spirit. That need not be the case. The Holy Spirit leads us in paths of testing because we cannot experience victory without the possibility of defeat. It is also the Holy Spirit who will bring to mind the appropriate resources of Scripture to help us overcome temptation— if we have placed those resources in our minds so the Spirit can remind us of them.

2. THE BEGINNING OF JESUS' MINISTRY 4:12–25

Matthew's introduction to Jesus' ministry has three sections: establishing Galilee as the center of that ministry in 4:12–17; calling the first disciples in 4:18–22; and a summary of Jesus' ministry in 4:23–25.

The imprisonment of **John** the Baptist signaled the beginning of **Jesus'** ministry. According to verses 12–13, **Jesus returned** from Judea **to Galilee** and then moved from **Nazareth** to **Capernaum,** which was to become the headquarters for His ministry. Capernaum was a strategic location on the northwest shore of the Sea of Galilee and near the main road from Damascus. Matthew describes this move to Capernaum as the fulfillment of Isaiah 9:1–2 (Matt. 4:14). This is the seventh event in his first four chapters that he describes as fulfilling Scripture.

The quotation in verses 15–16 comes from Isaiah 9:1–2 and identifies Jesus as the **great light** shining on **the people living in darkness.** Galilee did not have a good reputation among the most religious Jews living in Jerusalem. Galilee included the ancient Israelite tribal territories of **Zebulun and Naphtali.** These territories had been the northernmost outposts of Israel and most influenced by the Baal worship of Phoenicia. Frequently foreign invaders from Syria and Assyria occupied these territories, leaving their pagan influence. In the eighth century B.C., Isaiah had called this area **Galilee of the Gentiles.**

Matthew has already introduced the first worshippers of Jesus as Gentile Magi. Now Jesus begins His ministry bringing the **light** of God to **Galilee of the Gentiles.** No matter how Jewish Jesus was—nor how natural it should be for Jews to follow Him—Matthew insists that He welcomes Gentiles.

Verse 17 marks the beginning of Jesus' preaching ministry with a summary quotation of His message. Those opening words of **Jesus** are identical to John the Baptist's first words: **Repent, for the kingdom of heaven is near.** The importance of repentance and the meaning of the kingdom noted earlier in the comments on Matthew 3:2, also pertain here. Further, by this repetition, Matthew joins together God's message in the very Jewish context of John the Baptist's ministry to Pharisees and Sadducees with Jesus' message beginning His ministry in Galilee of the Gentiles. The first gospel declares to Jews and Jewish believers in Jesus, "Jesus, the Messiah, the fulfillment of Jewish hopes, has opened the door of the gospel to the Gentiles." Further, the good news and the demands of the gospel are the same for Jews and Gentiles alike.

That Jesus' first words are identical to John the Baptist's first words demonstrates John as a genuine forerunner of Jesus the Messiah. The emphasis on repentance and on the Kingdom also sets the stage for understanding the ministry of Jesus that Matthew is about to unfold: a call to repentance. It will invite us into the Kingdom.

The calling of the first four disciples in verses 18–22 then illustrates the appropriate response to Jesus' call to repentance and to the Kingdom. The abruptness of Jesus' demand on **Simon called Peter and his**

brother Andrew and **James son of Zebedee and his brother John** is difficult for many modern people. A previous generation of commentaries concluded that Jesus must have built relationship with these four through prior meetings and ministry. While that may have been true historically, this abrupt call to discipleship represents the radical demand of the kingdom of God: to let go of all human sources of security and all human aspirations and to embrace wholehearted obedience to God. Since repentance is a change of direction, the first four disciples powerfully demonstrate repentance. They turned **immediately** from their own business—fishing for money—to the business of the Kingdom, being **fishers of men.**

Jesus' first words to them, **Come, follow me,** characterize the call to discipleship (4:19). The following words, **I will make you fishers of men**, immediately turn their attention from the demand Jesus makes on them to the results that God desires in the lives of others. For Matthew, Jesus introduces the task of mission at the same time He creates the fellowship of the church. There can be no mistaking the centrality of mission for Jesus.

Matthew 4:23–25 presents a summary and overview of Jesus' ministry. Rather than describing specific events, these verses give a general statement of the patterns that will be described in more detail in the remainder of the Gospel.

Verse 23 identifies the primary location of Jesus' ministry as **Galilee.** This is no surprise, based on verses 12–16. It also identifies the three main activities that will constitute Jesus' ministry: **teaching . . . , preaching . . . , and healing**. Some scholars have suggested that Matthew organizes each of the major sections of this Gospel around one of these three central ministry activities. However, it is not always clear whether some sections are intended to represent teaching or preaching. What is clear is that Matthew will frequently hark back to this basic description of Jesus' ministry. Not only are these three activities central for Jesus, they also provide direction for His followers. From Matthew's perspective, ministry in the name of Jesus is **teaching . . . , preaching the good news of the kingdom, and healing every disease and sickness among the people.**

The impact of that three-pronged ministry was **large crowds** coming to Jesus from all the surrounding Jewish and Gentile territories (4:25). The response of the crowds was to follow Jesus. Their coming together creates the audience for Matthew's first large block of teaching material by Jesus, the Sermon on the Mount.

Part Two

The Authority of Jesus in Word and Deed

MATTHEW 5:1–9:38

The first major section of Matthew's gospel consists of a block of teaching in chapters 5 through 7 and a narrative collection of miracles stories in chapters 8 and 9. A common theme uniting the two parts is the authority of Jesus.

The first, longest, and best-known block of teaching material, the Sermon on the Mount, appears in chapters 5–7. Thousands of books and articles have been written about it. Despite the extensive study, there is no agreement about the outline or the purpose of the sermon. Clearly Matthew presented the sermon as a summary of Jesus' teaching about the kingdom of God. Its strategic placement immediately following Matthew 4:17 and 23–25, as well as the content of the sermon, demonstrate this. The concluding narrative frame indicates that the sermon establishes Jesus' authority as a teacher. Thus Matthew 5:1–7:29 presents Jesus' authoritative teaching in the Sermon on the Mount.

Following the large collection of teachings of Jesus in chapters 5–7, Matthew returns to a narrative of Jesus' ministry. However, the authority of Jesus remains central to Matthew's thought. This narrative, found in Matthew 8:1–9:38, presents Jesus' authoritative actions in ushering in the Kingdom.

5

THE BEATITUDES AND JESUS' TEACHING ON THE OLD TESTAMENT

Matthew 5:1–48

Matthew frames the Sermon with a narrative introduction in 5:1–2 and a narrative conclusion in 7:28–8:1. The sermon itself begins with blessings in 5:3–12 and ends with warnings in 7:13–27. Three major sections can be identified between the blessings and the warnings: Jesus' teaching on the Law in 5:17–48; Jesus' teaching on righteous devotion in 6:1–18; and Jesus' teaching on relationships with money, people, and God in 6:19–7:12.

1. THE NARRATIVE INTRODUCTION TO THE SERMON ON THE MOUNT 5:1–2

Matthew 5:1–2 provides the initial framework for the sermon. First, Jesus delivers the sermon **on a mountainside**. This contrasts with Luke 6:17, where Jesus teaches from "a level place." For Matthew, the *mountain* is the place of divine revelation. Like Moses who brought the Law from Mount Sinai, Jesus teaches from the mountainside. The statement that Jesus **sat down** also reflects a Mosaic motif. Sitting was the position for rabbis when they gave official teaching about the Law. Their seat was called the seat of Moses. To say that Jesus sat down claims both His authority to give genuine teaching from God and His connection to Moses.

A second important insight arises from the Greek form of the verb **teach** in verse 2. The verb tense suggests that Matthew did not regard the sermon as only a single event in Jesus' life. Rather, it presented the pattern of Jesus' typical teachings. Matthew has collected and organized the teachings Jesus customarily gave. This is consistent with observation of Luke's gospel. Much of the material in Matthew 5–7 can be found scattered throughout Luke. The Sermon on the Mount is a summary of the essential teachings of Jesus.

A third observation relates to the audience for the sermon. Verse 1 states that when Jesus **saw the crowds**, He went to the mountain. Then **his disciples came to him**, and He taught them. Should we understand the audience of the sermon to be the crowds or the disciples? This is not simply a historical question. Does the sermon teach a universal ethic applying to everyone (the crowds), or does it apply only to the devoted followers of Jesus (His disciples)? This question has been debated often through history.

2. THE BEATITUDES: THE GRACE OF THE KINGDOM 5:3–12

Other than the Lord's Prayer, the Beatitudes are the best known and most loved material in the sermon. But there has been significant disagreement about what **blessed** means. Often the Beatitudes have been viewed as the demands of the Kingdom. If one demonstrates poverty of spirit or meekness, the blessing will be admission into the Kingdom. Those who fall short of those virtues would be excluded from the Kingdom. It is more natural to understand the Beatitudes as effective words of grace. This view builds on the biblical understanding that words are effective causes of that of which they speak. To speak a blessing is to begin to put a blessing into effect. In this view when Jesus says, **Blessed are those who mourn, for they will be comforted**, the very words begin the comforting process. The word translated **blessed** is an exclamation of joy. It means, *Oh, the good fortune of . . .* or *Oh, how happy*. The very meaning of blessed suggests good news.

Another way of understanding the Beatitudes as effective words is to see them answering the question, "What is the Kingdom of God like?" The Beatitudes answer that the Kingdom is where the poor in spirit, the meek, the merciful, and the pure in heart are blessed. That immediately tells us that the Kingdom is very different from the kind of human society to which we are accustomed. It also brings us to see the Beatitudes as describing the characteristics we would like to experience in the Kingdom. Perhaps rather than describing the Beatitudes as Kingdom requirements, we could describe them as effective words of grace that portray the aspirations we have for life in the Kingdom.

Matthew's first beatitude, in verse 3, is **Blessed are the poor in spirit**. The first beatitude in Luke 6:20 blesses simply the poor. What do Matthew's words **in spirit** mean? Some see these words as evidence that Matthew spiritualizes the Beatitudes, turning them from economic issues to spiritual needs. While this may be true in part, it is not likely that Jesus disregards the extreme economic poverty of His time.

Extreme poverty devastates the human spirit as much as it decimates the pocketbook. Poverty destroys hope, as much now as in Jesus' time. Further, the word **poor** already had a long history of being used to describe those who in their financial poverty put all their faith and hope in God. The **poor in spirit** would be those whose poverty had removed all human hope and left them hoping that God would intervene on their behalf. The poor are promised that **the kingdom of heaven** (Matt. 5:3) comes to them.

Those who spiritualize the Beatitudes understand **those who mourn** (5:4) as those who grieve over their sins. This may be part of Matthew's intent, but its natural meaning is those who mourn the loss of loved ones and their dearest possessions. The good news for these grief-stricken people is that **they will be comforted**. The passive voice—will *be* comforted—is often used in the New Testament to speak of God without mentioning the divine name. Thus Jesus' good news is that God himself will comfort those who mourn.

The blessing of **the meek** (5:5) is easily misunderstood in contemporary society. Meekness did not mean weakness in the biblical world. The Septuagint version of the Old Testament describes Moses as a meek man in Numbers 12:3. Moses was not weak. Rather, meekness portrays the person who has learned to trust God. The word was often used in the Old Testament as a synonym for the poor. This third beatitude adapts Psalm 37:11 in the promise that the meek **will inherit the earth**. This suggests that God rewards the faithfulness of those who trust in Him rather than in themselves by fulfilling the ancient promises He made to His people.

The fourth beatitude blesses **those who hunger and thirst for righteousness** (Matt. 5:6). Matthew may spiritualize the words of Jesus here. Luke 6:21 blesses those who **hunger now**. Righteousness is an important term for Matthew. It speaks of right relationships with God and with other people. The word **thirst** intensifies the desire for righteousness that Jesus blesses. The promise is that these who intensely hunger for righteousness **will be filled**. The verb means being satisfied so that the hunger pangs disappear. Further, the passive voice indicates that God himself will satisfy this deep desire for righteousness.

Jesus next blesses **the merciful** (Matt. 5:7). Mercy is an important theme for Matthew. Twice (9:13; 12:7) he quotes Hosea 6:6: **I desire mercy, not sacrifice**. Mercy encompasses the ideas of both compassion and forgiveness. The promised blessing to the merciful is **mercy** from God. The passive voice again identifies God as the giver of mercy to those who are merciful.

The following beatitude blesses **the pure in heart** (Matt. 5:8). Psalm 24:3–4 describes a pure heart as the requirement for standing in God's holy presence. The Old Testament spoke often of ritual or cultic purity. To describe purity as a matter of the heart means that it deals with the intentions or the will of a person. The pure in heart are those who motives or intentions are unmixed. The promise of these people is that **they will see God**. Exodus 33:11 states, "The LORD would speak to Moses face to face, as a man speaks with his friend." Thus seeing God describes intimate relationship with Him.

The seventh beatitude blesses **the peacemakers** (Matt. 5:9). The blessing is not for peace-lovers, but for those who make peace or do the things that create peace. The Hebrew word for peace is *shalom*, which means total well-being rather than absence of conflict. This beatitude blesses those who do the work of bringing well-being or good into others' lives. The blessing is that the peacemakers **will be called sons**

of God. Again the passive voice of the verb suggests that God will call peacemakers His sons. Hebrew often used the phrase *son of* in an adjectival way. This means people who are called sons of God are godly people.

The eighth beatitude climaxes the promises of grace to suffering and oppressed people by blessing **those who are persecuted** (5:10). Matthew's interest in **righteousness** reappears in this beatitude as the reason for persecution. The promise echoes that of verse 3 by promising the persecuted the **kingdom of heaven**. Not only does the repetition of this promise mark the end of a set of beatitudes, all eight of the blessings in verses 3–10 are expressed in the third person: "blessed are those who . . ." The final beatitude repeats the concept of persecution but is expressed in second-person form: **Blessed are you . . .** While persecution and insults are not reasons most people rejoice, Matthew notes that those who suffer such persecution share the treatment of **the prophets who were before you** (5:12). The persecution is not the good news. The sharing of the ministry and fate of the prophets is the good news.

3. DISCIPLES AS SALT AND LIGHT IN THE KINGDOM 5:13–16

Verses 13–16 shift from the blessings of the Kingdom to the responsibilities of the Kingdom. Jesus uses two metaphors to describe believers as kingdom people. The metaphors of salt and light place disciples against the world rather than portraying them as part of the world.

Jesus does not explain His metaphor, **you are the salt of the earth** (5:13). Salt had at least three uses in the ancient world: it purified, preserved, and provided taste. Salt was often used to purify wounds because it was the closest agent to a disinfectant in ancient Palestine. Gangrene often set in when wounds were not cleansed with salt. Salt was also a preservative in an era before refrigeration. The use of salt to provide taste is still one of its functions in our society. It is important to notice that this teaching on salt follows the Beatitudes on persecution. Though the world might persecute His followers, Jesus instructs us to make the world a better place.

Jesus' teaching that His followers are to be **the light of the world** (5:14) makes a similar point. This metaphor views the world in terms of darkness, a common symbol for danger, fear, and evil. As light, disciples are to change the world by making it safe, secure, and good. While it is possible for the action of salt to be invisible, there is no such possibility for light. The Christian witness is to be purposeful and visible. That is the point of sharpening the metaphor to describe Christ's followers as a **lamp** (5:15) that has been **put on** a **stand.** Its purpose is to **give light to everyone**.

The theme of visibility extends to verse 16 as Jesus commands His followers to **let** their **light shine before men**. The Christian calling to be salt can be done without attention, but light will be noticed. However, the purpose of being light in the world is not to bring attention to ourselves, but to bring **praise** to our **Father in heaven**. Believers whose lives demonstrate the blessings of the Beatitudes will be salt and light in the world, and the result will be glory given to God by the world.

4. THE OLD TESTAMENT IN THE KINGDOM 5:17–48

The call to disciples to be salt and light in the world implies that Jesus' followers will be different than the world. In part, that difference is a difference in ethics. In the Jewish context in which Jesus and Matthew taught, one's ethics were the product of one's interpretation of the Law of the Old Testament. Matthew 5:17–20 presents a general introduction to Jesus' teaching on the Old Testament. Then Jesus gives six examples, sometimes called the Great Antitheses, of how His general teaching is applied in specific ethical issues.

JESUS AND THE OLD TESTAMENT 5:17–20

The relationship of Jesus and the Old Testament is a major concern for Matthew. His frequent quotations from the Old Testament, as well as motifs drawn from Moses and the Exodus, demonstrate this. Matthew is the only Gospel writer to include Jesus' statement that He had not **come to abolish the Law or the Prophets; . . . but to fulfill them** (5:17).

By speaking of both the Law and the Prophets, Jesus speaks of the Old Testament as a whole. The Jewish canon of Scripture had three major sections: the Law, the Prophets, and the Writings. Though modern Christians often see the Law and the Prophets as having very different functions, Jesus had a unified way of understanding them. This should warn us against embracing the Prophets and rejecting the Law. Second, Jesus uses the verb **fulfill** to describe His effect on both the Law and the Prophets. This tells us that He understood Scripture as the Word of God, but it was a word that could be filled with greater meaning. It is important to recognize that He saw himself fulfilling both the Law and the Prophets.

It is possible that the **commandments** in verse 19 refer to Jesus' teachings in this section of the sermon rather than to the Old Testament Law. However, in light of verses 17–18, it is doubtful that Jesus or Matthew

HISTORICAL CONTEXT

YODH

The **smallest letter** (5:18) of the Hebrew alphabet was *yodh*, which was written much like an apostrophe. It is easy to miss a *yodh* when reading a handwritten Hebrew manuscript. The least stroke of a pen (the "tittle" of the King James Version) was a tiny projection of the vertical line of a letter extending beyond the intersection with a horizontal stroke. This *horn*, as it was sometimes called, was the only distinction between two otherwise identical letters. Jesus' statement that heaven and earth will disappear before these tiniest parts of the Law strongly affirms the importance of the Old Testament in all its details.

intended later readers to place Jesus' words and the words of the Old Testament in opposition to each other. Both are words from God. The point of verse 19 is that the seriousness—or lack thereof—with which we approach the Word of God will be noted and will become the basis for our evaluation and position in the **kingdom of heaven**.

Jesus calls for His followers to demonstrate a **righteousness** that **surpasses that of the Pharisees and the teachers of the law** (5:20). The examples that follow in Matthew 5:21–6:18 make clear that this superior righteousness is a matter of having the Law written on people's hearts (Jer. 31:33) rather than simply maintaining outward observance. This greater righteousness produces disciples whose hearts for the Word of God match God's purpose in giving His Word.

KEY IDEAS

THE GREAT ANTITHESES

Matthew 5:21–48 contains what are often called the Great Antitheses. Six times some variation of the following pattern introduces a new subject:

> You have heard that it was said to the people long ago
> [Quotation from the Old Testament]
> But I tell you
> [Jesus' teaching on the subject]

These six antitheses contrast the letter of the Old Testament law with Jesus' interpretation of it. His teachings reveal the law of God written on our hearts by addressing the inner motivation of obedience to the commandments.

JESUS AND MURDER 5:21–26

The first illustration of Jesus' approach to the Old Testament comes with prohibition of **murder** (Matt. 5:21). The quotation is derived from the sixth of the Ten Commandments and is found in Exodus 20:13 and Deuteronomy 5:17. Murder is a more accurate translation of the Hebrew word used in the sixth commandment than the more general word *kill*. It describes the intentional taking of another's life, disregarding the truth that the gift of life belongs in God's hands. Jesus then declares that such disregard for the value of another person also appears when one **is angry with his brother** (Matt. 5:22).

Some translations describe this anger against a brother as "without cause." These words are missing in the oldest and best manuscripts of Matthew. They were added by a copyist who wanted to excuse someone. Unfortunately, we always think we have reason to be angry with another. The word **raca** was a contemptuous Aramaic word like *fool*, *idiot*, or *brainless*. It is a synonym of the word **fool** later in verse 22. Calling a person raca, or fool, is not so much a way of expressing anger at another, but disdain. The words illustrate the error of anger, which is that it treats another as someone far less than a person created in the image of God.

Jesus then demonstrates the importance of right relationships with and attitudes toward others. It is more important to **be reconciled to your brother** than it is to **offer your gift** (5:24) **at the altar** (5:23). Worship of God is meaningless as long as we live in broken human relationships. People matter so much to God that He requires that we mend our relationships with them before we come and offer our gift to Him. Right relationships are even more important than defending ourselves. The example of verse 25 describes one being taken **to court**. Jesus advises such a person to make right the relationship immediately while still **with him on the way**. The possibility of vindication in court is less important than reconciliation in relationships.

JESUS AND ADULTERY 5:27–30

Jesus then quotes the seventh of the Ten Commandments (Ex. 20:14; Deut. 5:18), which prohibits **adultery** (Matt. 5:27). His teaching here provides the clearest example of driving home the heart purpose of the Old Testament commandment. To look at another person **lustfully** is to commit **adultery** with that person in one's **heart** (5:28). Some interpreters argue that the Old Testament concerns about adultery were simply issues of the violation of another man's property rights over his wife. However, the Old Testament prophets' descriptions of idolatry—and especially of Baal worship as adultery—reveal a deeper understanding. The underlying assumption is that marriage was a covenant relationship like the covenant relationship between God and Israel. Such a covenant calls for mutual love, fidelity, and valuing.

Adultery is the violation of such covenant love, faithfulness, and valuing. To desire—sexually or otherwise—someone other than one's covenant spouse violates the mutual valuing implied by the covenant itself. Lust and the variety of pornographic entertainments available now—and in biblical times—undermines covenant mutuality. And Jesus makes it clear that the issue is ultimately a heart issue. Verses 29–30 make clear how important this truth is to Jesus. He raises the possibility that one's **right eye** or **right hand** might **cause** one **to sin.** If that were true it would be better to remove the offending body part because it is **better to lose one part of your body than for your whole body to be thrown into hell**. There can be no question of the importance of avoiding sexual sin.

However, Jesus had already taught that adultery exists first in the heart before it is expressed through one's body. Thus there is a very real sense in which one's eye or hand does not cause one to sin. One's heart is the cause of sin. One cannot tear out one's heart, but the evil within a heart can be removed. Jesus' point comes very near to the teaching on circumcision of the heart found in Deuteronomy 10:16; 30:6; and Romans 2:29.

JESUS AND DIVORCE 5:31–32

The third ethical issue raised by Jesus is **divorce** (Matt. 5:31). Matthew will include a fuller presentation of Jesus' teaching on divorce in 19:3–12. It appears here because it is closely associated with the teaching on adultery. The Old Testament text that Jesus quotes is the popular rendition of Deuteronomy 24:1. The passage begins, "If a man marries a woman who becomes displeasing to him because he finds something indecent about her . . ." The rabbis of Jesus' day debated what indecent thing could legitimately cause a wife to be displeasing to her husband. Some suggested such trivial matters as being a poor cook or not being as physically attractive as another woman. Jesus considers **marital unfaithfulness** (Matt. 5:32) the only indecent thing that might justify a divorce.

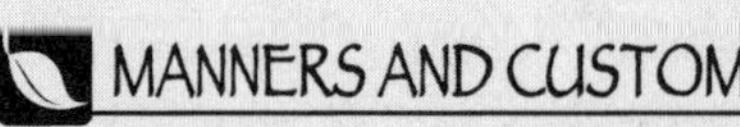

The quotation from Deuteronomy 24:1 states that **anyone who divorces his wife must give her a certificate of divorce**. The **certificate of divorce** was a legal document in which a husband relinquished his rights to the wife he was divorcing. In Jewish society this would allow the woman the possibility of remarriage. Jewish culture was structured in such a way that every woman was legally dependent on some man—a husband, father, or brother. For women whose fathers or brothers would not or could not support them, the only options were remarriage or illicit relationships with other men.

Jesus describes remarriage in terms of adultery. When divorcing a woman put in her a position in which only remarriage or illicit relationships were possible, the man had **caused** the woman **to become an adulteress** (5:32). Further, marrying a **divorced woman** is described as an act of **adultery**. Further details will come in 19:3–12, but it is clear that Jesus saw the marriage relationship as permanent. Judaism of that time expected divorce in response to marital infidelity. Jesus never commands divorce and portrays it as a step toward adultery, which He has clearly condemned in verses 27–30.

JESUS AND OATHS 5:33–37

Jesus next addresses the reliability of a person's word. This section is often more difficult for contemporary Christians to understand. First, the quotation from the Old Testament, **do not break your oath** (5:33), is not an exact quotation from any known passage of the Old Testament. Rather, it appears to be a paraphrase from putting together Leviticus 19:12; Numbers 30:2; and Deuteronomy 23:21–23. In some ways the warning comes close to the ninth commandment, the prohibition of giving false testimony against a neighbor. Second, many modern believers tend to lump together oaths, cursing, and obscene language. This text deals only with making an oath to certify that one is telling the truth. Third, we fail to understand the role of such oaths in the society of Jesus' time.

In that culture, some people felt free to lie unless they had sworn by God's name that they were telling the truth. Most Jews tried to avoid pronouncing God's name, and, as a result, they developed substitute expressions that caused the listener to think of God, but did not require the speaker to pronounce the divine name. Perhaps the most common substitute was the word **heaven** (Matt. 5:34). To swear **by heaven** would cause the listener to think the person was swearing by God's name and thus committed to telling the truth, but in reality, since God's name had not been pronounced, the speaker was able to lie.

Jesus' response is clear and understandable: **Do not swear at all** (5:34). He forbids us to swear by God's name or by any substitute for God's name, whether that substitute be heaven or **earth** (5:35) or **Jerusalem** or one's **head** (5:36). None of these substitutes is acceptable. What is acceptable is telling the truth and being a person of such integrity that no oath is necessary to validate one's word. **Yes** must mean **yes, no** must mean **no** (5:37). Lack of such integrity in our words is not the result of our cleverness but of the work of Satan (**the evil one**).

JESUS AND RETALIATION 5:38–42

The fifth antithesis addresses the subject of retaliation. Jesus quotes a common Old Testament saying: **Eye for eye, and tooth for tooth** (5:38).

These words appear in Exodus 21:24; Leviticus 24:20; and Deuteronomy 19:21. Though most modern people hear these words expressing the right for revenge, in their Old Testament context they served to *limit* the amount of retaliation a person could seek.

In contrast, Jesus instructs His followers to not seek to repay evil with evil. This is the meaning of the phrase **Do not resist an evil person** (Matt. 5:39). The point is not to stand idly by while evil runs rampant. Rather, one should not retaliate in kind to mistreatment (see Rom. 12:17–21). Christ then gives four examples of this new pattern of living. The first instructs us to turn the other cheek to someone who **strikes you on the right cheek**. A blow to the right cheek would be given with the back of the hand. Back-handed slaps were expressions of contempt wounding one's pride more severely than one's cheek. Jesus' instruction is to let the insult go and cheerfully prepare for another.

Suing for a **tunic** or **cloak** (Matt. 5:40) did happen. Amos 2:6 speaks of people being sold into slavery for a pair of sandals for failing to pay their debts. The tunic was an undergarment, and so to sue for it was extremely mean-spirited and stingy. The cloak was an outer garment that doubled as overcoat and blanket at night. Exodus 22:26–27 forbids an Israelite to take a cloak to pay a debt. Jesus taught we should not respond by demanding our rights when someone is mean-spirited to us. During the Roman occupation, troops could demand a local citizen carry a soldier's pack for **one mile** (Matt. 5:41). Jesus tells His followers that when such a demand is made, the pain of the insult can be defused by cheerfully carrying the pack for two miles. The final illustration speaks to the natural human response that resists giving anything away. In contrast followers of Christ will not **turn away** from a person wanting **to borrow** from them (5:42).

JESUS AND LOVE FOR ENEMIES 5:43–48

The final antithesis sharpens the point of the previous paragraph from refraining from retaliation to actual love for an enemy. Jesus quotes from Leviticus 19:18: **love your neighbor** (5:43) and then supplies a popular conclusion from His time—that loving your neighbors implies that you

hate your enemy. No Old Testament text commands hatred for enemies, though Psalm 139:21–22 extols hatred of those who oppose God. In contrast, Jesus commands that we **love** our **enemies and pray for those who persecute** us (Matt. 5:44).

The basis for Jesus' audacious command to love our enemies is that such is God's own nature. Loving our enemies qualifies us to be counted as authentic children of our **Father in heaven** (5:45). The illustrations of God's love for enemies instruct us regarding Jesus' meaning. God's love for enemies is shown by the fact that He grants sunshine to **the evil and the good**. God **sends rain on the righteous and the unrighteous**. In the basic necessities of life, God does not discriminate between those who love Him and those who hate Him. The Greek word used for love is *agape*, which means to seek the best for the other. God gives the good gifts of sun and rain to people regardless of their response to Him.

To refuse such love—to friend and foe alike—is to be like **the tax collectors** who only **love those who love** them (5:46). Tax collectors were usually Jews who profiteered at their countrymen's expense through collecting the taxes for the Romans. They were especially hated and seen as most unethical persons. To **greet only your brothers** was to behave no better than the **pagans** (5:47). Hating your enemies puts you on their level.

Verse 48 concludes both the paragraph on love of enemies and the whole section of the ethical antitheses. The way to demonstrate a righteousness that "surpasses that of the Pharisees and teachers of the law" (5:20) is by being **perfect as** our **heavenly Father is perfect**. Modern readers are sure perfection is impossible. How can we hear these words of Jesus as meaningful to us?

First, most scholars believe that Jesus is paraphrasing the Old Testament command to be holy as God is holy (see Lev. 19:2). Thus the perfection being described in Matthew 5:48 is holiness. Second, as the conclusion of the sixth antithesis, the perfection that is asked for is a perfection of love, which is demonstrated by loving one's enemies. What Jesus asks for is not perfect performance of all God's laws but a heart willing to love those who seem unlovable.

Third, as the conclusion of all six antitheses, the perfection of verse 48 is a heart seeking God's will in all human relationships. The antitheses

LIFE CHANGE

ATTAINING PERFECTION

The biblical word for *perfect* means functional rather than absolute perfection. This implies a perfection that can improve and grow rather than being static. A rosebud may be perfect as a rosebud, but it will achieve another level of perfection as a fully developed and beautiful rose. To be perfect is to be what God desires us to be at each stage of our spiritual journey. That perfection will grow and develop through years of relationship with Christ.

cover a range of ethical issues, but all are relational. The person who commits to pursuing God's will in all these relationships is perfect as God is perfect.

6

DEVOTION AND MONEY IN THE KINGDOM

Matthew 6:1–34

Following the discussion of Jesus and the Law in 5:17–48, the sermon shifts to the subject of devotion in 6:1–18. Matthew then turns to a disciple's relationship to money in 6:19–34.

1. DEVOTION IN THE LIFE OF A DISCIPLE 6:1–18

Matthew begins his treatment of devotion in the life of a disciple with an introduction in verse 1. He then treats giving to the needy in verses 2–4, prayer in verses 5–15, and fasting in verses 16–18.

Verse 1 introduces the section by warning about how one does **acts of righteousness**. The word **righteousness** connects the audience to 5:20, where Jesus had taught that His followers' righteousness should surpass that of the Jewish leaders. It also sets the context in which giving to the needy, prayer, and fasting are to

HISTORICAL CONTEXT

ORAL TRADITION

The three sections on the life of devotion in Matthew 6:2–18 share a common structure:

When you [verb] do not [verb] as the hypocrites do

To be honored/seen by men

I tell you the truth, they have received their reward in full.

But when you [verb]—Jesus' instructions

So that your [devotion] may be in secret.

Your Father who sees in secret will reward you.

The repetition of this pattern was characteristic of good oral teaching. It was a way to make remembering great amounts of material easier.

be understood in the following verses. Jesus warns His disciples not to perform acts of righteousness **to be seen by** people. Righteous acts done to be seen are no longer righteous and gain **no reward from** the **Father in heaven.**

GIVING TO THE NEEDY 6:2–4

The Greek word for giving **to the needy** in verse 2 literally means a merciful deed. It regularly referred to almsgiving or acts of compassion. Such acts were important in Jesus' time. Medical science was still at the stage of superstition. There were no government programs for social welfare. Many children were orphaned or became blind at or shortly after birth. Begging was the only means of support for handicapped persons. Unless people were merciful and generous in giving to beggars, hundreds of children and adults would have starved. The Old Testament taught that God cared for these people, and Judaism taught the appropriate response to God's goodness was to give alms to people in such need.

Jesus commands the continuation of this practice in verse 3. He objected to giving to the needy for the purpose of being seen and **honored by** people. It is not clear whether announcing a gift to the needy **with trumpets** (6:2) was an actual practice or a figure of speech. Regardless, drawing public attention to one's merciful deeds is hypocrisy. The goal becomes attention rather than compassion.

The expression **I tell you the truth** (6:2) translates an expression, *Amen, I say to you.* The word *amen* is a Hebrew word used in the Old Testament as a response to a word from God. Jesus often introduced His teachings with this word. By this He claimed to be speaking a word from God.

He further states that when people give to the needy to be seen, **they have received their reward in full** by being seen. Matthew uses the Greek verb for *paid in full.* This word was written over hundreds of papyrus bills found in excavations in Egypt. What a picturesque expression! When people give to the needy to be seen, God stamps paid in full and gives no further reward.

Jesus assumes in verse 3 that His followers *will* **give to the needy.** The expression **do not let your left hand know what your right hand is doing** means that you do not arrange or choreograph your actions so they are seen and recognized. Jesus does not forbid planning to perform acts of mercy but forbids such acts of mercy being a performance. The purpose is that **your giving may be in secret** (6:4). The goal of helping another should never be attention to oneself as the helper, but simply aid for the person in need. The promise is that giving to the needy in secret will be seen by our Heavenly Father and rewarded.

PRAYER 6:5–15

Jesus' treatment of prayer has four sections. Verses 5–6 are parallel in thought and structure to the teaching on the treatment of giving to the needy in verses 2–4. Verses 7–8 give further comments on prayer. Verses 9–13 contain what is usually called the Lord's Prayer. Verses 14–15 conclude the section with a statement on forgiveness.

Verse 5 forbids praying **to be seen by men**. Persons might well pray while **standing in the synagogues** or while **on the street corners** not bringing attention to themselves. Praying in the synagogue would be indoors. Praying on the street corners would be outdoors. Jesus' examples illustrate a range of possible places; however, the issue is not the place but the purpose. The **hypocrites** Jesus condemned **love to pray** in ways that cause them to be seen. When the purpose is to be seen, the **reward** comes from being seen and that reward is payment **in full**.

Rather than praying to be seen, Jesus instructs His followers to **pray** in their **room** with the **door** closed (6:6). With that pattern, being seen by people is not the motive. One should not interpret too literally the command to pray in one's room. Many of Jesus' listeners lived in one-room houses. There was no separate room in which they could pray. The point is that prayer is to be done in ways that do not draw attention to the one who is praying.

Another pattern of prayer to be avoided is **babbling like pagans** (6:7). The use of **many words** implies such babbling is the constant repeating of particular phrases. Probably the issue is not repetition of phrases in prayers as much as the assumption of many that they can manipulate God with the right phrases. This assumption fails to understand the nature of

God. He **knows** our **need before** we **ask him** (6:8), and His love is committed to seeking what is best for us. We do not have to persuade God to do good things for us; nor will the right phrases force Him to do something that is not good for us.

The Lord's Prayer, found in 6:9–13, may be the best known and most prayed of all the prayers in the Bible. Many scholars believe a shorter form, found in Luke 11:3–4, is more likely to have been the prayer Jesus taught His disciples. This is possible but not certain. The use of the plurals our, us, and we make it clear that the prayer in Matthew is intended for use in public. The first three petitions deal with relationship with God. The next four petitions deal with life and relationships on earth.

Addressing God as **Father** (Matt. 6:9) reflects Jesus' intimate relationship with God. The fact that He instructs His followers to address God this same way means that a similar relationship with God is possible for us. It also points to an understanding of the Church as the family of God. The first petition calls for the holiness of God's **name**. Ezekiel 36:16–32 demonstrates what is at stake in the sanctity of God's name. Israel had profaned God's name through their sins. God pledged to sanctify His name by restoring Israel. Their return from captivity and the purification of their hearts would bring honor to God's name. To pray that God's name be **hallowed** or sanctified is to pray that God's people will bring honor to His name by living holy lives.

The second petition prays God's **kingdom come** (Matt. 6:10). Because the Kingdom was another name for the messianic age, a petition like this was common in Jesus' time. The evidence the Kingdom had come would be the complete obedience of God's people. This can be seen in the third petition that God's **will be done on earth as it is in heaven**. Since God's will is done completely and perfectly in heaven, this petition calls for total obedience on earth. The second and third petitions interpret each other.

The fourth petition asks God for the basic material needs of life. **Bread** (6:11) was the normal and often only form of sustenance for the poor. It was the main course for the two meals eaten each day by Jews. The meaning of the word translated **daily** is uncertain. It may mean *necessary for survival, for the current day,* or *for the next day.* The prayer asks for this bread **today**, which suggests that one must trust God day by day for the necessities of life. Jesus' inclusion of this petition shows that His followers should bring their material needs to God in prayer.

Jews often described the commandments as obligations owed to God. This led them to speak of sins as **debts** (6:12) accruing by failure to meet their obligations to God. The Greek word **forgive** literally means to *let go of* or *release*. Forgiveness is letting go of obligations owed in a relationship. The condition for receiving forgiveness from God is granting forgiveness to **our debtors**: those who have sinned against us. Verses 14–15 amplify this point and make it clear that forgiveness from God will be forfeited if we refuse to forgive those who have offended us. This theme will be developed at greater length in 18:21–35.

Jewish prayers often asked God for deliverance from the power of sin, guilt, and **temptation**. The temptation mentioned in verse 13 could be any testing of a disciple's faith by enticement or disobedience. Falling into temptation would bring disrepute to God's name and be contrary to the first petition of the prayer. Some debate whether the prayer asks for deliverance **from the evil one** or from evil. The difference is not important since enticement to evil comes from the evil one, and the resulting disobedience has no place in a disciple's life.

FASTING 6:16–18

The final devotional practice Jesus addressed is fasting. Matthew 6:16–18 follows the pattern of phrases found in verses 2–4 on giving to the needy and, in verses 5–6, on prayer. The behavior Jesus

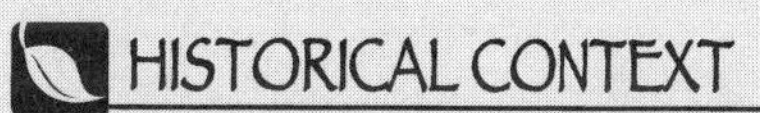

Readers of most modern versions who are familiar with the traditional form of the Lord's Prayer notice that those versions lack the final benediction: "For thine is the kingdom, and the power, and the glory, forever. Amen." These words are missing in the oldest and best manuscripts of Matthew. This does not mean we are in error to pray them. All Jewish prayers concluded with a benediction like that. It would not have been necessary for Jesus to have told the disciples to use such a benediction, nor for Matthew to have written it. From earliest times the benediction would have been part of the Lord's Prayer. Eventually, when Matthew was being copied in the Gentile world, a scribe added the conclusion that the Church had always used.

warns against is disfiguring people's **faces to show men they are fasting** (6:16). Ancient documents suggest that many Jews fasted regularly on Mondays and Thursdays. An early Christian document commands Christians to fast on Wednesdays and Fridays to distinguish themselves from the Jews.

Jews occasionally fasted for long periods of time—up to ten to forty days. The physical changes in a person's appearance could not help but be noticed as such long fasts progressed. Jesus poked fun at people who fasted one day and then used makeup so it would look as if they had fasted for many days. If their goal was being noticed as fasting, they would receive **their reward in full** when they were noticed (6:16).

Jesus assumes His followers *will* fast. **When you fast** your grooming and appearance should not draw attention to your fast (6:17). The point is that it **not be obvious to men that you are fasting** (6:18). Few Christians today would use makeup to communicate piety in fasting. Rather, a testimony service or conversation offers the opportunity to mention casually that we have been fasting. When we do so, God pulls out His stamp in heaven and marks paid in full.

2. MONEY IN THE KINGDOM 6:19–34

Matthew 6:19–34 has two main sections, and the issue of money or security is prominent in both sections. The first section, verses 19–24, has three parts, with the first and last focusing on money and security. The second section, verses 25–34, consists of a poetic call to trust God and a concluding exhortation.

Verses 19–21 develop the idea of where one's treasures are stored. Jesus forbids His followers to **store up ... treasures on earth** for them-selves (6:19). He notes that both the natural process of decay (**moth and rust destroy**) and human greed (**thieves break in and steal**) make it impossible to keep our material treasures secure. However, it is possible to create spiritual treasures that never decay or tempt someone to steal them. Jesus does not specify what constituted **treasures in heaven** (6:20) because the concept was familiar in Judaism. Jewish preaching spoke of righteousness as a treasure in heaven. Heaven and the kingdom of God itself were also treasures in Jewish thought. The Sermon on the Mount as a whole, and 6:1–18 specifically, both instruct us about such treasures.

The question of how one acquires treasure in heaven is answered in verse 21: **where your treasure is, there your heart will be also**. One could reverse the order of the phrases. It is equally true that where one's heart is, there one's treasure is found. We can talk about a heart for God, but if the investment of our time, money, and energy is given to our career, then the career is our treasure, not God. Our lips can say what they wish, but our hearts reveal where our treasures are.

At first glance, verses 22–23 seem to go in another direction. They speak of the eye as **the lamp of the body** (6:22). Ancient people did not think of light entering the eye from the outside, but rather of light coming out of one's eye like a lamp. These verses should be understood in relation to the Hebrew text of Proverbs 22:9; 23:6; and 28:22. Proverbs 28:22 describes the person who chases after wealth as having an *evil eye*. Proverbs 23:6 advises against eating the food of a person with an evil eye. The modern versions show that a person with an evil eye is stingy and does not share. Proverbs 22:9 blesses the person with a good or bountiful eye because that person will share with the poor. So when Jesus speaks of **eyes** that **are good** (Matt. 6:22), He is speaking of a generous person. In contrast, **eyes** that **are bad** (6:23) point to a person who is stingy. Verses 22–23 call on the disciple to be generous because the true source of security is not wealth but God.

Verse 24 draws the conclusion, **No one can serve two masters**. These **masters** that Jesus place in conflict for our devotion are **God and Money**. The Greek word translated **Money** is *mammon*, which is actually a Hebrew phrase meaning, *that in which one trusts*. That in which one trusts is one's security. The conclusion is that you cannot trust both God and a material source of security. Ultimately, one's trust can only be placed in one of those two options.

The second section, treating money in the life of the disciple, appears in verses 25–34. This passage is one of the most powerful texts on trusting God in the entire Bible. Its placement, following Matthew 6:19–24, challenges every disciple to trust in God rather than in material resources for ultimate security. The section begins with **therefore** (6:25), which connects these verses with the preceding treatment of money in the life of a disciple.

The key word in verses 25–34 is **worry,** which appears six times in these verses. Worry is anxiety expressed as fearfulness. Jesus' instruction to **not worry about your life** (6:25) does not forbid taking care or giving thought to the future. Rather, it calls the disciple to live without fear regarding what we often call the basic necessities of life. Concern for what one **will eat or drink** and what one **will wear** shows that the issue is survival. The majority of the ancient world lived on the edge of death. Food, clothing, and shelter were the basic and, in most people's minds, the only necessities for life. Most of Jesus' first audience and Matthew's first readers did worry a great deal about these matters. The first step in overcoming worry about these necessities is to recognize that **life is more important than food**.

Jesus' first illustration appeals to **the birds of the air** (6:26). Birds do not engage in the basic survival activities of planting, harvesting, and storing food against future need. Despite this lack of forethought, God **feeds them**. Jews spoke of birds as worthless things. Jesus' logic is that since God takes care of birds, disciples can trust God to take care of them because they **are much more valuable than** the birds.

Verse 27 challenges translators. The Greek words translated **single hour** and **life** can also be translated a *single cubit* and *height*. A cubit is eighteen inches. No one can **add** eighteen inches to his or her height. The question of whether worry can add an hour to one's life fits the context of Jesus' discussion about worry and life. Modern medicine might suggest that worry could subtract hours from one's life; it certainly will not add to life.

Jesus' second illustration addresses the question of worrying about clothes. He points to **the lilies of the field** (6:28), which engage in none of the activities by which clothing is created. However, those lilies have a **splendor** (6:29) that not even **Solomon**, the wealthiest king of Old Testament history, could equal. Following the typical Jewish argument from lesser to greater already employed in verse 26, Jesus points out that since **God clothes the grass of the field,** He will **much more** clothe those who trust in Him (6:30).

The word **so** in verse 30 indicates a conclusion to Jesus' arguments. Don't **worry** (6:25). Questions of **what** to **eat or drink or wear** are questions asked by **pagans**—literally *Gentiles*—not by believers (6:31). To **run after these things** is to ignore the fact that God **knows** we **need them**. It also expresses a lack of trust that God will provide those things. The antidote to such lack of trust is to **seek first** God's **kingdom and his righteousness** in the confidence that God will supply **all these things as well** (6:33). Choosing to **worry about tomorrow** will not take care of tomorrow, for each tomorrow **has enough trouble of its own** (6:34). Only trusting God will securely take care of tomorrow.

Making Priorities

Learning to trust God rather than trying to provide for our own security may be the biggest challenge facing Western Christians today. Our culture teaches us to measure our worth by the possessions and status we can acquire. Making God's kingdom the priority of our lives feels like we are not doing the things that make us worthwhile. But only such a radical commitment to God's agenda for the world, as well as for our lives, will enable us to discover the blessing of God taking care of all our needs.

7

PROBLEMS IN THE LIFE OF THE KINGDOM

Matthew 7:1–29

Chapter 7 concludes the Sermon on the Mount. If Matthew 6:19 34 dealt with the relationship of disciples to money, Matthew 7:1–12 will deal with the relationship of disciples to others and to God. Verses 13–27 provide a series of warnings about the life of discipleship, and 7:28–29 gives the closing narrative frame for the sermon.

1. PROBLEMS IN RELATIONSHIP WITH OTHERS 7:1–6

The transition from the end of Matthew 6 to chapter 7 abruptly shifts from money to treatment of one's neighbor. People easily misunderstand the command to **not judge** (7:1) because the word translated **judge** had at least two meanings in New Testament Greek. Positively the word could mean to analyze, evaluate, or decide. Negatively, it could mean to condemn. The negative meaning is in mind in verse 1. Verses 2–6 clearly ask the reader to evaluate and make decisions about other persons. Jesus' point is that the person who regularly condemns others will find himself or herself condemned by God. The passive voice **will be judged** in verses 1–2 should be understood as a divine passive, indicating God as the actor and judge. That God would **measure** people **with the measure** they **use** has already been implied in 6:14–15 regarding forgiveness. If we want to be judged fairly, we must judge others fairly.

The human tendency is to magnify one's virtues and the other's faults. Jesus points this out in verses 3–5 with the humorous comment about **the**

speck of sawdust in a **brother's eye** and **the plank in** one's **own eye**. The repetition of **brother** in verses 3–5 suggests Christ is concerned with a condemning spirit in the Christian community. Jesus does not mean that His followers never analyze the behavior or attitude of others. Rather, His followers are to first judge their own behavior and attitude.

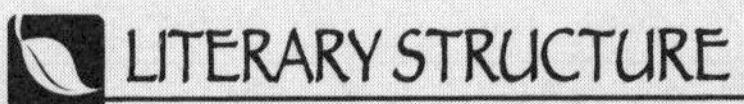

CHIASM

Jesus structured the phrases of His teaching in verses 3–5 in the form of a chiasm. In this structure, the first phrase corresponds to the last, the second to the second to last, and so forth. The center phrase is the point of emphasis or teaching. The following phrases reveal the chiasm in verses 3–5:

A   the speck of sawdust in your brother's eye

  B   the plank in your own eye

    C   first, take out

  B'   the plank of your own eye

A'   the speck from your brother's eye

Because the words **first take out** (7:5) are the center of the chiasm, they are Jesus' main teaching point.

When one's own behavior or attitude has been corrected, a person is better able to analyze another's. One is also more inclined to show mercy after dealing with the reality of one's own faults. John Wesley comments that one should not judge a brother "without full, clear, certain knowledge, without absolute necessity, without tender love."

The function of verse 6 concerning dogs and pigs in the sermon is debated. Some interpreters see it as an independent saying unconnected to either the verses preceding or following. However, it is best to see verse 6 as a concluding and balancing statement to verses 1–5. If verses 1–5 are interpreted too literally—refusing to judge others—Jesus' followers will fail to set and enforce moral standards in the community of faith. **Dogs** were not pets in the ancient world but roamed in packs of wild wolf-like creatures, scavenging scraps of food. They were regarded as fearless and vicious. As a result, one would never **give** them **what is sacred**. Dogs would **tear you to pieces**. A person must understand the danger of dogs. Likewise, **pigs** were considered vicious and dangerous. Even a single pig could **trample** a person **under** its **feet**. Pigs would destroy precious **pearls**. The follower of Jesus must be wise enough to discern the people who are dangerous to the community and to make sure the love and grace of the community is not destroyed by such persons.

2. PROBLEMS IN RELATIONSHIP WITH GOD 7:7–12

Matthew 7:7–11 forms a unit marked by the first word *ask* in verse 7 and the next to last word in verse 11, which is also *ask*. These verses deal with the generosity of God. Verse 12 concludes the main body of the Sermon on the Mount.

Three commands—**ask, seek, knock**—form the structure of verse 7. The Greek verb form of each command is present tense, indicating the follower of Jesus is to *continually* and *persistently* make requests. One might interpret verse 7 as commanding that we request help from other people in the community of faith. However, there are three indications that Jesus is dealing with prayer offered to God. First, seeking and knocking were common Jewish metaphors for prayer. Second, the passive verb **will be given** is a divine passive meaning that God will respond to one's prayer. The divine passive also appears in response to knocking when Jesus says **the door will be opened to you.** Finally, the beginning **ask** in verse 7 is balanced by the **ask** in verse 11, which clearly refers to prayer.

Verse 8 amplifies the promises of verse 7. The word **for** indicates that the reason disciples continually and persistently ask is because God can be counted on to answer. **Everyone who** continually and persistently **asks receives.** The verb **receive** is also present tense in the Greek text, indicating a continual and consistent receiving. Everyone **who seeks finds. Finds** is again present tense in the Greek text. God promises a life of finding when we live a life of seeking. With knocking, the response shifts to a future tense, **the door will be opened.** Having established God's pattern of consistent gracious response in the present, Jesus notes that we can count on that grace in the future.

Jesus then gives two examples from family life to encourage His followers to be persistent in asking. If a child asked **for bread**, no parent would instead **give . . . a stone** (7:9). Loaves of bread in ancient Palestine often resembled the common stones found lying around. No parent would mock a child by giving something worthless when the child had asked for the basic sustenance of life. Likewise, if the child asked **for a fish**, the parent would not **give him a snake** (7:10). No parent would give a child something harmful when the child asked for something good.

The teaching point appears in verse 11. Compared to God the Father's holy love, the best of parental love seems **evil**. Jesus assumes in that culture that parents are good and generous toward their children. If that is the case, **how much more** loving and generous the **Father in heaven** will be. God will respond to our requests with **good gifts**. God is generous and loving toward us. We can ask, seek, and knock in complete confidence.

Verse 12 contains what is often called the Golden Rule: **do to others what you would have them do to you**. Some interpreters point out that while earlier teachers had taught essentially the same truth in negative form, Jesus was the first to articulate it positively. Whether Jesus was the first to give a specific teaching is less important than the fact that He taught this truth. More important is that Jesus says that living in consideration of others **sums up the Law and the Prophets**. This reference brings to a conclusion the body of the Sermon on the Mount that began in Matthew 5:17, where Jesus declared His teachings fulfilled the Law and the Prophets. Treating others as you would wish them to treat you sums up all the ethical teachings Jesus has given in the Sermon on the Mount.

3. PROBLEMS IN THE LIFE OF THE KINGDOM 7:13–27

The final section of the Sermon on the Mount consists of a series of warnings that provide a negative counterpart to the Beatitudes with which the sermon began. Matthew 7:13–14 contrasts two ways of approaching life. Verses 15–23 warn against false prophets. Jesus then presents the parable of the wise and foolish builders in verses 24–27. The common theme in these passages is the importance of obedience. Heeding Christ's words and following His example is not optional for entry into the Kingdom.

Verses 13–14 contrast the narrow and wide gates, drawing on the image of the gates of a city. A modern person might suppose that the **wide gate** signifying accessibility would be favored. However, the world of Jesus was more concerned about security, and thus the **narrow gate** is superior because it limits those who can enter. The fact that Jesus commands His followers to **enter through** the narrow gate points to the kingdom truth the metaphor conveys. He is calling for the obedience to His teachings that will show that disciples genuinely belong to the Kingdom.

The metaphor shifts in verse 13 from gates to roads. This turns the focus to the Jewish concept of the two *ways*, a more traditional translation than roads: the way of life and the way of death. The roots of this teaching are found in the Wisdom Literature of the Old Testament. The phrase *the way of life* was used by the Jews to describe all its teaching on obedience to God, moral and ethical living, and right relationships with other people. Jesus points to this by speaking of the narrow **road that leads to life** (7:14). On the other hand, the way of death described a pattern of disobedience that disregarded moral and ethical living and right relationships with others. Jesus calls this **the road that leads to destruction** (7:13). Because disobedience is so easy, this way is readily accessible and thus can be described as a **broad** road. Because obedience is difficult, the life of obedience is not easily accessible. It is a **narrow** road.

Even in the Old Testament, the two ways were represented in the teachings of the prophets. True prophets taught the way of life; **false prophets** taught the way of death (7:15). One could evaluate the validity of the prophets' messages by comparing their teachings to what was known about the two ways. That is Jesus' point in verse 16 when He states, **by their fruit you will recognize them**. Good fruit—**grapes** and **figs**—does not come from **thornbushes** or **thistles**. A **good tree bears good fruit** (7:17), which means true prophets produce lives characterized by obedience. On the other hand, **a bad tree bears bad fruit**. This means that the fruit of false prophets' ministries will be people characterized by disobedience. These categories cannot be mixed. It is as impossible for a false prophet's ministry to consistently produce people who are virtuous and obedient to God as it is for **a bad tree** to **bear good fruit** (7:18). The statement in verse 19 that promises **every tree that does not bear good fruit** will be **cut down and thrown into the fire** seems parenthetical. It is Jesus' reminder that God will not allow false prophets and their harmful effects to continue unpunished forever. Ultimately, there will be accountability for obedience and disobedience.

The danger of being deceived by false prophets appears in verses 21–23. It is clear that neither religious words such as **Lord, Lord** (7:21) nor impressive religious signs of success such as prophesying, casting out **demons** (7:22), or working **many miracles** guarantee the genuineness of a person. Regardless of what a prophet may say or do, that prophet will be judged on conformity to the will of God. The question is whether a person **does the will of** the **Father who is in heaven**. When such obedience is lacking, Jesus will speak the damning word of judgment—**I never knew you** (7:23)—despite a sparkling record of ministry and miracles.

Verses 24–27 present the parable of the wise and foolish builders. The bubbly children's song about the wise man and foolish man may distract us from the serious spiritual warning of these verses. The **wise man** is the one **who hears** the words of Jesus **and puts them into practice** (7:24). The result of such obedience is security—**the house** does **not fall** in the midst of the storms and trials of life. The **foolish man** is the one who hears the words of Jesus **and does not put them into practice** (7:26). The result of such disobedience is destruction as verse 27 so picturesquely portrays. The first meaning of Jesus' parable here refers to His Sermon on the Mount. Obedience to the sermon will bring security in the storms of life. Disobedience to the sermon will result in destruction. The point of the parable of the wise and foolish men is to provide an evangelistic conclusion to the sermon. The parable invites us to a life of obedience.

4. THE NARRATIVE CONCLUSION TO THE SERMON ON THE MOUNT 7:28–29

Following the conclusion of Jesus' teachings in the Sermon on the Mount, Matthew provides his own concluding editorial comments in verses 28–29. These verses form the literary counterpart to the opening narrative frame for the sermon in Matthew 5:1–2. The words **when Jesus had finished** (7:28) mark the end of the first block of teaching material: the Sermon on the Mount. These words will reappear at the end of each block of teaching material in Matthew's gospel. The author notes that **the**

crowds were amazed at his teaching. The reason is that Jesus **taught as one who had authority, and not as their teachers of the law** (7:29). By the time of Jesus, Jewish teachers always supported their teachings by appealing to earlier authorities. Virtually every paragraph of the *Mishnah*—the collection of the oral tradition put in written form about A.D. 200—quotes from one or more rabbis from an earlier period. Jesus' authority is most clearly demonstrated in the sermon by the Great Antitheses, which contrast the traditional interpretations of the Old Testament with His own.

The authority of Jesus' teaching in the Sermon on the Mount is not simply a matter of form. In the sermon, we discover God speaking to us, judging our thoughts, and discerning the intentions of our hearts (Heb. 4:12). We find ourselves constantly confronted with the deception of our religious games. The sermon has more than just the ring of truth; it penetrates with conviction into our own hearts and calls us to new levels of commitment to Christ. We cannot genuinely hear the sermon and live as we did before.

8

MIRACLES TEACHING JESUS' IDENTITY AND LIFE IN THE KINGDOM

Matthew 8:1–34

Like the Sermon on the Mount, the material in chapters 8 and 9 appears to be collected by Matthew to teach important truths rather than simply to tell the story in chronological order. These chapters consist primarily of miracle stories and, in 8:1–17, focus on Jesus' identity. Those described in 8:18–34 give teaching in narrative form on the meaning of discipleship.

1. MIRACLES REVEALING JESUS' IDENTITY 8:1–17

Matthew 8:1–17 contains two miracle stories: the cleansing of a leper in verses 1–4 and the healing of the centurion's son in verses 5–13. The section concludes in verses 14–17 with a brief summary and interpretation of Jesus' healing ministry.

THE CLEANSING OF A LEPER 8:1–4

The opening verse of this section provides a transition into the narrative of the miracle stories. Jesus had taught the sermon on the **mountainside** (8:1). The **large crowds** had been with Him there and had testified to His authority. Will Jesus' authority follow Him as the crowds do? The first answer comes from the encounter with **a man with leprosy** (8:2).

MANNERS AND CUSTOMS

LEPROSY

There is often confusion about the exact nature of the disease described in the Bible as leprosy. The Old Testament instructions regarding leprosy, and the examples from both Old and New Testaments, suggest that the biblical term included a wide variety of skin disorders. The modern medical term refers to a more devastating disease that attacks the nerves and muscle tissues of the extremities, often resulting in paralysis and significant disfiguring. Most of the symptoms and biblical examples of leprosy are not so severe.

The Old Testament regarded leprosy as ritual uncleanness. Because of this, and the fear of the spread of these skin disorders, Leviticus 13–14 prescribes the strict isolation of lepers. Because of their outcast state, and their threat to both health and ritual cleanness, lepers were feared and avoided as much as possible by the Jews of Jesus' time.

The social isolation and destructiveness of leprosy can be seen in these verses. The leper's first words, **if you are willing, you can make me clean** (8:2), reveal his awareness of being outcast. By Jewish social expectations, Jesus could have easily refused to even talk with the leper. The language of making **clean** or cleansing rather than the language of healing appears twice in verse 3. It reflects the Old Testament understanding of leprosy as causing ritual uncleanness. That Jesus would say, **I am willing**, demonstrates an amazing compassion for the leper. It also shows His authority over both the disease and ritual uncleanness. In contrast to the Old Testament's assumption of gradual improvement, the man was cleansed **immediately**. Jesus' command in verse 4 is to **go** and **show** himself **to the priest and offer** the offering as prescribed in Leviticus 14:10–11. This is consistent with Matthew's understanding that Jesus fulfilled the Law rather than destroyed it (Matt. 5:17).

The story of the cleansing of the leper is also found in Mark 1:40–45. Most interpreters believe Matthew had access to Mark's account. Two changes that Matthew makes from the text found in Mark are instructive. Mark 1:40 describes the leper as coming to Jesus "begging him on his knees." Matthew replaces these words with a single word—**knelt**—in verse 2. The particular Greek word Matthew used for **knelt** regularly means *to worship*. It is the same word used in Matthew 2 to describe the Magi worshipping Jesus. This small editorial change by Matthew points to Christ's identity as the Son of God who is worthy of worship. The other change has a similar motivation. Mark 1:40 has no title by which the leper addresses Jesus. In Matthew 8:2, the leper calls Jesus **Lord**. Matthew frequently adds the word Lord or changes Mark's title of teacher to Lord. This pattern reveals Matthew's desire that we correctly understand Jesus' identity as Lord.

THE HEALING OF THE CENTURION'S SON 8:5–13

Jesus' journey from the mountainside takes Him back to **Capernaum** (8:5), the city identified in verse 4:13 as His home and center of His ministry. There He meets a **centurion . . . asking for help**. The centurion would have been part of the Roman army and a Gentile. Within Jewish traditions, the leper would have been excluded from the people of God because of his disease; the centurion by his nationality. He, too, addresses Jesus as **Lord** (8:6) and reports that his **servant** is **paralyzed and in terrible suffering**. Jesus' response in verse 7 is translated as a statement in almost all English versions of the New Testament: **I will go and heal him**. It is also possible to translate Jesus' words as a question: "Am I to come and heal him?" This translation actually fits better with the centurion's response in the following verse. The question should not be understood as indignant nor as a rebuff of this Gentile soldier. Rather, Jesus asks him to be clear about what he wants. He forces the centurion to express his faith more clearly.

The centurion recognizes that the implication of his request for help would be asking Jesus to come to his house to heal his servant. To do so would render Jesus ceremonially unclean according to the Jewish law. The fact that Jesus touched the leper shows that He was not concerned with such contamination. However, the centurion recognizes the dilemma and offers an alternative by suggesting that Jesus simply speak a **word** (8:8) and heal his servant at a distance. For Matthew, the centurion's offer is very important. As a military officer, the centurion understood **authority** (8:9). He can speak a command and expect that it will be carried out. The clear implication of verse 9 is that Jesus is also a man of authority. If He is truly Son of God, a word will be as effective as a visit in healing the servant. At its heart, this miracle acknowledges Jesus' identity.

Jesus' response is astonishment (8:10). The Gentile soldier had demonstrated more **faith** than anyone of Jewish descent whom Jesus had met. In this context, faith means confidence in who Jesus is as the one who can heal by a word at a distance. Verses 11–12 indicate that many Gentiles will enter the **kingdom**, while many Jews **will be thrown outside** because of their lack of faith. These verses are a powerful affirmation of Jesus' openness to the evangelization of Gentiles.

However, the significance of the verses goes beyond the Jewish-Gentile hostilities of the first century. In our time, many from the Third World will enter the Kingdom, while many from the missionary-sending countries of Europe and North America will be left out because we have not had enough faith to trust Jesus for all our needs. Verse 13 records the words Jesus spoke to accomplish the miracle and concludes the account with simple declaration that the centurion's **servant was healed at that very hour**. Through his account of this healing, Matthew focuses attention on Jesus' authority and identity.

THE EXTENT AND PURPOSE OF JESUS' HEALING MINISTRY 8:14–17

The final paragraph in the opening section of Matthew 8 briefly describes the healing of Peter's mother-in-law, gives a summary statement of an evening of healings, and notes the way Jesus' ministry fulfilled a prophecy of Isaiah. These three elements continue Matthew's focus on Jesus' authority and identity. His description of the healing of **Peter's mother-in-law** portrays Jesus entering the house, seeing the sick mother-in-law, and healing her with a touch (8:14). In the parallel account of Mark 1:30, the disciples tell Jesus about the sick woman. In contrast the initiative shown by Jesus in Matthew 8:14–15 portrays Him as a person of authority. After Jesus' touch, the **fever left** the woman, **and she got up and began to wait on him** (Matt. 8:15). The English translation veils the overtones of the Greek verbs. One might catch these overtones by translating, *She was raised and ministered to Him.* The verb *raised* is the word used throughout the New Testament for the resurrection of Jesus and for the resurrection hope of the followers of Christ. The verb *ministered* (*diakoneo* in Greek) suggests that Peter's mother-in-law became a disciple who entered ministry. These verbs anticipate the worship and ministry given to Jesus the risen Lord following His resurrection. They point to Jesus' identity.

Verse 16 does not describe a specific act of healing but summarizes an **evening** of healing ministry. Matthew divides the evening's work into two categories: the exorcism of demons and the healing of **the sick**. Not only are the afflictions distinct, but so are Jesus' saving actions. By separating the categories, Matthew has elevated the authority of Jesus. He drives **out the** demonic **spirits with a word**, but heals the sick with a touch. Further evidence of Jesus' authority is the fact that His deliverance is offered to **many**.

Matthew then observes that this healing ministry took place **to fulfill what was spoken through the prophet Isaiah** (8:17). This is the first time since 4:14–16 that we find a fulfillment quotation. The reference comes from Isaiah 53:4 and identifies Jesus as the Suffering Servant of Isaiah 53. Thus, this first section of Matthew 8 portrays Jesus in aspects of His power and deity but also in aspects of His humility and humanity.

2. MIRACLES TEACHING LIFE IN THE KINGDOM 8:18–34

Matthew 8:18–34 contains two sections. Jesus dialogues with two would-be disciples in verses 19–22, and verses 23–27 describe the stilling of the storm. However, these two passages belong together as a unit in Matthew's mind. Verses 28–34 narrate the healing of the Gadarene demoniacs.

TEACHING DISCIPLESHIP BY WORD AND DEED 8:18–27

Verse 18 begins the section with Jesus' **orders to cross to the other side of the lake**. The follow-up statement about getting into the boat does not appear until verse 23. Thus verses 19–22 are inserted into the narrative about crossing the sea. In these inserted verses, two would-be disciples promise to follow Jesus. In both instances, Jesus seems to rebuff them with a harsh reply. Verse 19 introduces a **teacher of the law** who promises, **Teacher, I will follow you wherever you go.** One might suspect that, from the negative light in which teachers of law have been cast thus far in Matthew, this one will not be a likely candidate to truly follow

Jesus. His addressing Jesus as **Teacher** rather than Lord confirms that he is not prepared to actually follow **wherever** Jesus might lead. Christ's reply points out that **foxes have** lairs **and birds have nests** (8:20). However, following Jesus commits one to a Master who **has no place to lay his head.** The teacher of the law neither answers nor follows Jesus.

Immediately **another** would-be **disciple** seems to commit to follow Jesus but asks permission to **first go and bury** his **father** (8:21) before pursuing the life of discipleship. To most modern readers this request seems most reasonable, and Jesus' harsh reply, **let the dead bury their own dead** (8:22), is hard to understand. It is likely that the man's father was not yet dead. In Jewish culture of that time, the final obligation of a son to his father was to bury him. There was not embalming in Galilee at that time, so burial was done within a few hours of death. Had the father actually been dead, the son would have been busily making the arrangements for the burial rather than conversing with Jesus. The request to first bury his father was a request to postpone the decision about discipleship until all future family obligations were completed.

The key word in verses 19–22 is *follow*. It reappears in verse 23 when Matthew says Jesus **got into the boat and his disciples followed him.** This statement resumes the story that began in verse 18. Matthew immediately describes **a furious storm** (8:24) sweeping **over the boat.** In contrast to the fury of the storm, **Jesus was sleeping** calmly. The distress of the disciples appears in their cry: **Lord, save us! We're going to drown!** (8:25). Their cry contains several clues that suggest Matthew views the storm theologically. First, the cry, **We're going to drown**, paraphrases the Greek text. Literally, the disciples cried, *We are perishing*, or *We are lost.* The Greek verb is the word often used in the New Testament for spiritual ruin. Their request fits this understanding, for they pray, *Save us.*

Jesus responds: **You of little faith, why are you so afraid?** (8:26). He then rebukes **the wind and the waves,** and the storm becomes **completely calm.** In the parallel account in Mark 4:35–41, Jesus calmed the storm first and then spoke with the disciples about their fear and lack of faith. That is the natural and preferred order. Matthew's reversal of the order implies that he is interpreting the storm and its calming in spiritual and theological terms. He envisions the journey on the sea by boat as corresponding to the journey of life. Matthew 7:24–27 tells us that storms will come to the followers of Jesus. Here, the storm may particularly represent the crisis of persecution and opposition to faith. The disciples' natural response is fear. However, Jesus had commanded in verse 18 that they would go to the other side. The disciples' fear has become a lack of faith in Jesus' command to go to the other side. Matthew understands that when we journey with Jesus, we will arrive safely at the destination to which He takes us.

The statement in verse 26 that He **rebuked the wind and the waves** points to Jesus' authority and power over nature. Such authority and power ultimately belong to God. The question and exclamation of verse 27—**What kind of man is this? Even the winds and the waves obey him!**—emphasize this truth. No man can command the wind and the waves. By this question, Matthew points his readers to think about the deity of Christ.

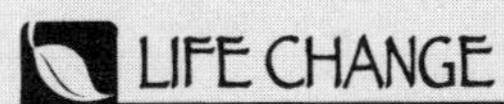

Matthew's interpretation of the stilling of the storm invites us to hear this story as a promise in the storms of our lives. But it is not simply a promise to remove all fearful and difficult times from our lives. Rather, it is a promise that Jesus is able to take us safely to the final destination. The Christian journey offers no protection from the tragedies and painful circumstances of life. Those times will come, and they may well rock our boat. What they can not do to the person of faith is sink our ship. We can live in confidence that Jesus will carry us through.

THE AUTHORITY OF JESUS OVER EVIL 8:28–34

Matthew connects this paragraph dealing with the two demon-possessed men to the journey across the sea with the opening phrase of verse 28: **When he arrived at the other side**. This connecting phrase tells us that verses 28–34 have implications for our understanding of the life of discipleship.

The **two demon-possessed men . . . were so violent that no one could pass that way** (8:28). They pose a similar danger to Jesus and the disciples as that of the storm in the preceding paragraph. However, these two demoniacs know the answer to the question of verse 27: "What kind of man is this?" With no introductions or possible lines of communication, they address Jesus as **Son of God** in verse 29. Their recognition of Jesus' true identity is also revealed by their asking if Jesus had **come** to **torture** them **before the appointed time**. Judaism taught that demons were free to work until the coming of Messiah and the end of this present evil age. The men's question points to Jesus' identity as the Messiah and the fact that His ministry was ushering in the end of the present age. In verse 31 the subject shifts from the demon-possessed men to the **demons**. They understood Jesus' coming as an assault on their power, and they offer terms of compromise: **If you drive us out, send us into the herd of pigs.**

Some question why Jesus would destroy the pigs that represented the livelihood of their owners. However, as Matthew presents the case, the demons initiated their departure into the pigs. In fact, they posed the question in such a way that Jesus could send them into the pigs or not expel them from the men. Clearly the men were more important to Jesus than were the pigs, and He sent the demons into the pigs, who self-destructed by running **into the lake** (8:32). When this had been reported, **the whole town** came out to ask Jesus to **leave their region** (8:34).

Readers locked into a modern and secular worldview will not understand the significance of this conflict with evil. Matthew has edited away many of the details told in Mark and Luke to focus our attention on the encounter between Jesus and the demonic powers of evil that had become incarnate in the two men. As Messiah and Son of God, Jesus has arrived in a world controlled by evil. His very arrival confronts and challenges evil, which must give way before His divine power and authority. The disciple who believes will trust and obey this Jesus. Those who fear the new life cling to the patterns of domination established by evil, and they beg Jesus to leave. It is as true today as it was in the first century.

9

MIRACLES REVEALING JESUS' AUTHORITY

Matthew 9:1–38

Matthew 9 continues the pattern of teaching about Jesus' authority and its meaning for discipleship. The question of authority predominates the three paragraphs found in Matthew 9:1–17. The faith of a disciple is the focus of Matthew 9:18–34. The final paragraph, Matthew 9:35–38, summarizes the Gospel to this point and sets the stage for chapter 10.

1. THE AUTHORITY OF JESUS 9:1–17

Three paragraphs form the first section of Matthew 9. Verses 1–8 describe the healing of a paralytic. Verses 9–13 relate the calling of Matthew, and verses 14–17 conclude with Jesus' response to a question about fasting.

JESUS HEALS A PARALYTIC 9:1–8

Jesus' healing of a paralytic is best known from its version in Mark 2:1–12. The story of four friends who carried a paralyzed man on a stretcher and let him down through the roof is a favorite of many Christians. Matthew, however, makes no mention of the pressing crowd that blocked the man's entry through the door. The details of the friends carrying him to the roof, opening a hole, and letting him down in front of Jesus are all missing in Matthew, who cuts away every detail not necessary to provide a context for the words of Jesus.

The healing is set in **his own town**, Capernaum. The reference to the boat and the journey across the sea (Matt. 9:1) continues the narrative sequence that began in 8:18, when Jesus gave orders to go to the other side. Matthew quickly introduces the **men** who carry a **paralytic, lying on a mat** to Jesus (9:2). Jesus' first observation is the **faith** of the men who brought the paralytic to Him.

Jesus' first words in this paragraph are **Take heart, son; your sins are forgiven**. These words immediately raise the question of Jesus' authority to forgive sins. The response **of the teachers of the law** rejects such authority for Jesus with the complaint, **This fellow is blaspheming!** (9:3). The charge of blasphemy shows that the Jewish teachers of the law considered Jesus' action of forgiving sins to be a claim to be God. Matthew accepts Jesus' claim because he begins verse 4 with the words, **knowing their thoughts**. Judaism ascribed the ability to know people's thoughts to God. Jesus would not know their thoughts if He were not God.

The question of verse 5—**Which is easier to say, "Your sins are forgiven," or to say, "Get up and walk?"**—puts the teachers of the law in an impossible bind. Neither option is easier to say—or accomplish. Only God can forgive sins; only God can heal a paralytic. Jesus then forces the issue in verse 6 by commanding the paralytic, **Get up, take your mat and go home.** The purpose of healing the paralytic is **so that** the teachers of the law **may know that** Jesus **has authority on earth to forgive sins**. This is a clear claim to Jesus' divine nature. The claim would have been meaningless had not the paralytic gotten up and gone **home** (9:7). The crowd, which

---

MANNERS AND CUSTOMS

SIN VERSUS SICKNESS

Modern thinking often separates spiritual and physical needs so that we see no connection between forgiveness of sins and physical healing. First-century Judaism would have assumed a connection, as John 9:2 shows. In the first century, before healing could take place, the healer had to determine the sin that caused the illness. That sin had to be dealt with in order to deal with the physical symptom of the illness. Jesus rejects such a simplistic connection between sin and sickness in John 9:3, but that does not mean there is no connection. The healing of the paralytic does not depend on connecting sin and sickness, but the teachers of the law and the crowds would have assumed such a connection.

Matthew did not mention at the beginning of the story, now responds **with awe** and praise to **God** (9:8). Their response to Jesus is the appropriate response to God. Matthew then notes that their praise is that God **had given such authority to men.** Thus the account of the healing of the paralytic ends with the theme of Jesus' divine authority.

THE CALL OF MATTHEW 9:9–13

The following paragraph reports the call to discipleship of a tax collector named Matthew and a meal with tax collectors and sinners. Though the teachers of the law would not accept Jesus' claim to be able to forgive sins, Matthew will now illustrate what forgiveness of a sinner looks like. Because Mark 2:14 and Luke 5:27 record the same incident using the name Levi for the tax collector, much of Christian tradition has assumed that the change from Levi to Matthew in the first Gospel was the signature of the author.

Matthew worked **at the tax collector's booth** (Matt. 9:9) in Capernaum. Historical evidence suggests that he would have been a customs officer, collecting import and export taxes on trade goods crossing the frontier between the territories of Herod Antipas and Herod Philip. Rome had divided the region between Antipas and Philip following the death of their father, Herod the Great, in 4 B.C. Though the division solved a political problem for Rome, it divided territory that the Jews considered one. Jews were taxed when they did business with Jews in the other region. They saw such taxes as Roman robbery of money that rightfully belonged to them. The Jews hated the tax collectors as instruments of Rome. The hatred increased when the tax collector was a Jew, as Matthew was.

The kindest word Jews used for tax collectors was *sinner*. Thus, the call to Matthew to **follow** Jesus was inviting a sinner to discipleship. Such an invitation implies the forgiveness of sins. That Matthew **got up and followed him** meant that he received that forgiveness. Verses 10–13 make this clear. In Jewish culture of that time, eating with another person was to enter into a covenant of friendship, accepting and affirming the worth of that person. To eat with **tax collectors and "sinners"** (9:10) meant accepting them as they were.

For the teachers of the law, Jesus' eating with sinners made *Him* a sinner. For Jesus, eating with sinners offered forgiveness and grace to them. Thus the **Pharisees'** question, **Why does your teacher eat with tax collectors and "sinners"?** (9:11), meant *Don't you know that by eating with those sinners He becomes a sinner himself?* From the Pharisees' point of view, Jesus' eating with the sinners completely disqualified Him from forgiving sins as He had claimed the right to do in the preceding paragraph. Jesus' response in verse 12 shows the radical difference of His perspective from that of the Pharisees. He was the Divine Physician. The sick needed His ministry, and their return to spiritual health—rather than congratulating the righteous—was His calling.

Verse 13 sternly challenges the Pharisees to learn to read the Scriptures. The words **go and learn** were a rabbinic expression implying that the hearers were superficial in their interpretation of a scripture passage. It meant, *Go, think more deeply, study, and meditate until you arrive at the true meaning.* The passage under discussion is Hosea 6:6: **I desire mercy, not sacrifice.** Jesus sees this verse as meaning that God desires forgiveness of sinners more than He desires right rituals devoted to Him. As a result, Christ can summarize the purpose of His ministry as **not** calling **the righteous, but sinners.** Like the Pharisees, Jesus' modern followers need to learn to read Hosea 6:6 as He did.

GREAT THEMES

HOLINESS

The Pharisees thought sin was contagious and would contaminate anyone who came into contact with it. Their view can be supported by the spiritual failure of many through history. However, Jesus regarded His holiness as contagious and able to bring grace to sinners. His example suggests that the Church develop a more positive view of the power of holiness to influence others for the good. This must be done, however, without naively ignoring sin's power.

FASTING FOR JESUS' FOLLOWERS 9:14–17

The teachers of the law had challenged Jesus over the forgiveness of sins in Matthew 9:3. The Pharisees had challenged Jesus' eating with tax collectors and sinners in 9:11. The challenge now comes from **John's**

disciples (9:14), who ask, **How is it that we and the Pharisees fast, but your disciples do not fast?** Fasting was one of the hallmarks of Judaism in the ancient world. Some fasted because they feared demons could enter food and, thus, enter and possess a person. Fasting reduced the odds of demon possession. Other Jews fasted as an expression of penance or mourning for their sins. Many fasted hoping to be forgiven of their sins. Assuming that the disciples of John the Baptist were correct, it was an unusual thing that Jesus' disciples did not fast. The question was both normal and accusing.

Jesus' answer is a rhetorical question: **How can the guests of the bridegroom mourn while he is with them?** (9:15). By asking the question with the verb *mourn* rather than the verb *fast*, Jesus focuses attention on the role of fasting as mourning for one's sins in an effort to gain forgiveness. The unspoken answer is that if Jesus is able to forgive sins, His followers do not need to fast to gain forgiveness; they need only ask Him for that forgiveness. However, the force of the question provides the obvious answer. The guests of a bridegroom cannot fast while the wedding celebration is still in process. The implication is clear. Jesus portrays himself as the Messiah presiding at the messianic banquet. His followers cannot fast at such a kingdom celebration. However, Jesus has already instructed His followers to fast (Matt. 6:16–18). Should His disciples fast or not? The issue is timing. They do not fast while He is with them, but **the time will come when the bridegroom will be taken from them; then they will fast.**

Both the question of John's disciples and Jesus' answer suggest something new and unusual is taking place in His ministry. Jesus acknowledges that newness with two brief parables. Verse 16 declares that **No one sews a patch of unshrunk cloth on an old garment.** Before clothing was made with preshrunk material, the first washing would cause it to shrink. If one patched a tear in an old garment with cloth that had not been washed (and thus shrunk), at the first washing the patch would shrink, **making the tear worse**. The point is that old and new are not compatible.

Verse 17 makes the same point with a parable about **new wine** in **old wineskins**. Newly made leather wineskins can expand with the expansion of new wine. But once the wineskins are old, their elasticity is gone.

If new wine is put in them, its expansion will burst the wineskins. Through these two parables, Jesus tells John's disciples that His ministry is new and unique. The old explanations and theologies would not be adequate to explain Him. A follower of Jesus must discern the times and recognize the ways in which Jesus does not fit old religious categories. Refusing to believe that He could forgive sins as well as refusing to accept His eating with tax collectors and sinners was to cling to the old categories no longer adequate to explain Jesus.

2. THE FAITH THAT BRINGS HEALING 9:18–34

Matthew returns to healing stories in 9:18–34. Like Matthew 8:1–17, the theme of these miracles is the faith of the one seeking the healing. Matthew 9:18–26 combines the account of the raising of a ruler's daughter and the healing of a bleeding woman. Verses 27–31 describe the healing of two blind men, while verses 32–34 relate Jesus' giving speech to a demon-possessed mute man.

RAISING A DEAD DAUGHTER AND HEALING A BLEEDING WOMAN 9:18–26

Matthew, Mark, and Luke all tell of the raising of the daughter of a ruler with the healing of a bleeding woman sandwiched between the beginning and ending of the account of the daughter. Comparison with the parallel account in Mark 5:21–43 and Luke 8:40–56 shows how drastically Matthew can edit out interesting details that he does not view as necessary to the main point. In the parallels, we learn that the man was a ruler of a synagogue and that his name was Jairus. In the parallels, Jairus came desperately seeking Jesus' help because his daughter was deathly ill. On the trip to Jairus's house, the message came that she had died. Matthew has compressed all those details into a single plea from the ruler for Jesus to come so that his daughter who has died can live (Matt. 9:18). Verse 19 notes that **Jesus . . . and . . . his disciples** went with the ruler.

Embedded in the story of the journey to the ruler's house is the healing of **a woman who had been subject to bleeding for twelve years** (9:20). The mention of twelve years confirms the seriousness of the sickness and thus the difficulty of curing it. The Greek text suggests that the woman's problem was a menstrual disorder, perhaps a light flow throughout the month. Leviticus 15:25–26 indicates that such a condition made the woman and everything she touched ritually unclean. She **came up behind** Jesus **and touched the edge of his cloak.** Her desire to touch Jesus reflects a magical view that healing power would flow from Him to her by that touch. Matthew rejects this magical view by asserting that Jesus **healed** the woman with a word (Matt. 9:22). Matthew also omits from the parallel accounts Jesus' question about who touched Him and the comment that power had gone out of Jesus when the woman touched Him. Matthew's account suggests that Jesus has the power to discern the woman's thoughts and needs no information to understand what has happened. By compressing the account, Matthew highlights Jesus' statement that it was the woman's **faith** that **healed** her.

Resuming the journey, verse 23 tells us that **Jesus** first encountered **flute players** in the ruler's house. That culture expected funerals to hire flute players to play shrill notes as well as mourners to shout out expressions of grief. The mention of the flute players shows the finality of the girl's death. The funeral was about to begin when Jesus arrived. His statement in verse 24, **The girl is not dead but asleep,** seemed ludicrous and the crowd **laughed at him.** But by simply taking the girl's hand, Jesus raised her from the dead. No wonder then that **news of this spread through all that region** (9:26).

HEALING TWO BLIND MEN 9:27–31

Matthew 9:27–31 describes the healing of two blind men. Two blind men are also healed in 20:29–34, which appears to be parallel to the healing of blind Bartimaeus described in Mark 10:46–52 and Luke 18:35–45. The other Gospels have no parallel for this account in Matthew 9. The way Matthew presents the miracle shows that this healing teaches discipleship.

The first indication that discipleship is on Matthew's mind is the way he introduces the **two blind men** (9:27). They *follow* Jesus. This verb is the characteristic word describing what disciples are to do. Their first words contain a confession of faith as they address Jesus as **Son of**

David. Though this title is clearly taught in Matthew's genealogy in chapter 1, this is the first time the title appears in his Gospel. Some Jewish groups used the title **Son of David** with a particularly militaristic messianic content. The two blind men correctly understand that Jesus is Messiah, but they do not understand that His messiahship will call Him to be a suffering servant rather than a victorious general.

Jesus' response to their confession is to ask if they **believe that** He is **able to do this** (9:28). The question directly raises the question of their faith. Their positive response is, **Yes, Lord**. Their use of the title **Lord** indicates a progression in faith from the title **Son of David** they had used earlier. Jesus approves their growing faith by touching **their eyes** (9:29) and restoring **their sight** (9:30). Though He **warned them** to not spread the news, they immediately did just that and **spread the news about him all over that region** (9:31).

HEALING THE MUTE MAN 9:32-34

The final specific healing miracle recorded in Matthew 8 and 9 is the healing of a mute man in 9:32–34. The Greek word describing the man who **could not talk** (9:32) was used for both deaf and mute persons. Matthew also notes that the man was **demon-possessed**. Deafness, muteness, and other diseases were often considered the result of demon possession in the ancient world. Matthew's interest at this point is not in the exorcism of the demon but in the final result. **When the demon was driven out** is a dependent clause. The main sentence affirms that **the man who had been mute spoke** after the demons were driven out.

There are two responses to this healing. **The crowd** is **amazed** and points out that nothing comparable **has ever been seen in Israel** (9:33). The crowd acknowledges the newness of Jesus' ministry and shares the amazement that has attended the recent miracles Jesus has performed. On the other hand, **the Pharisees** (9:34) accuse Jesus of driving **out demons** by the use of demonic power. Matthew does not develop this accusation here. That development will occur in verse 12:24. At this point, Matthew simply notes the shadow of disbelief from the Pharisees in contrast to the faith that has brought healing and life to a ruler's daughter, a bleeding woman, two blind men, and a demon-possessed mute.

3. CONCLUSION AND TRANSITION 9:35–38

Matthew 9:35 is almost identical to the summary of Jesus' ministry found in 4:23. The repetition of this summary suggests that Matthew viewed chapters 5–9 as a single section showing the authority of Jesus both in teaching and in healing. It is clear in this section that titles of Jesus, such as Son of David, Son of Man, and even Lord, do not provide adequate insight into His full identity. Only by hearing Him teach and by experiencing His healing can one realize the genuine identity of Jesus Christ, the Son of God.

Verse 36 describes Jesus' motivation for healing as **compassion.** Modern Christianity tends to think of Jesus' compassion as the main motivation for all His miracles. That may be true, but the Gospels do not frequently mention His compassion. Verse 36 is one of the places affirming compassion as a reason for the healing miracles. However, the verse does not identify the sicknesses and diseases of the people as the reason for Jesus' compassion. Rather, it was the disruption of their lives and the loss of God's peace that moved Jesus. He saw the people as **harassed and helpless, like sheep without a shepherd.** His ministry was not just to heal but to restore hope.

To accomplish that goal Jesus introduces a new metaphor for ministry, that of harvesting. He notes in verse 37 that the **harvest is plentiful but the workers are few.** His point is that there is much to do in ministry but few to do that work. He then commands the disciples to pray that God would raise up workers for the ministry that was needed (9:38). Matthew 10 will name the apostles and present Jesus' teaching on how His followers are to minister. Thus 9:35–38 not only concludes Matthew 5–9, it also introduces Matthew 10.

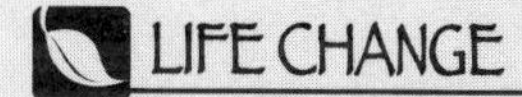

THE MINISTRY OF HOPE

Jesus' healing ministry responded to people who were harassed and helpless. That healing was His response to people's emotional disintegration reveals an important truth. People can endure horrible sickness if they have hope. People who are deeply discouraged and depressed suffer illness much more frequently than happy persons. A ministry of hope and encouragement may well be the first step toward physical healing. Even when we can't provide physical healing, we can offer hope.

Part Three

Mission in the Face of Rejection: Precept and Example

MATTHEW 10:1–12:50

The third major section of Matthew consists of a block of teaching material on mission and a narrative collection of incidents in Jesus' life that demonstrate the beginning of hostility against Him. Jesus' teaching on mission appears in 10:1–11:1 and portrays the mission of the disciples as the extension of Jesus' own ministry. This includes both the activities of ministry and a pattern of rejection. Chapters 11 and 12 then portray a pattern of emerging resistance to Jesus' ministry. This pattern begins with questions about Jesus and moves to conflict with Jewish leaders.

10

JESUS' TEACHING ON MISSION

Matthew 10:1–11:1

Jesus' teaching on mission in 10:1–11:1 has four main sections. Matthew 10:1–4 introduces and commissions the twelve apostles. In verses 5 15, Jesus instructs the disciples on a mission to the **lost sheep of Israel**. Verses 16–39 collect Jesus' teaching on persecution. Finally, 10:40–11:1 brings the mission teaching to a conclusion.

1. AUTHORIZING AND INTRODUCING THE TWELVE APOSTLES 10:1–4

Matthew 9 concluded with a prayer for God to "send out workers into his harvest field." The opening verses of chapter 10 move toward the answer to that prayer. Verse 1 declares that Jesus **called his twelve disciples to him**. This is the first mention of the **twelve disciples**. The number twelve symbolizes the twelve patriarchs and the twelve tribes of Israel. Jesus' selection of twelve disciples figuratively portrays His ministry as beginning a new Israel.

Verse 1 also states that Jesus **gave** these disciples **authority to drive out evil spirits and to heal every disease and sickness**. This equips the disciples to extend the ministry He has begun. Jesus demonstrated authority over evil spirits in chapter 9. The words "heal every disease and sickness" quote exactly the words used to describe Jesus' own healing ministry in Matthew 4:23 and 9:35. Jesus authorizes the disciples' ministry to extend His ministry.

The Gospel of Matthew uses the word **apostles** only once, here in verse 2. The use of this word to describe **the twelve** links the disciples' mission during Jesus' ministry with the apostles' post-resurrection ministry. The word also highlights the Twelve representing Jesus in their ministry. The Hebrew word behind **apostle** speaks of a person sent to represent the sender. From a Jewish perspective, apostles were authorized to speak for and act on behalf of their sender.

The Zealots were the "fourth sect of Jewish philosophy," according to Josephus. Their zeal for freedom led to the name Zealots as well as to violent actions against Romans or Roman sympathizers. Their fierce independence made it difficult for them to cooperate with other Jewish groups or even with others sharing most of their resentment against foreign occupation. A rebellion in A.D. 6 led by Judas the Galilean drew the Zealots together and eventually, in A.D. 66, they instigated the revolution known as the First Jewish War.

The **names of the twelve** are listed in verses 2–4. The first four—**Peter, Andrew, James,** and **John**—have already been introduced in Matthew 4:18–22. Peter, James, and John appear as the inner circle among the Twelve. **Matthew** appears in all lists of the Twelve, but only here is he described as **the tax collector**, an obvious reference to his call in 9:9. Perhaps most amazing is the listing of **Simon the Zealot** and Matthew the tax collector together. Tax collectors were collaborators with the Romans. They worked for and with the Romans against their fellow Jews. Zealots hated collaborators and were as violent against them as against the Romans. That Matthew and Simon coexisted in the same group is testimony to Jesus' leadership and the power of the gospel to unite people of radically different political persuasions.

2. THE MISSION TO ISRAEL 10:5–15

The remainder of chapter 10 consists of **instructions Jesus** gave the **twelve** (10:5) for their mission. Though verse 5 states that Jesus **sent out** the Twelve, Matthew never describes their actual mission. Rather he has collected Jesus' teachings about mission into this block of teaching. The first instructions are disconcerting. Jesus forbids the Twelve from ministry **among the Gentiles or . . . Samaritans. Rather**, they are instructed to go **to the lost sheep of Israel** (10:6).

This anti-Gentile approach seems out of place from the Jesus who loved the world. It is at odds with the pro-Gentile approach in the opening chapters and the Great Commission at the end of Matthew. The Gospels portray Jesus as welcoming individual Gentiles during His earthly ministry, but just as clearly He focuses His efforts on Jews. This is not a matter of prejudice but of strategy. God's strategy from Genesis 12 on has been to the Jew first and then to the Gentile. Jews must first enter the Kingdom themselves if they are to offer it to Gentiles. Believers must be revived and empowered before they evangelize the world.

The **message** the Twelve are to **preach** is the message of Jesus and John the Baptist (Matt. 4:17; 3:1). They are to announce that **the kingdom of heaven is near** (10:7). Evidence for the arrival of the Kingdom will be seen as they **heal the sick, raise the dead, cleanse** lepers, and **drive out demons** (10:8). These are exactly the miracles Jesus performed, according to Matthew 8 and 9. Again the disciples' ministry extends the ministry begun by Jesus. The principle is, **Freely you have received, freely give.** The disciples had freely received the grace of the Kingdom through Jesus' ministry. It was not given for them to possess or keep for themselves. It was given for them to give away.

Verses 9–10 continue the theme that the disciples' ministry will be modeled after that of Jesus. They are forbidden to **take along any gold or silver or copper.** Jesus has taught that His followers are "not to store up treasures on earth" but "treasures in heaven" (6:19–20). He has already said that He has "no place to lay his head" (8:20). So His followers must enter ministry without providing for their own security. Even basic needs like a **bag for the journey, or extra tunic, or sandals or a staff** are forbidden (10:10). They must trust God to provide rather than managing those needs themselves. The reason they can trust God is that **the worker is worth his keep.**

That does not mean ministry will be easy. Whenever they arrive at a **town or village**, they must **search for some worthy person there and stay at his house** (10:11). Finding such a worthy person will be risky. When they arrive at the **home**, they are to **give it** their **greeting** (10:12).

This common cultural custom of the time began with the greeting *Shalom*, meaning *peace*. **If the home is deserving**, their greeting of **peace** was to remain. The word *deserving* in verse 13 is the same Greek word as *worthy* in verse 11. The worthy person or deserving home is the one that welcomes the disciple. If the home is not deserving, the disciple's **peace** is to **return**.

This means that village by village the traveling disciple must seek lodging and support. The disciple will experience rejection and hostility as well as welcome and sustenance. The disciple was to collect no guilt for the decisions of others regarding the message of the Kingdom. When a **welcome** or listening ear was refused, the disciple was to **shake the dust of** his **feet when** leaving **that home or town** (10:14).

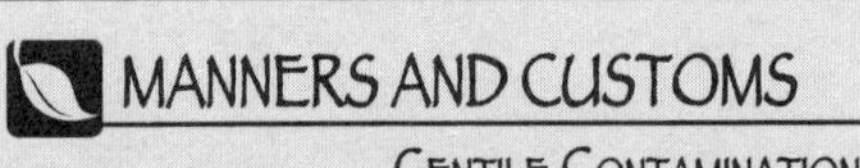

Walking in the ancient world, one inevitably collected dust on one's feet, sandals, and the lower part of one's robe. Devout Jews returning to the land of Israel from pagan territory would shake or wipe the dust off their sandals and shake the dust from their robes so that the Holy Land would not be contaminated by Gentile dirt. Ironically, Jesus instructs His followers to respond to Jewish rejection of their message by treating those Jews as if they were Gentiles.

Though the disciples were to break off their ministry to those who rejected them, **judgment** was to be left to God (10:15). **Sodom and Gomorrah** were legendary in Judaism for their wickedness. Part of the wickedness of those cities was their rejection and mistreatment of the messengers sent from God (Gen. 19). To reject the disciples' ministry was to reject Jesus and His ministry. Because He is greater than the messengers to Sodom and Gomorrah, the judgment on the villages who reject Him by rejecting His disciples will be greater than the judgment awaiting Sodom and Gomorrah.

3. MISSION IN THE FACE OF PERSECUTION 10:16–39

The instructions about how to respond to rejection in Matthew 10:13–15 lead naturally into the theme of persecution in 10:16–39. Jesus treats persecution in five sections. Verses 16–23 warn the disciples to be prepared for persecution. Verses 24–25 point out that Jesus was persecuted, so His followers should expect persecution also. Verses 26–31 urge courage in the face of the fear and persecution. Matthew 10:32–33 deals with confessing and denying Jesus, and verses 34–39 deal with the division that discipleship brings.

READINESS FOR PERSECUTION 10:16–23

Though verse 16 may conclude the subject of verses 5–15, it is better understood as a transition verse. Jesus sends His disciples into such a hostile environment that He characterizes it as **sending . . . sheep among wolves.** The details of the danger will follow, but at this point Jesus counsels wisdom: **be as shrewd as snakes and as innocent as doves.** Some believe this was a popular proverb of that culture comparable to *a stitch in time saves nine* in North American culture. It is more likely the two parts were both proverbial, but that Jesus put them together. A balance of prudence and purity must describe the followers of Jesus. His disciples must be insightful enough about evil to not be taken in by it, but innocent enough about evil to not prejudge people caught in its snares.

Verses 17–18 warn that the disciples will soon face charges in **the local councils** and floggings in the **synagogues.** They will **be brought before governors and kings** in order to witness **to them and to the Gentiles** (10:18). The book of Acts shows that all this and more happened to early Christians even before Matthew's gospel was written. Clearly Jesus anticipated persecution against His followers from both Jews and Gentiles. Though the disciples are to **be on . . . guard** (10:17), there is no guarantee that being on guard will actually protect them from the persecution.

Verse 19 assumes that persecution *will* happen. Jesus says, **when they arrest you,** not if they arrest you. The Greek word translated **arrest** in the New International Version is the same word used throughout the New Testament to describe Judas's betrayal of Jesus. In the face of such betrayal, the disciple is to **not worry about what to say or how to say it.** The early followers of Jesus were often of a lower social class and might be tongue-tied before governors or kings. But Jesus promises that **the Spirit** of God will speak **through** them (10:20). Though God will supply the words for them to speak when needed, He does not promise that their lives would be preserved or that they would be set free. The promise is that they will be able to defend the message of the Kingdom, not that they will be able to defend themselves.

The picture of persecution darkens in verse 21. Early Christianity, whenever it first was preached in a culture and an age, caused family divisions. Jewish culture was then—and still is—strongly oriented by family ties. When a member of a Jewish family began to follow Jesus, severe consequences—some of them leading to death—could occur. As a result **brother** could **betray brother to death** or a parent could betray a **child**.

Verse 22 promises that everybody **will hate** Jesus' followers. This hatred will be the result of the radical claims of the Kingdom on people's lives. Sinful people always resist the call to total obedience to God. The more clearly one sounds the call to holy living, the more hatred that person should expect. Fidelity to the demands of the Kingdom, not obnoxious personalities and witness methods, will bring the opposition. However, the issue is not persecution or popularity. The issue is obedience and, as a result, Jesus promises that the one **who stands firm to the end will be saved.**

The persecution of which Jesus warns should not be expected to be occasional or sporadic. Rather it will be the pattern of Christian witness. As a result verse 23 warns, **When you are persecuted in one place, flee to another.** Because the mission of the disciples in Matthew 10 is to **the lost sheep of Israel** (10:6), the followers of Jesus should continue to witness to Jews in every period of history. The exact meaning of Jesus' words **you will not finish going through the cities of Israel before the Son of Man comes** is not clear. Whether it speaks about the timing of the second coming of Christ can be debated. However, the effect of the verse is to commission Christ's followers to witness to the Jewish people until the end of time.

PERSECUTION AS IMITATION OF CHRIST 10:24–25

Verses 24–25 form a small paragraph in the larger treatment of persecution. Superficially these verses are a truism. **A student is** never **above his** or her **teacher** (10:24). A slave is never **above his** or her **master.** But it is the context and assumption of persecution that give meaning to these statements. If Jesus was persecuted and people resisted His ministry, His followers should expect to be persecuted and have people resist their ministries. **It is enough for** the disciple **to be like** the **teacher** or **like** the **master**. Since people accused Jesus of obtaining His power for ministry from Satan (Matt. 9:34), the **members of** Jesus' **household** should expect the same.

Matthew views discipleship as the imitation of Christ. That is attractive to us when we think of Jesus' miracles, great teachings, and compassion. But the imitation of Christ also includes suffering. For followers of Christ, the validation of discipleship is not escape from persecution but being counted worthy to share in His sufferings. Only by dying to self can a believer become one with Jesus and joyfully participate in the mission of announcing and demonstrating the total obedience that characterizes the Kingdom.

COURAGE IN THE FACE OF PERSECUTION 10:26–31

Because Jesus suffers persecution before His disciples, this authorizes Him to command them to **not be afraid** when they suffer. Verses 26–27 promise the ultimate triumph of truth and righteousness. The words **There is nothing concealed that will not be disclosed** are paralleled by the next phrase: **[nothing] hidden that will not be made known** (10:26). This parallel structure is typical of Hebrew poetry, and the two lines have the same meaning. Some hear these words fearful of some forgotten sin being exposed. This is not Jesus' intent. He promises that the evil motives and wickedness of the persecutors will someday become public. God may wait as late as the judgment to expose their sin, but persecutors will not be able to hide their sin forever. God does not let evil and injustice go on indefinitely, but eventually brings it to light and to judgment. Then those who have been persecuted will be vindicated before God and before the world.

Verse 28 declares that Jesus' followers should **not be afraid of those who kill the body but cannot kill the soul.** At first glance it appears that Jesus views the person as a dichotomy of body and soul along the lines of Platonic philosophy. However, the second part of the verse makes it clear that He does not envision a never dying soul, for He warns the disciples to **be afraid of the One who can destroy both soul and body in hell.** One's body is the outward expression of the whole person who is described by the word **soul.** Persecutors only have access to the body—they have no access to the whole person, what Paul calls the *inner man* in 2 Corinthians 4:16 (NASB). Issues of the heart, mind, spirit, and will can be tested but not destroyed by persecutors.

The second part of Matthew 10:28 is more difficult. It is not immediately clear whether Jesus has God or Satan in mind as the One who can destroy both soul and body. The following verses suggest that it is God who should be feared. The capitalized *One* in the New International Version agrees with this. **Sparrows** were among the cheapest of all foods (10:29). **Two** were **sold for a penny.** The penny was about one-sixteenth of a daily wage. Proverbially, sparrows were considered worthless, but **not one of them** falls **to the ground** apart from God's knowledge and His **will.** However, the least disciple is **worth more than many sparrows** (10:31). Even the **hairs** of a disciple's **head are all numbered** (10:30). If God gives such attention to the worthless sparrows and the hairs of a person's head, how much more will He be concerned with Jesus' followers. So, though a disciple should fear God because He can destroy both soul and body, that disciple need not be terrified, because a God who cares for the sparrows will give much greater care to His people.

CONFESSING AND DENYING CHRIST 10:32-33

The persecution, which has been in view since verse 16, comes from resistance to the witnessing mission of Jesus' disciples. Verses 32–33 remind us that such a witness is not optional; it is necessary for the follower of Christ. Jesus declares in verse 32, **Whoever acknowledges me before men, I will also acknowledge him before my Father in heaven.** Verse 33 states the proposition negatively: **Whoever disowns me before men** will be disowned by Me **before my Father in heaven.**

The Greek word translated **acknowledge** means to say the same thing. It is often translated *confess,* but it means to agree with. People who acknowledge or agree with and accept God's call upon their lives will be identified with Christ's acknowledgment of them before God. People who deny or claim they do not know Christ will find their denying identity rising up to haunt them when Christ denies knowing them to God. The degree of allegiance to Jesus disciples demonstrate under persecution will be the degree to which Christ identifies himself with them at the time of judgment before God.

THE DIVISIVENESS OF FOLLOWING JESUS 10:34–39

Jesus returns to the theme of the division of families that discipleship brings. This theme first appeared in verse 21. Though Christians often speak and sing of the peace Christ brings, Jesus claims the contrary in verse 34. He states that He **did not come to bring peace, but a sword.** The result of the preaching of the Kingdom will be adult children set **against** their parents (10:35). **The members of** a person's **own household will be enemies** (10:36). This does not come about through a lack of love but because of the radical demands of discipleship.

To be **worthy** of Jesus, one must love Him more than **father or mother**, more than **son or daughter** (10:37). Many close-knit families cannot accept Jesus' radical demand of supreme allegiance. The call of God to kingdom obedience must have priority above every other allegiance. If it does not, the other allegiance is one's true god. To be **worthy of** Jesus requires the disciple to **take his cross and follow** (10:38). But such commitment is well worth the price, for **whoever loses his** or her **life for** Jesus' **sake will find it** (10:39). On the other hand, the person who tries to find life apart from such radical commitment to Christ will lose it. The price of persecution is a price worth paying.

4. THE REWARDS OF THE MISSION 10:40–11:1

The final section of the mission instructions in Matthew 10 speaks of the ways followers of Christ may be received positively. Persecution is not the only response to witness. Some receive the witness to the Kingdom gladly. Jesus notes that such a welcome to the disciple's witness should not be credited to the disciple, as if it were a matter of personality or technique that brought the positive reception. Rather, the one **who receives you receives me** (10:40). To receive the disciples' witness is to receive Christ himself, and that is to be open to God himself.

Further, whatever reward there is for discipleship is shared by those who give the positive reception to the good news of the Kingdom. If a disciple is called to witness as a **prophet**, those who accept the prophet's message will share in the **prophet's reward** (10:41). Likewise, if a disciple is called to witness as a **righteous** person, those who receive the righteous one will share in a **righteous** one's **reward.** Rewards are not handed out in the Kingdom on the basis of titles or success rates. Rewards are given to those who faithfully support and give witness to the Kingdom in their lives. Even one who **gives even a cup of cold water** to support the ministry of a disciple will receive the appropriate **reward** (10:42).

Matthew 11:1 contains the characteristic phrase marking the end of a teaching discourse in his Gospel: **after Jesus had finished**. Matthew then points out that Jesus turned from teaching the **twelve disciples** to **teach and preach in the towns of Galilee**. After instructing the disciples on their ministry, Jesus continues with His.

11

QUESTIONS AND UNCERTAINTY ABOUT JESUS

Matthew 11:2–30

Turning from mission teachings in chapter 10, Matthew narrates a series of events that raise questions about Jesus. Doubt, dissatisfaction, and outright opposition are the themes in chapters 11–12. Chapter 11 has three sections: 11:2–19 focuses on three questions; 11:20–24 condemns three Galilean cities for their lack of repentance; and 11:25–30 explains the rising doubts about Jesus.

1. QUESTIONS FROM AND ABOUT JOHN THE BAPTIST 11:2–19

The first section of chapter 11 is built around three questions and their answers: verses 2–6 work with the question of John the Baptist as to whether Jesus is the coming one; verses 7–15 ask the crowd what they went out to see when they went to see John the Baptist; and verses 16–19 ask to what this generation should be compared.

ARE YOU THE ONE WHO WAS TO COME? 11:2–6

The first expression of doubt about Jesus appears in verses 2–6 from an unexpected source. The question of whether Jesus was truly the Messiah came from **John** the Baptist **in prison** (11:2). Matthew has already mentioned John's arrest in 4:12. The account of John's death will come in Matthew

14:1–12. Herod Antipas had imprisoned John at his isolated fortress of Machaerus on the east side of the Dead Sea. Matthew tells us John **heard** of the works of **Christ**. Matthew's readers have read of these works in chapters 8 and 9. The word *Christ* should be translated *Messiah* here. John has heard of the messianic ministry of Jesus and asks about His messiahship.

John **sent his disciples to ask** Jesus a question (11:2–3). The Gospels imply a close relationship between the disciples of John the Baptist and those of Jesus. John 1:35–51 indicates that some of Jesus' disciples had first been disciples of John. Communication between the two could have happened easily through their disciples. John asked, **Are you the one who was to come, or should we expect someone else?** (11:3). The expression **the one who was to come** was a messianic title in the time of Jesus. Psalm 118:26; Daniel 7:13, 9:25–27; and Malachi 3:1 describe the Messiah as the one who is coming. Thus, John's question was "Are you really the Messiah? If not, we must return to waiting."

It should not be surprising that John the Baptist doubted Jesus' messiahship. A wide diversity of messianic hopes existed in Jesus' time. Militaristic, political, priestly, and spiritual understandings of the Messiah competed for people's commitment. If John was hoping for a militaristic Messiah, he naturally would question Jesus' ministry because it failed to challenge Roman domination. At the least, John could have expected the Messiah to set him free from prison. Instead Jesus seems to have used John's imprisonment as an opportunity to expand His own ministry.

Jesus replies, **Go back and report . . . what you hear and see** (Matt. 11:4). John's disciples are to report what the readers of this Gospel have heard in the teaching sections (Matt. 5–7; 10) and the miracles described in chapters 8–9. Jesus provides a summary: **The blind receive sight, the lame walk, those who have leprosy are cured, the deaf hear, the dead are raised, and the good news is preached to the poor** (11:5). One should note the similarity of this list to the tasks in 10:8 that Jesus assigns His followers in their ministry. Matthew also expects the reader to connect this list to the preceding chapters. The blind receiving sight was described in 9:27–30. The lame walking pointed to the paralytic mentioned in 9:1–7. The 8:1–4 passage recounted the curing of leprosy. The raising of the ruler's daughter provides an example of the dead being raised. There is no mention of deaf hearing in chapters 8–9, but the Greek word for *deaf* is the same word used for the *mute* man in 9:32–33. The Sermon on the Mount and the teaching about mission provide an example of the poor having the good news preached to them.

Jesus does not seem to answer John's question—unless one knows the Old Testament well. The description of the miracles in verse 5 includes almost exact quotations from Isaiah 26:19; 29:18; 35:5–6; 42:18; 53:4; and 61:1—passages that were clearly understood to be messianic prophecies by the Jews. Without directly claiming to be the Messiah, Jesus pointed to the Scriptures that explained what He was doing in messianic terms. Matthew 11:6 speaks a blessing on John or anyone else who can accept Jesus' understanding of messiahship.

WHAT DID YOU GO OUT TO SEE? 11:7–15

With the departure of **John's disciples, Jesus** (11:7) asked a series of questions designed to cause the listeners to examine their own motivation for being interested in John. Had they gone **out into the desert to see . . . a reed swayed by the wind?** Some suggest this simply asks if the crowd had gone out to see scenery. However, it is more likely that Jesus knew His listeners did not regard John as a political person easily swayed one way or another by people's opinions.

Further, they had not gone **out to see . . . a man dressed in fine clothes** (11:8). The Greek word translated **fine** can also mean soft. Since kings and rich people were the only ones wearing soft and fine clothing, Jesus was pointing out that John the Baptist's listeners knew that he was not wealthy or part of the government. The real reason people had gone out to see John was that they knew he was a **prophet** (11:9). However, Jesus and Matthew want it to be clear that John was **more than a prophet**.

The distinctiveness of John was that he was the **messenger** prophesied in Malachi 3:1 (Matt. 11:10). The messenger of Malachi 3:1 prepared the way for the Lord to come among his people. The parallel passage in Malachi 4:5 names the messenger as Elijah. These two passages became the basis for Jewish expectation that Elijah would return as the forerunner of the Messiah. If John the Baptist is Elijah, the forerunner of the Messiah, and if John prepared the way for Jesus, then Jesus must be the Messiah.

This logic makes clear that John the Baptist was a major pivot point in salvation history. As such, no Old Testament prophet was **greater than John the Baptist** (Matt. 11:11). But the person **least in the kingdom . . . is greater than** John, who is only the forerunner of the Messiah who would transform human history. Such a radical transformation would not take place without resistance, and Jesus describes a violent reaction to it in verse 12. This verse is difficult to translate and interpret. The New International Version translates it, **the kingdom has been forcefully advancing**, which suggests the triumphant progress of the Kingdom against great spiritual resistance. In this light, that **forceful men lay hold of it** means strong and wise people join forces with the Kingdom.

It is more likely that Jesus saw the Kingdom creating violent conflict with the present power structures of the world. Thus the Kingdom suffers violence and violent people seize the Kingdom and its representatives. Such violent opposition was the very reason John the Baptist was in prison and would soon be killed (Matt. 14:1–12), as well as Jesus and many of His followers.

This was not clear because Jesus and John stood at the pivot point of salvation history. **All the Prophets and the Law prophesied until John** (11:13), which means the entirety of salvation history came to its climax at that time in John's ministry. In fact, according to verse 14, John was **the Elijah** prophesied in Malachi 4:5 as the forerunner of the Messiah. While such a message is familiar to present-day Christian listeners, it would have been mind-boggling to the crowd listening to Jesus that day. It is no wonder Jesus concluded with one of His common phrases: **He who has hears, let him hear** (11:15). His message would require spiritually tuned ears to hear and understand.

HOW DO WE UNDERSTAND THIS GENERATION? 11:16–19

The generation of Jesus and John faced the most challenging choice of human history. While they experienced the marvelous evidences of the

Kingdom firsthand, they did not have the benefit of hindsight to enable them to understand what God was doing as well as later Christians would.

So Jesus asks how to understand **this generation** (11:16). Their lack of responsiveness led Him to **compare** them to **children** playing **in the marketplaces**. One group wanted to play a make-believe wedding: **We played the flute for you**. However, the other children refused to play: **you would not dance**. The first children responded with another game, pretending to be at a funeral: **we sang a dirge**. Once again, however, the others refused: **you did not mourn**. These children's games (11:17) represented historical reality. Like the children proposing to play funeral, John the Baptist came preaching judgment. There was nothing festive about his approach, **neither eating nor drinking** (11:18). But the crowds rejected John's ministry, claiming, **he has a demon.**

On the other hand, like the children wanting to play wedding, Jesus had come **eating and drinking** and presenting the Kingdom as a party. But the crowds were equally unresponsive to Him, and they created their checklist of condemnation: **a glutton and a drunkard, a friend of tax collectors and "sinners"** (11:19). That generation found John's demands too hard and Jesus' grace too embracing of sinners. It was easier to complain about the messengers than to respond in obedience to the call to the Kingdom. However, Jesus affirms the truth of His message. **Wisdom is proved right by her actions** was probably a proverbial saying. The point is that the message of the Kingdom is proved right by its evidence, not by the fickle responses of the crowds.

2. JUDGMENT ON THREE UNREPENTANT CITIES 11:20–24

Such rejection of the Kingdom could not go without consequences. The **miracles** mentioned in verse 20 are the signs of the Kingdom narrated in Matthew 8–9 and mentioned by Jesus in 11:4–5. Because the miracles were Kingdom signs, the appropriate response would have been to **repent**, as both John and Jesus urged with their first words in the Gospel: "Repent, for the kingdom of heaven is near" (Matt. 3:2; 4:17).

Jesus announced judgment for failure to repent on the cities where He had ministered. **Bethsaida** (11:21) was located on the north shore of the

Sea of Galilee, a few miles east of Capernaum, and was the home of several disciples (see John 1:44; 12:21). **Korazin** is only mentioned here and in the parallel passage in Luke 10:13, but historical evidence suggests it was also a fishing village on the north shore of the Sea of Galilee, located between Bethsaida and Capernaum.

Jesus' words—**woe to you**—were an expression of grief such as might be exclaimed at a funeral. They portray the spiritual death of these villages that rejected the Kingdom. They are more deserving of judgment than **Tyre and Sidon**. These cities were part of ancient Phoenicia and were noted for their idolatry. Isaiah 23; Ezekiel 26–28; and Amos 1:9–10 promised judgment on Tyre and Sidon for their arrogant pride. The Jewish people had long resented the power and arrogance of Tyre and Sidon, but Tyre and Sidon **would have repented long ago** had they seen the miracles done by Jesus. As a result the villages of Korazin and Bethsaida will suffer far more **on the day of judgment than** will Tyre and Sidon (Matt. 11:22).

Jesus then turns His attention to **Capernaum**, the headquarters for His ministry. Verse 23 quotes portions of Isaiah 14:13 and 15. In their original context, these verses spoke of the arrogant self-exaltation of the king of Babylon, who claimed to be equal to God. Such pride is prelude to a great fall. Capernaum was the place where God most directly revealed himself in the kingdom miracles performed by Jesus. For the residents of Capernaum to refuse to repent was to set themselves up as equals to and rivals of God. Their judgment will be worse than what God sent on **Sodom** (Matt. 11:24).

3. THE MYSTERY OF RESPONSE TO JESUS 11:25–30

The final paragraph of Matthew 11 has two sections. Verses 25–27 contain a thanksgiving prayer of Jesus. Verses 28–30 graciously renew Jesus' invitation to the Kingdom.

JESUS' PRAYER OF THANKSGIVING 11:25–27

A logical question often asked is, how could people who had such direct contact with Jesus as Capernaum, Korazin, and Bethsaida refuse to repent and so reject the gospel? In verse 25 Jesus answers: God has **hidden these things from the wise and learned, and revealed them to little children**. It is not intellectual expertise, or even wisdom in the practical matters of life, that explains people's response to the Kingdom. In fact, there is no explanation other than the mystery of human freedom that God has chosen to give us.

It is possible Jesus was suggesting that if any person becomes like a little child, that person can understand the mystery of divine revelation. By refusing to become like little children, some people refuse the gospel. It is more likely that Jesus' comment is ironic. Infants may understand basic relational matters like love and trust in more profound ways than adults do, but these infants are unable to communicate such knowledge. Thus the mystery of human responsiveness to the gospel is known only to God and the persons making their choices. This has always been God's plan (11:26).

Verse 27 makes the point that no one **knows** Jesus **except the Father**. All of chapter 11 has dealt with the question of knowledge of Jesus. John the Baptist had lost clarity on Jesus' identity. Korazin, Bethsaida, and Capernaum failed to recognize His significance. Only God truly knew and understood Jesus. Thus the knowledge of Christ is a gift that only God can give. Likewise knowledge of God is given to us by Christ.

A GRACIOUS INVITATION 11:28–30

Following discussion of His rejection and the mystery of knowing Him, Christ issues one of the most gracious invitations to the Kingdom recorded in all Scripture. The invitation is directed to those who **are weary and burdened** (11:28). The Greek words speak of grinding toil and desperate burdens. The invitation to people, so crushed by life's load, is to **come to** Jesus who **will give** them **rest.** The word **rest** suggests renewal and refreshing. Jesus did not promise the burdens would go away. He did not promise that people would never be weary again. Rather, He promised renewal and refreshment on the journey of life.

Verse 29 makes clear that this invitation is extended to those who have not yet responded to the call of Jesus to discipleship. The phrase

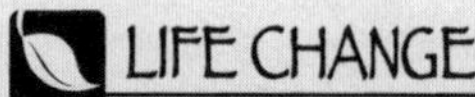

LIFE CHANGE

JOY IN DISCIPLESHIP

When Christ renews and refreshes us from our weary burdens in the journey of life, the discipline of obedience to Him becomes a joy. We discover that the disciplines of discipleship set us free. Habits, thoughts, and friends that kept us in bondage in the past cannot continue to control us when we discover the freedom of living in the discipline of Jesus' yoke. His yoke fits and enables us to pull our weight in the Kingdom.

learn of me could be translated, *become my disciples*. Though chapter 11 has focused on those who doubted and rejected Jesus, the chapter concludes with the renewed invitation to discipleship.

The key expression in this invitation is **take my yoke**. The word **yoke** was used in Judaism in a figurative way to signify submission, discipline, duty, and obedience. Jews used the word with reference to the Law and the commandments. To become a student of the Law, one took on the yoke of the Torah. Such disciplined commitment was not dreary bondage. Rather, submitting to the yoke of the Law brought freedom and life. Jesus states in verse 30 that His **yoke is easy**. The word **easy** is normally translated *kind*. This is a way of saying that Christ's yoke fits. As a well-fitting yoke does not chafe or irritate the ox, Jesus' easy yoke offers the grace of fulfillment and meaning to those who follow Him.

12

CONFLICT WITH JUDAISM

Matthew 12:1–50

The unifying theme in Matthew 12 is conflict with Judaism. Verses 1–21 contain two Sabbath controversy stories, while Jesus' response to accusations of the Pharisees occupies verses 22–45. The chapter concludes with distance between Jesus and His family.

1. SABBATH CONTROVERSIES 12:1–21

Matthew's first Jewish readers would have naturally contrasted Jesus' gentle or easy yoke (11:28–30) with the yoke of the Torah that the Pharisees insisted upon. That contrast appears in the Sabbath controversy stories found in 12:1–14. Matthew concludes the section with a lengthy quotation from Isaiah that prophesied the gentle ministry of Jesus.

THE LORD OF THE SABBATH 12:1–8

Matthew quickly sets the stage for conflict with the Jewish leaders by describing Jesus and His disciples passing through a grain field on the Sabbath. Because the **disciples were hungry** they **began to pick some heads of grain and eat them** (12:1). Deuteronomy 23:25 permitted this as long as they did not use a sickle to cut the grain. The issue is whether such work should be permitted on the Sabbath and who has the authority to answer that question. The Pharisees declare that the disciples' activity is **unlawful on the Sabbath** (12:2).

The accusation was a serious charge. At one level, it charged the disciples with being unpatriotic and desecrating one of the supreme Jewish symbols. At another level, it charged Jesus with teaching against the Law,

HISTORICAL CONTEXT

SABBATH

Sabbath observance was one of the major identity markers of Judaism in Jesus' time. Even in the Old Testament, Sabbath observance made Israel unique by connecting the nation to the God who observed Sabbath after Creation. Failure to keep the Sabbath was one of the reasons Israel had fallen to her enemies and had been taken into captivity, according to Jeremiah 17:27 and Nehemiah 13:15–18. Antiochus Epiphanes had forbidden Sabbath observance as part of his effort to destroy Judaism in the second-century B.C. Christians often fail to recognize that for most Jews, Sabbath was a joy and delight, a time of celebration, an affirmation of the holiness of God, and a defense against falling into disregard for God and His world.

the supreme gift of God to Israel given at Mount Sinai. Jesus does not deny their charge directly but answers it scripturally. Matthew clears Jesus of the accusation that He spoke against the Law and shows that the issue is a matter of proper interpretation of Scripture. He set the question in the context of Jesus' authority to interpret the Sabbath commandment.

Jesus' response comes in three parts. The first is to remind the Pharisees of **what David did when he and his companions were hungry** (12:3). He alludes to the event described in 1 Samuel 21:1–6, when David and his men were hungry, as they fled from Saul, and **ate the consecrated bread** reserved **only for the priests** (Matt. 12:4). Jesus' point goes beyond David doing something unlawful for his men, so sometimes the law can be broken for hungry people. Rather, David was the prototype of the Messiah and, when an urgent situation occurred, he was not condemned for taking liberties with the Law. Here Jesus claims that, as the Messiah, He is greater than David and thus has even greater authority to interpret the Law.

Jesus' second response notes that the responsibilities of the priests in the Temple services cause them to break the Sabbath every week, yet they are guiltless (12:5). If the details of Sabbath observance can be set aside by the requirements of Temple worship, then it is even more appropriate to relax those requirements in the very presence of God incarnate. That is the point of the comment in verse 6 that **one greater than the temple** was present. The purpose of the Temple service was to bring people into the presence of God. Jesus brought the presence of God into people's lives.

The third response appeals to Hosea 6:6: **I desire mercy, not sacrifice**. The words of Matthew 12:7, **If you had known,** suggest that the Pharisees were poor interpreters of Scripture. They should have read Hosea 6:6 and understood that God's desire for loving kindness is greater than His desire for ritual fulfillment. Thus Jesus and His disciples are not disregarding the Law but are pursuing its actual intent in contrast to the narrow legalism of the Pharisees. The conclusion is that Jesus is **Lord of the Sabbath** (Matt. 12:8). The word **Lord** claims authority for Jesus to create, direct, and use the Sabbath as He sees fit.

HEALING A SHRIVELED HAND ON THE SABBATH 12:9–14

The theme of conflict with the Jewish leaders intensifies in the following paragraph. Matthew notes that Jesus **went into their synagogue** (12:9). There He met **a man with a shriveled hand** (12:10). The exact nature of the man's problem is not certain. The Greek text says that he had a dry or dried up hand. Some suggest his hand muscles had atrophied; others propose that the problem was dried skin caused by working in lime; while still others think of his hand as paralyzed or simply so stiff it could not move. Regardless of the exact nature of the problem, a man's inability to use his hand meant the loss of the ability to work and thus to support his family.

The Pharisees are also present in the synagogue, **looking for a reason to accuse Jesus**. Perhaps they had set up the encounter between Jesus and the man with the shriveled hand, suspecting that Jesus would heal the man. The question **Is it lawful to heal on the Sabbath** is the key to understanding Matthew's purpose. In the context of Matthew 12:8, it is the most appropriate question to ask the Lord of the Sabbath. Who other than the Lord of the Sabbath is qualified to answer?

The Pharisees were divided among themselves about whether it was lawful to heal or even pray for a sick person on the Sabbath. Jesus turned the question from the healing of a person to the issue of rescuing an animal fallen **into a pit on the Sabbath** (12:11). Pits were often dug near villages to capture prowling wild animals. However, **sheep**, which were the major economic resources of villagers, could also fall into the pit. The Essenes argued that one could not remove a sheep fallen into a pit on the Sabbath without incurring guilt. The Pharisees disagreed, and Jesus took advantage of their position on this issue.

Jesus' argument follows a typical Jewish technique of arguing from lesser to greater. His use of this technique appears in the words **how much more** (12:12). A human being is infinitely **more valuable than a sheep**. If it is lawful to rescue a sheep on the Sabbath, how much more will it be lawful to help a human being. In this argument, we see Jesus not only as Lord of the Sabbath but also Lord of the Law. The evidence of His authority to interpret the Law is confirmed by His healing the man's hand (12:13). Matthew notes that the healing is not partial or temporary. Rather, the man's hand **was completely restored, just as sound as the other.** The healing that should have been an occasion for rejoicing, however, became another benchmark in the growing opposition to Jesus. The **Pharisees** left, plotting **how they might kill Jesus** (12:14).

THE SCRIPTURAL MANDATE FOR JESUS 12:15–21

The threat of death causes Jesus to withdraw from the Pharisees. However, Matthew is clear that opposition from Jewish leaders did not lessen Jesus' popularity. Rather, **many followed him, and he healed all their sick** (12:15). Matthew does not say whether these healings took place on the Sabbath or not, but clearly this paragraph flows out of the two Sabbath controversy stories. Jesus instructed those who were healed **not to tell who he was** (12:16). This instruction reflects the growing conflict with the Jewish leaders. Jesus would not be deterred from healing, but neither would He seek confrontation with those who object to His healing. The instruction also assumes that those who were healed knew Jesus' identity. For Matthew, it is the identity of Jesus as Lord of the Sabbath that authorizes His healing ministry on the Sabbath.

Interpretation of Scripture had been central to the argument between Jesus and the Pharisees in the Sabbath controversies. Matthew has one other scripture passage he wants to introduce to explain why Jesus would heal on the Sabbath. Isaiah 42:1–4 was not one that entered into the actual interchanges between Jesus and the Pharisees, and so Matthew introduces it as Scripture fulfilled by Jesus' ministry (Matt. 12:17).

With all the Scripture quotations cited by Matthew, this text of Matthew 12:17–21 is the longest. It is a paraphrase of Isaiah 42:1–4, which is now considered the opening lines of the Servant Songs of Isaiah. These songs found in Isaiah 42:1–9; 49:1–13; 50:1–11; and 52:13–53:12 give concentrated emphasis to the Servant of the Lord. The Servant Songs identify the servant as **my servant**. In contrast to the Pharisees who rejected Jesus and accused Him of breaking God's Law, God himself calls Jesus **my servant whom I have chosen** (Matt. 12:18). Rather than being a blasphemer or an enemy of God, as the Pharisees suggested, Jesus was anointed by God to the ministry He was performing.

The second line of the quotation—**the one I love, in whom I delight**—clearly points the reader back to the words from heaven at Jesus' baptism: "This is my Son, whom I love; with him I am well pleased." Thus, through the Isaiah 42 quotation, Matthew is able to declare that the ministry that God inaugurated for Jesus at His baptism is now unfolding through His healing ministry, even though it is opposed by the Pharisees. The further statement, **I will put my Spirit on him**, would remind readers of the descent of the Spirit on Jesus at His baptism. These words also provide important context for accusations that will emerge in subsequent verses. The statement that the servant **will proclaim justice** could be translated *will preach righteousness*. Thus, Matthew 12:18 provides clear scriptural vindication for Jesus' preaching ministry that has focused on righteousness in the chapters leading up to this text.

Verses 19–20 frame Jesus' identity negatively. He does **not quarrel or cry out**. This is the reason Jesus withdrew when the Pharisees began to plot His death. He would not force conflict, though He would not change His message or ministry. The following line notes that **no one will hear his voice**. Though He proclaimed justice, He was not heeded. Thus, Matthew even sees in Scripture the Pharisees' rejection of Jesus' message. The prophetic statement in verse 20 that **he will not break a bruised reed** or **snuff out a smoldering wick** affirms the gentleness of Jesus' ministry.

The poor, afflicted, and sick will benefit by His gentle touch. By quoting this portion of Isaiah 42:3, Matthew explains why Jesus was more concerned with the sick, the needy, the sinners, and the tax collectors than He was with the Jewish religious leaders like the Pharisees.

Matthew could have easily concluded the quotation at that point. What Matthew 12:21 omits and what it includes from Isaiah 42:4 are very instructive for Matthew's first audience: Jewish believers being pressured to abandon the mission to the Gentiles. Matthew concludes the quotation in verse 21 with the words **in his name the nations will put their hope.** The word *nations* could easily be translated *Gentiles*. Thus, in the midst of conflict between Jesus and Jewish leaders, Matthew affirms the scriptural mandate for the Gentile mission. But this reference to the hope of the Gentiles is the last phrase of Isaiah 42:4. Any reader familiar with Isaiah 42:4 would have known that the verse begins, "He will not falter or be discouraged." The servant Messiah would not be discouraged until His ministry accomplished all God had intended—including bringing the gospel of the Kingdom to the Gentiles. If Jesus would not falter, neither should His disciples be discouraged in the face of opposition.

2. ACCUSATIONS BY THE PHARISEES 12:22-45

The next major section of Matthew 12 is built around accusations and demands by the Pharisees. Verses 22–37 center on the accusation that Jesus cast out demons by the power of Satan. Verses 38–45 respond to the demand that Jesus perform a miraculous sign.

DEMONS CAST OUT BY BEELZEBUB 12:22-37

The immediate cause of the Pharisees' accusation against Jesus was His healing of a **blind and mute** man (12:22). As was common in that time, the man's blindness and dumbness were attributed to demon possession. Matthew does not specifically mention that Jesus cast out the demon(s), but the statement that He healed the man assumes the defeat of the demonic powers. One must understand that assumption to follow the argument of the remainder of this section. The crowds **were astonished** (12:23) at Jesus' victory over the demonic and wondered if such power signified that

Jesus was the Messiah. The title that appears in verse 23 is **Son of David**, which was a common messianic title in first-century Judaism.

The reality of Jesus' power and of the miracle itself could not be questioned. The only question the **Pharisees** can raise is the source of Jesus' power. Verse 24 presents their answer to that question: **It is only by Beelzebub, the prince of demons, that this fellow drives out demons.** The Greek text, and almost all modern translations of verse 24, speak of Beelzebul rather than Beelzebub. Beelzebul had become a synonym for Satan by New Testament times. The Pharisees charged Jesus with casting out demons by the power of Satan. To accuse Jesus of being associated with Satan was to accuse Him of sorcery, a charge that reappears in later Jewish literature about Jesus. The charge was serious because the *Mishnah* prescribed the death penalty as punishment for sorcery.

Verses 25–26 present Jesus' first argument against the accusation of the Pharisees. Since demons were considered under the control of **Satan**, to cast out demons by the power of Satan would be a case of Satan fighting or being **divided against himself.** Using a brief parable, Jesus compared the matter to political and military scenes people understood. A **kingdom** or a **city** or even a **household divided against itself will not stand.** To fight with oneself leaves one vulnerable to the enemy outside. Thus the charge that Jesus casts out demons by working with Satan himself is ridiculous. Satan would never agree to such an arrangement because it would weaken his power exercised through the demons.

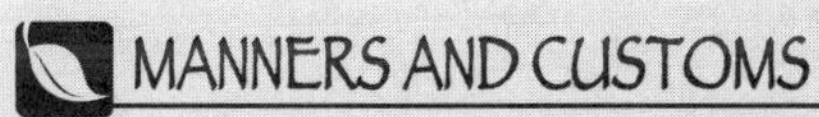

MANNERS AND CUSTOMS

BEELZEBUL

Beelzebul is a Hebrew word meaning *lord of the dwelling* or *lord of the heights*. A few scholars argue for *lord of the dung* as the meaning. The term was used of a god in several of the cultures surrounding Israel. By New Testament times, the word had become an alternative title for Satan. The Hebrew word Beelzebub appears in 2 Kings 1:2, 3, 6, and 16 for a god of Ekron and means *lord of the flies*. It was probably a sarcastic variation on Beelzebul even then. Mysteriously, the Syriac, Latin, and a few English versions read Beelzebub instead of Beelzebul.

Jesus then turned the argument on its head. If they wanted to argue that He cast out demons by demonic power, then what was the power by which the Pharisees cast out demons (12:27)? He does not argue that the

Pharisees cast out demons by the power of Satan. Jesus assumed that the defeat of the demons was always the work of God. Rather, His point was that there was no more reason to accuse Him of casting out demons by the power of Satan than to accuse themselves of doing the same. If, however, it is **the Spirit of God** by which Jesus drove out demons, **then the kingdom of God has come** (12:28). The construction of the Greek sentence in verse 28 shows that there is no question but that Jesus drove out demons by the power of the Holy Spirit. One might translate, *Since I drive out demons by the Spirit of God, then the kingdom of God has come upon you.* The defeat of the evil spirits is clearly a sign of the presence of the Kingdom.

Verse 29 presents another brief parable describing the matter. Jesus portrays Satan as **a strong man** who must first be tied up before one can enter his **house and carry off his possessions**. Thus Jesus portrays himself and His ministry as a process of robbing Satan. Both the casting out of demons and the healing of those in need were expressions of Jesus stealing Satan's possessions and carrying them off. For the Pharisees to attribute His work to Satan is perverted indeed. Because they refuse to stand **with** Jesus in the battle against evil, they are **against** him (12:30).

Jesus describes blasphemy against the Holy Spirit as the unforgivable sin in verse 31. The sentence structure declares **every sin and blasphemy** as forgivable except blasphemy against the Spirit. The severity of this statement can be seen by the reiteration of it in verse 32. Any **word** spoken **against the Son of Man**—that is against Jesus himself—can be **forgiven**. But any word spoken **against the**

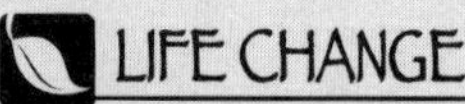

Many believers worry about committing the unforgivable sin. They should not. Matthew 12:31–32 describes the unforgivable sin as blasphemy against the Holy Spirit. It is to become so perverted as to label good as bad and bad as good. When that happens, there is no conscience left by which one may recognize his or her sin, repent, and be forgiven. It is not that God is unwilling to forgive. The problem is the conscience is so seared that it cannot repent. Worry about sin indicates a healthy conscience. Believers need to learn to live with confidence in God's gracious forgiveness and the faithfulness of His Spirit to convict them when they have sinned.

Holy Spirit will not be forgiven. The seriousness of this issue is that forgiveness of such a sin is impossible both **in this age** and **in the age to come.** The meaning of this strong statement must be understood in relation to its context. According to verse 28, the Holy Spirit is the power by which Jesus drives out demons. The blasphemy against the Holy Spirit must refer to the Pharisees attributing that work of Jesus through the Holy Spirit to Beelzebul.

Verses 33–37 present a brief sermon applying the truth that Jesus has just taught. The call to **make a tree . . . and its fruit . . . good** follows both on the teaching in Matthew 7:16–20 and teaching on the unforgivable sin. The coming of Jesus—then and now—calls for a decision to commit oneself to either the Kingdom (good) or to the powers of Satan (bad). Verse 33 calls for the hearer to choose between these alternatives. The choice will reveal the nature of one's **heart**—whether it is good or bad. Once the choice is made, the fruit will be good or bad. The fact that **a tree is recognized by its fruit** means that the Pharisees who **are evil** cannot **say anything good** (12:34). One's **mouth** reveals one's **heart**.

The result is that a person **brings** either **good** or **evil things out of the good** or **evil stored up** within that person (12:35). Jesus sees a certain inevitability to this. One is either good or evil. As a result, a person produces good or evil things in one's life, and one's words will ultimately reveal both the source and the results as good or evil. But this is not a matter of predestination, because verse 36 calls on people **to give account . . . for every careless word they have spoken.** Careless or idle words reveal careless and idle hearts. One cannot give account of words **on the day of judgment** without owning up to one's commitments and heart. Because words reveal the heart, they are sufficient evidence to acquit or condemn a person on the judgment day (12:37).

THE DEMAND FOR A MIRACULOUS SIGN 12:38–45

The way in which words reveal hearts is then illustrated by the demand of **some of the Pharisees and teachers of the law,** asking Jesus to provide them with **a miraculous sign** (12:38). Many modern Christians take the desire for miraculous signs as positive indications of faith. In this case, Jesus interpreted the request as evidence of a **wicked and adulterous generation**. One must wonder what further sign the Pharisees desired from Jesus. He has already cleansed a leper, healed many people, cast out demons, raised the dead, and preached righteousness. His ministry has given ample evidence that He is the Messiah, Servant of the Lord, and Son of God. The fact that all these signs have been given—and the Pharisees ask for another—indicates their evil and unrepentant hearts.

HISTORICAL CONTEXT

Signs

The NIV added the word **miraculous** as an adjective modifying *sign* in Matthew 12:38–39. Jesus' point is not the miraculous but the use of signs for proof of truths that need to be taken by faith. Deuteronomy 13:1–3 associates signs with false prophets. Matthew 24:24 declares that false prophets will deceive people with signs and miracles. Matthew 7:22–23 warns against people trusting in miracles rather than in obedience. Satan had demanded signs from Jesus in the temptation account in Matthew 4:1–11. This pattern suggests that the request for signs reveals the Pharisees to be allied with Satan or functioning as false prophets.

Jesus responds that it is **a wicked and adulterous generation** that **asks for a miraculous sign** (12:39). The only sign Jesus will grant the Pharisees is **the sign of the prophet Jonah.** Verse 40 describes the sign of Jonah and illustrates that the main point of the sign is not something miraculous but a pattern that points to the work of God. In the same way **Jonah was three days and three nights in the belly of a huge fish**—likewise Jesus **will be three days and three nights** in the tomb **in the heart of the earth.** This clearly refers to the coming death and resurrection of Jesus. Jesus seems willing to drop the sign value of the miracle healings, casting out demons, and raising the dead that He has performed in His ministry. Instead He looks to His death and resurrection as the supreme evidence of His identity and purpose. The resurrection will prove beyond a shadow of doubt that His ministry was not accomplished in partnership with Satan.

The evidential values of the sign of His death and resurrection will be clear **at the judgment** (12:41) when the people **of Nineveh will stand** in condemnation of the **generation** of Jesus' time. The people of Nineveh **repented at the preaching of Jonah.** If **one greater than Jonah** should come, surely the people who heard would repent. But the Pharisees did not repent at the ministry of Jesus who is the one greater than Jonah. Likewise **the Queen of the South** will **condemn** Jesus' **generation**. The Queen of the South refers to the Queen of Sheba described in 1 Kings 10:1, who came from far away to **listen to Solomon's wisdom** (Matt. 12:42). Though Solomon was a son of David, Jesus is a **greater** Son of David. The accusations and demands from the Pharisees had come in reaction to the people who responded to the healing of the blind and mute man by confessing Jesus as Son of David (12:23).

Verses 43–45 develop a parable to present a warning to the Pharisees with regard to the danger in which their evil hearts have placed them. The parable speaks of **an evil spirit** who **comes out of a** person and seeks a new home (12:43). When the spirit **does not find** a home, it returns **to the house** or the person it **left** (12:44). When it finds the house **swept clean and put in order**, it finds **seven other spirits more wicked than itself, and they go in and live there** (12:45). Though the parable describes the actions of an evil spirit, the teaching point is the condition of the house, which represents the person the evil spirit left. The problem is that **the final condition of that man**—the house—**is worse than the first**.

The parable warns the Pharisees that their encounter with Jesus and His message has offered them an opportunity to repent of the evil of their hearts and lives. If they persist in their opposition to Jesus—calling good evil and blaspheming the Holy Spirit—their evil condition will multiply, perhaps sevenfold, to the point that they can no longer repent. Their final condition will be far worse than their first condition.

3. THE TRUE FAMILY OF JESUS 12:46–50

On the surface, the brief account of Jesus' family seeking to speak with Him and His response to them seems to be simply a human interest story from the events of Jesus' life. However, Matthew's placement of this exchange at the end of chapter 12 is quite strategic.

Verse 46 describes **Jesus still talking to the crowd** when **his mother and brothers** arrive and stand outside, waiting **to speak to him.** When a person told Jesus His family waited outside, He responded with a rhetorical question: **Who is my mother, and who are my brothers?** (12:48). He answered His own question by **pointing to his disciples** and saying, **Here are my mother and my brothers** (12:49).

This paragraph emphasizes the separation between Jesus and His earthly family. Twice they are described as standing outside. When Jesus becomes aware of their presence, He ignores their desire to speak to Him and rejects them as His family by claiming that His disciples are His family. This unexpectedly harsh response to His family must be understood in the context of the conflict with Judaism that Matthew 12 unfolds. The Pharisees and the Essenes were the closest theological families to Jesus and His disciples. But this chapter has been about the growing distance between Jesus and these Jewish groups. The separation from His earthly family symbolizes the separation from the Jewish religious leaders under whose ministry He had grown up.

Jesus defines His family in terms of obedience: **Whoever does the will of my Father in heaven is my brother and sister and mother** (12:50). This statement reminds Matthew's readers of the importance of obedience in Jesus' teaching in the Sermon on the Mount, especially in 7:15–27. It also defines the Kingdom entrance requirement Jesus preaches. Obedience to the will of God—rather than arguing about the Law and accusing Jesus of being in a league with Satan—will be the marker of Jesus' family of faith.

Part Four

The Variety of Responses to Jesus: Teachings and Examples

MATTHEW 13:1–17:27

The fourth major section of Matthew begins with a block of parables demonstrating the variety of responses that people make to the Kingdom. This collection of parables appears in 13:1–53. The following narrative portion of this section also demonstrates a variety of responses to the Kingdom: the rejection of Jesus' hometown in 13:54–58; the death of John the Baptist; the disciples' response to Jesus' walking on the water; Jesus healing a Canaanite woman's child; Peter's confession of Jesus as the Messiah; and the frustrations of discipleship. Matthew 13:54–17:27 demonstrates a wide variety of ways people respond to Jesus. Though some responses continue the pattern of rejection of Jesus begun in Matthew 11–12, other responses demonstrate faith and obedience.

13

JESUS' PARABLES TEACHING THE KINGDOM

Matthew 13:1–53

A natural question, following the doubt and rejection of Jesus described in Matthew 11–12, is how people could reject or doubt Jesus after seeing His authority demonstrated in both His teachings and His miracles. The third collection of Jesus' teachings in 13:1–52 appears designed to answer that question by demonstrating that Jesus understood there would be a variety of responses to the Kingdom. This third teaching block consists of parables, interpretations of parables, and discussion of Jesus' purpose in teaching by means of parables.

1. THE VARIETY OF RESPONSES TO THE KINGDOM 13:1–30

Jesus appears to operate with a Hebrew concept of parables. The Hebrew word for parable is *mashal*, which was used of many kinds of sayings—from proverbs to illustrations to word plays to allegories. Twentieth-century scholarship on parables witnessed a journey that came almost full circle. The result is that the interpreter has many methods available to interpret a parable. The variety of kinds of parables suggests that a variety of ways of interpretation is also needed.

Matthew's collection of parable teachings begins with the story of the sower in 13:1–9. This is followed by a discussion of the purpose of parables in 13:10–17. The interpretation of the parable of the sower appears in 13:18–23. The second major parable in the collection is the parable of the weeds found in 13:24–30. The similitudes of the mustard seed and the yeast are inserted in 13:31–35 before Matthew returns to give the interpretation of the parable of the weeds in 13:36–43. Two more similitudes, of the hidden treasure and of the pearl, appear in 13:44–46. The parable collection concludes with the story of the net and closing comments in 13:47–52.

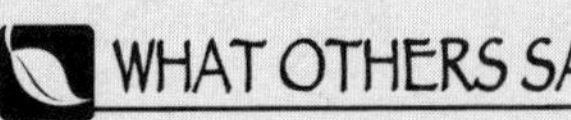

PARABLES

For the majority of Church history, parables were interpreted as allegories, that is, theological truth told in code via stories. At the beginning of the twentieth century, Adolf Jülicher proposed that every parable of Jesus had one and only one point of teaching. For the first half of the twentieth century, that one point was thought to be some truth about the kingdom of God. By mid-century, increasing attention was given to the literary form and function of parables. Similitudes, illustrations, examples, proper parables, and allegories are all structured differently and have different functions for the teacher. By the final quarter of the twentieth century, scholars of parables had become open once again to multiple points of comparison and even multiple meanings arising from a parable. Some parables are now understood as allegories once again.

THE PARABLE OF THE SOWER 13:1–9

This parable of the sower is also found in Mark 4:1–9 and Luke 8:4–8. Though the most common title is the parable of the sower, it is often called the parable of soils, and occasionally it has been called the parable of the seed. The parable is introduced by a brief narrative framework in verses 1–2. The statement that these teachings through the parables took place **that same day** as the conflict with the Pharisees described in chapter 12 shows that the parables answer further questions from the accusations and demands of the Pharisees. That Jesus taught **by the** side of the **lake** and was so pressed by the crowd that **he got into a boat** to continue is a common theme in the Gospels (see Luke 5:1–3; Mark 4:1–2). The statement that He **sat in** the boat (Matt. 13:2) describes Jesus in the official teaching position for Jewish rabbis, as He was for the Sermon on the Mount (5:1).

Matthew's comment that Jesus **told** the people **many things in parables** appropriately introduces this collection in chapter 13. It suggests that the parables in this chapter are only representative examples of the larger body of Jesus' parable teaching. The sentence also sets up the question of the purpose of the parables that will receive special attention in the next paragraph.

The parable, like many Jesus told, is set in the agricultural world of ancient Palestine: **a farmer went out to sow his seed** (13:3). While ancient farmers threw the seed more accurately than moderns might imagine, some seed would inevitably fall **along the** beaten **path** at the edge of the field (13:4). This path would be beaten into a hard surface by the many farmers who walked it on the way to their fields. As a result, the seed would not penetrate the dirt, and **the birds** could easily come and eat it off the path. Other seeds would fall **on rocky places where** the **soil was shallow** (13:5). Many places in Palestine have only a thin layer of soil over rocky shelves that may be quite large. Because the soil is shallow, the heat of the sun causes the seed to germinate **quickly,** but with so little depth of soil, the plant is **scorched** and withers away almost as quickly (13:6).

Other seed would be scattered **among thorns** (13:7), which seem to have the ability to survive in any conditions and to choke out the young wheat that has been sown. However, much of the **seed fell on good soil** (13:8). Whether the soil was naturally good or the farmer had worked hard for many years to improve the quality, most fields had enough good soil for the farmer to expect the possibility of a good crop. Everything in the parable, up to the harvest, was very typical of

MANNERS AND CUSTOMS

FARMERS

Unlike the customs of rural North America, the farmers of Jesus' world did not live on their farms. Rather they lived in villages and walked out to the plot of ground they farmed. Because of the primitive agricultural technology, and the division of the land through the process of inheritance, the farms were small, consisting of only a few acres. To plant, the farmer carried the seed in a bag slung over his shoulder and *broadcast* the seed. That is, he would take a handful of seed from the bag and, swinging his arm while opening his hand, he scattered the seed in a wide arc across the ground. After scattering the seed, the farmer would plow the field with a primitive wooden plow that would scratch a small amount of earth over the seeds.

farming experience in Jesus' time. None of His audience would have been surprised by the variety of soils and the resulting loss of the crop from the seed sown in bad soil. What would have surprised them was the harvest Jesus described in verse 8: **a hundred, sixty or thirty times what was sown.** In Jesus' time a good crop for farmers in Palestine was about *ten-fold.* This amazing harvest must be a significant part of the teaching point of the parable.

Jesus concluded the parable with an enigmatic exhortation: **He who has ears, let him hear** (13:9). Matthew used the same words back in 11:15, and they will appear again in 13:43. The words challenge the listener to think through and understand the parable. Part of the power of parables as a teaching instrument is that they have the ability to shed light on the subject from a variety of angles. The teacher of parables will not be satisfied if the listener jumps too quickly to a conclusion of the meaning. One must allow time for the words of the parables to soak in until the meaning becomes clear. It is also likely that Jesus and Matthew wanted to play on the meaning of the word **hear.** In Hebrew the word meant both to listen and to obey. The exhortation is not just to listen but also to obey the truth that pondering the parable finally yields.

JESUS' PURPOSE IN TEACHING WITH PARABLES 13:10–17

Jesus' challenge to truly hear the parables and obey them reveals that parables are not as easily understood as some people think. That is why we must learn—before we read the interpretation of the parable of the sower—Jesus' purpose in teaching in parables. We may suppose that Matthew does not follow a strict chronological order here, for Jesus no longer seems to be in the boat. Rather, the disciples give words to the question Matthew wants Jesus to answer at this point: **Why do you speak to the people in parables?** (13:10).

Jesus' answer has been difficult for the modern Western mind to understand. His opening words in verse 11 suggest that the subject of parables is **the kingdom of heaven.** That the parables primarily deal with the Kingdom has become widely accepted in gospel scholarship. But Jesus' statement that **the knowledge of the secrets of the kingdom has**

been given to the disciples, **but not to** the people runs counter to North American assumptions about learning. The implication of Jesus' answer is that parables are not easy to understand, and so they enable insiders like the disciples to be given the secrets of the Kingdom while keeping outsiders in the dark. This does not mean the outsiders are bad people. It simply means they cannot understand the parables on their own. They will need to come to Jesus and be taught the meaning of the Kingdom.

In the economy of the Kingdom, the rich get richer and the poor get poorer. The disciple who **has** knowledge of the secrets of the Kingdom **will be given more** until he has **an abundance** (13:12). The passive voice of **will be given** indicates that God is the one who gives. The knowledge with which the disciple began was a gift of grace, and God would increase His investment in that disciple. On the other hand, **whoever does not have, even what he has will be taken** away. Persons without spiritual insight into the Kingdom will fall into deeper spiritual darkness. This concept appears again in Matthew 21:43 and in the parable of the talents in Matthew 25:29.

Verse 13 resumes the answer to the question of why Jesus speaks **in parables**. It is because of the hard-hearted condition of the people. The final two lines of verse 13 paraphrase Isaiah 6:9: the people see but **do not see;** they hear, but **do not hear or understand**. Having alluded to Isaiah 6:9, Jesus—or Matthew—then quotes the totality of Isaiah 6:9–10 in Matthew 13:14–15. This quotation from Isaiah clarifies that it is not the harsh judgment of God that prevents the people from understanding Jesus' parables. Rather, it is their own hard-heartedness. Verse 15 particularly places the blame on the hearers, because their **heart has become calloused; . . . and they have closed their eyes**. Had the people's choice been **otherwise they might** have seen **with their eyes,** heard **with their ears,** understood **with their hearts, and** turned. The word *turned* could equally well be translated *repented*. Had the people repented, God would have healed them. Thus Jesus spoke in parables because parables drove hard-hearted people away and drew open-hearted people near.

Verses 16–17 are directed to the disciples who asked the question about the purpose of parables. The disciples have blessed **eyes because they see** and blessed **ears because they hear**. They are not like hard-hearted Israel that rejected the prophets, but they have been open to hear Jesus. Once again it is likely that Jesus intends the word **hear** to have its double meaning from Hebrew—to hear and to obey. **Many prophets and righteous men** of both the Old Testament and intertestamental eras **longed to see . . . and to hear what** the disciples saw and heard but did not have that opportunity. When God graciously granted people the opportunity to learn the secrets of the Kingdom by hearing the teaching of Jesus, then those people should have taken advantage of that opportunity.

THE INTERPRETATION OF THE PARABLE OF THE SOWER 13:18–23

The interpretation of the parable of the sower builds on the explanation of the purpose for the parables. The opening word of verse 18 in the New International Version text, **Listen**, is the same Greek word as the word *hear* used frequently in verses 13–17. Thus the exhortation is to listen to, understand, and obey the teaching of the **parable of the sower**. The **seed sown along the path** and eaten by the birds is compared to persons who hear **the message of the kingdom and** do **not understand it** (13:19). The pattern of hearing and not understanding echoes the use of those words in verses 13 and 15 above. Because of this, the blame is not completely placed on the **evil one**, who, like the birds, **snatches away what was sown in** their **heart**. The evil one does not control the listener's heart. Each person chooses his or her response to the Kingdom out of the heart.

The **seed that fell on rocky places is** compared to a person **who hears the word and at once receives it with joy** (13:20). Receiving the word **at once with joy** is analogous to the seed that sprang up quickly because the soil was not deep. However, such a person **has no root** and thus **lasts only a short time**. This is because **he quickly falls away** under the pressure of **trouble or persecution . . . because of the word** (13:21). The wording of this sentence reflects the circumstances of the Church by Matthew's time. Persecution is prompted by the preaching of the word of the gospel. The expression **fall away** also reflects the painful reality of persons in Matthew's time who abandoned the faith under the pressure of persecution.

The portion of the parable about **the seed that fell among the thorns** is compared to a person **who hears the word, but the worries of this life**

and the deceitfulness of wealth choke it, making it unfruitful (13:22). Again the application of the parable assumes a time in the life of the Church when people respond to the gospel and then stumble because of the busyness of their schedule and the pressures of their work. The final phrase, **make it unfruitful**, suggests that such persons may not completely abandon the faith, but they fall short of Kingdom expectations. On the other hand, there are also those who hear **the word**, understand it, obey it, and become fruitful disciples. Such persons are the bumper crop of the work of Jesus and the Church.

This interpretation of the parable is clearly allegorical. The seed is compared to the message about the kingdom of God, and each soil is compared to a human heart reflecting rejection or receptivity to the gospel. Because of these allegorical details, many interpreters in the first half of the twentieth century argued that this interpretation did not come from Jesus. They saw it as an allegorical interpretation developed by the early church or by Matthew and presented as words of Jesus. More recent scholarship has taken a more moderate position. One might ask why Jesus was not allowed to tell an allegory or give an allegorical interpretation to a parable when the early church was allowed to do so. There are evidences of Matthew's choosing words in these verses to fit the picture of persecution in his time. However, there is no reason Jesus could not have told the parable of the sower as an allegory with the interpretation found in Matthew 13:18–23. In fact, there is no reason Jesus could not have told the parable several times with different purposes and different interpretations.

THE PARABLE OF THE WHEAT AND THE WEEDS 13:24–30

The parable of the wheat and the weeds appears only in Matthew's gospel. It begins by comparing **the kingdom** to **a man who sowed good seed in his field** (13:24). The agricultural context is similar to the parable of the sower, but it is not developed in the same way. Verse 25 turns the plot sharply by describing an **enemy** who comes by night and sows **weeds among the wheat**. While such an evil attack on a farmer might have happened on occasion, there is no way that it could be described as a typical occurrence. Thus Jesus has developed the parable as an allegory from the beginning. The description of the antagonist as the **enemy** who comes working in the darkness suggests already that this is a parable about Satan. As the parable unfolds, this terrible attack becomes known only after **the wheat** had **sprouted and formed heads** and **the weeds also appeared** (13:26). The weeds were a kind of ryegrass called darnel, which was widespread in the Middle East. It looked like wheat in the early stages and frequently harbored a fungus that was poisonous.

Only after the darnel has grown several weeks can it be distinguished from the wheat. When that took place, **the owner's servants** reported the widespread weeds in the field (13:27). The owner quickly recognizes this as the work of **an enemy** (13:28). The **servants** ask if they should **pull up** the weeds. The owner recognizes that the wheat and the weeds are interwoven in their root systems, so to pull up **the weeds** would **root up the wheat with them** (13:29) The strategy will be to **let both grow together until the harvest** (13:30). At that point the **harvesters** will separate **the wheat** and **the weeds**. The weeds will be bundled to be burned. The wheat will be gathered into the owner's **barn**.

2. THE POWERFUL EFFECT OF THE KINGDOM 13:31–35

Separating the parable of the weeds and its interpretation are two brief parables and a further explanation of why Jesus used parables. The two brief parables of the mustard seed and the yeast are technically similitudes. Rather than telling a story about a particular person or event, a similitude offers a comparison between the Kingdom and a general truth or reality. The similitude works by inviting the listener to accept the comparison in order to see the application. The comparison of verse 31 is not between the **kingdom** and a certain **mustard seed**. It compares the Kingdom with every mustard seed. Jesus says, "The Kingdom is like a mustard seed." The listener responds, "OK, how?" If the comparison is skillfully made, the listener cannot back out and reject the application.

Jesus describes the mustard seed as **the smallest of all your seeds** (13:32). The Greek text does not include the word **your**, which the New International Version—alone among modern translations—inserted as explanation of Jesus' language. Technically, the mustard seed is not the smallest of all seeds as Jesus said. However, it was the smallest of all seeds known in ancient Palestine. The point of the similitude appears to be the contrast between the tiny seed and the large **tree** it becomes when it is fully grown. Like the mustard seed, the Kingdom begins small, but when its final growth is realized, it will be the **largest** reality of all. The comment that **the birds of the air** will **come and perch in its branches** may simply emphasize the impressive growth of the mustard bush. However, the rabbis often dismissively described Gentiles as birds of the air. Jesus may also be teaching that Gentiles will participate in the Kingdom also.

The parable of the **yeast** may have a similar point—that the Kingdom is small in its beginning but powerfully influential in its full growth (13:33). The New International Version seems to understand significant growth to be the point when it describes the flour simply as **a large amount** rather than translating literally as three *sata* of flour. Three *sata* would be between three and four and a half pecks, or about a bushel, of flour. This much flour could produce about a hundred loaves of bread. So the point of the parable may be the great contrast between the small amount of yeast and the large amount of bread produced.

However, another line of understanding is possible. The New International Version and several modern translations state that the woman **mixed** the yeast into the flour. The Greek text states that she hid the yeast in the flour. It may be that Jesus' point is the hidden nature of the Kingdom. The work of the Kingdom is often unobserved, but its effect enables great changes in the world. This leads Matthew to insert another comment on Jesus' use of parables, declaring that Christ said nothing **without using a parable** (13:34). It is not surprising, then, that Matthew notes this practice fulfills Scripture and quotes Psalm 78:2. There, the psalmist declares that he will speak **in parables** and will **utter things hidden since the creation of the world** (Matt. 13:35). By use of the psalm, Matthew is able to emphasize the hidden nature of the Kingdom again. He can also describe Jesus' parables as truths built into the universe from the beginning of creation.

3. THE JUDGMENT OF WRONG CHOICES IN THE KINGDOM 13:36–50

Though various responses to the Kingdom are possible, not all responses are equally appropriate. The interpretation of the wheat and the weeds speaks of the judgment that will come upon evil people who do not belong in the Kingdom. The parables of the hidden treasure and the pearl in 13:44–46 show the importance of choosing the Kingdom above every competing value. Finally, the parable of the net speaks again of the judgment of God against those who choose against the Kingdom.

THE INTERPRETATION OF THE PARABLE OF THE WHEAT AND THE WEEDS 13:36–43

Verse 36 provides a brief narrative transition by which Jesus leaves **the crowd and** enters **the house.** As the **disciples** raised the question of the purpose of Jesus' speaking in parables in 13:10, here they ask for an explanation of the **parable of the weeds.** The explanation shows Jesus' skill in constructing the allegory. **The one who sowed the good seed is the Son of Man**—Jesus himself (13:37). The **field** represents **the world, and the good seed** that grew into the wheat **stands for the sons of the kingdom** (13:38). **The weeds are the sons of the evil one, and the enemy is the devil** (13:39). **The harvest** represents the judgment at **the end of the age.**

The unusual expression, **the sons of the kingdom,** to describe the outcome of the ministry of Jesus suggests that He was envisioning the Church. The allegory is then a frank admission that the Church that will arise from Jesus' ministry, death, and resurrection will be quickly attacked by Satan. The result will be a Church in which sons of the Kingdom and sons of the evil one exist so similarly and are so closely intertwined in the life of the Church that it is difficult to distinguish between them. Jesus suggested that His followers not expend a great deal of energy trying to root the sons of the evil one out of the Church. Violent efforts at purifying the Church could be counterproductive by harming believers. Though willing to identify the sons of the evil one, Jesus was also willing to wait until the final judgment to bring about their destruction.

Verses 40–43 provide a clear allegorical picture of the final judgment. The statement that the **weeds** will be **pulled up and burned in the fire** (13:40) echoes the statement in the parable itself in 13:30. Jesus then declares that the **angels** will be sent **out** to **weed out** the evildoers (13:41). They will be thrown **into the fiery furnace, where there will be weeping and gnashing of teeth** (13:42). The reference is clearly to the sons of the evil one, but verse 41 envisions a final judgment larger and more comprehensive than just the condemnation of sinners. Jesus declares that **everything that causes sin and all who do evil** will be judged. In contrast to this judgment of destruction, **the righteous will shine like the sun in the kingdom of their Father** (13:43). The interpretation closes with the exhortation found back in 13:9: **He who has ears, let him hear.** The repetition of this phrase following the discussion of 13:10–17 places added responsibility on those who hear.

THE PARABLES OF THE HIDDEN TREASURE AND THE PEARL 13:44–46

Like the parables of the mustard seed and the yeast, the hidden treasure and the pearl form a pair. The themes of hiddenness and smallness are shared by both sets of the parable pairs. The new element of teaching for the parables of the hidden treasure and the pearl is the immense value of the Kingdom.

Describing the **kingdom** as **like treasure hidden in a field** (13:44) would have been less mysterious than it would be today. There were no safe places for deposit of money as we now have in banks and other safety deposit possibilities. As a result people often buried treasure in the ground. Often the person who buried the treasure died before retrieving it, and it remained lost until discovered by some fortunate person stumbling upon it. Such a person would naturally hide **it again,** and sell **all he had,** and buy **that field** so he could own the treasure.

The word **again** that begins verse 46 indicates that the parable of the pearl makes a similar point as the parable of the hidden treasure. Pearls were highly valued in the ancient world. There is some evidence that pearls were even more highly valued than gold. A pearl **merchant**

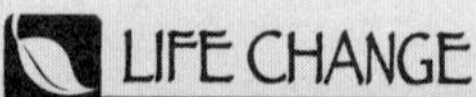

LIFE CHANGE

THE SUPREME VALUE OF THE KINGDOM

Occasionally Christians today are distressed that the person who found the treasure did not try to find the rightful owner. They see questionable ethics in the man Jesus praised. The point of the parable is not to tell us what to do when we find treasures hidden in a field—a fairly rare occurrence for most of us. Rather, the parable uses what any person of the ancient world would have done to illustrate how we should respond to the discovery of the Kingdom. Whatever the price, we should relinquish everything we have in order to enter the Kingdom. Its value is far superior to any human currency or human values.

would have the ability to recognize a pearl **of great value** compared to other pearls (13:46). Finding such a marvelous pearl, the merchant would have **sold everything he had and bought it**. Again the central point is that the Kingdom is of such great value that it is worth relinquishing everything a person has to enter into it.

Though the central point of both parables is the same, the parable narratives set up two different scenarios for entering the Kingdom. The pearl merchant was actively seeking the most valuable pearl, while the treasure was found accidentally. It does not matter whether one is actively seeking the Kingdom or seems to stumble upon it. In either case, the Kingdom is of such infinite worth that the only wise decision is to give up everything in order to become a part of the Kingdom.

THE PARABLE OF THE NET 13:47–50

The parable of the **net** begins with the words **once again** (13:47). This suggests the parable repeats the message of one of the earlier parables. The main point of the parable of the net is very similar to that of the parable of the weeds. The background of the parable shifts from the agricultural world to the world of fishing. The image of a net being **let down into the lake** and catching **all kinds of fish** would have been easily understood by the people who lived around the shores of the Sea of Galilee. When a net **was full, the fishermen** would pull **it up on the shore**, collect **the good fish in baskets, but** throw **the bad away** (13:48).

Jesus moves then to the interpretation in verse 49. **At the end of the age the angels will come and separate the wicked from the righteous.** The wicked will be thrown **into the fiery furnace, where there will be weeping and gnashing of teeth** (13:50). Verse 50 is virtually identical to verse 42, which describes the judgment in the interpretation of the parable of the weeds. The point of the parable of the net is that the community of faith will find itself to be a mixture of good and bad people. While that is not a comfortable position for the Church, it will never be completely remedied until the final judgment. The difference between the two parables is the cause of the mixed nature of the Church. In the first, the weeds are the work of Satan. In the parable of the net, it is simply part of the nature of reality. Both parables highlight the fact that the Kingdom and the Church belong to God. As much as human members would like to make their own judgments about who is good and bad, only God is qualified to make that judgment, and He will at the last day.

4. THE CONCLUSION OF JESUS' TEACHINGS WITH PARABLES 13:51–53

Jesus' question in verse 51 is astounding: **Have you understood all these things?** Even more astounding is the disciples' reply: **Yes.** The **all things** refers to the mysteries of the Kingdom taught in chapter 13. To understand these things requires more than simply intellectual comprehension. It requires obedience and becoming fruitful in kingdom life. Because obedience and fruitful living are significant elements of discipleship for Matthew, one would hope that the disciples would answer positively.

Several scholars suggest that verse 52 describes the ideal Christian for Matthew or was even an autobiographical testimony by the disciple. The New International Version **every teacher of the law** is unfortunate because it implies one of the teachers of the law trained by the Pharisees, whom Matthew consistently portrays in a bad light. Rather, Jesus is referring to His own disciples, using the Greek word for scribe. As disciples of the Pharisees became scribes of the Pharisees, so Jesus' disciples are

LIFE CHANGE

FINDING SPIRITUAL TREASURES

The new treasures are Kingdom treasures, the kinds of theological teachings Jesus has been providing in Matthew's gospel. The old treasures are the teachings of the Old Testament and traditional Jewish ethical commitments. Matthew himself was surely one of the finest scribes discipled for the Kingdom. A wise disciple brings the resources of the Old Testament and the riches of the gospel together. The constant challenge of Christian discipleship for us is to bring together the priceless treasures of the theological traditions of the Church and the fresh winds of the Spirit that blows in every generation.

scribes **instructed about the kingdom**. The Greek word translated **instructed** here is the verb form of the noun *disciple*. Thus these Christian scribes have been discipled in the Kingdom. Jesus compares them to **the owner of a house who brings out of his storeroom new treasures as well as old.** The words **when Jesus had finished** mark the end of the teaching section making use of parables (13:53).

14

JESUS PROVIDES LIGHT IN THE DARKNESS

Matthew 13:54–14:36

The teaching material in Matthew 13 used a series of parables to portray a variety of ways people might respond to the Kingdom. After the pattern of rejection that emerged in Matthew 11–12, one might well ask what hope there was that the people living in darkness would see a great light through Jesus—Matthew's hopeful declaration in 4:16. The parables of Matthew 13 suggest the light and darkness exist together, and the narrative materials following offer reasons to hope. He points to the growing darkness by describing Jesus' rejection in His hometown in 13:54–58 and the death of John the Baptist in 14:1–12. Then, in 14:13–36, Matthew presents the light of a Jesus who supplies the needs of people and overcomes the power of nature.

1. JESUS REJECTED IN HIS HOMETOWN 13:54–58

In contrast to the profitable teaching of the disciples through the parables, Jesus returned **to his hometown** and **began teaching the people in their synagogue** (13:54). The phrase **their synagogue** suggests there will be opposition. The people of Nazareth will show themselves to be among the ones who see and do not see, who hear and do not hear (13:13). Their question of **where** Jesus acquired **this wisdom and these miraculous powers** appears to be sarcastic and mocking. They only recognize Him as

the carpenter's son, the child of **Mary**, and the sibling of **his brothers James, Joseph, Simon and Judas**, and of **all his sisters** (13:55–56).

Verse 57 states that his hometown **took offense at him.** The Greek word translated here as taking offense is the same word that was used in 13:21 to describe people who fall away under the pressure of persecution. Thus the people of Nazareth are seed falling on rocky places. By responding with a proverb that **a prophet is without honor in his hometown and in his own house**, Jesus placed himself in the long train of Old Testament prophets rejected and dishonored by Israel. Jeremiah was a conspicuous example. He was from Anathoth (Jer. 1:1) yet the people of Anathoth threatened to kill him (Jer. 11:21). It is possible that Jesus intended the proverb to point specifically to Jeremiah and thus to raise the threat that Jesus' own people would kill Him. It is no wonder Matthew concluded with the comment that Jesus **did not do many miracles there because of their lack of faith** (Matt. 13:58).

2. THE DEATH OF JOHN THE BAPTIST 14:1–12

Though Jesus had faced growing opposition from the Pharisees, both His teachings and His miracles caused His popularity to increase among the common people. **The reports about Jesus** had even come to **Herod the tetrarch** (14:1). Herod was aware of Jesus' rapidly increasingly popularity, but was as confused about the true identity of Jesus as the Pharisees had been in Matthew 12. He feared that Jesus was **John the Baptist . . . risen from the dead** (14:2). The idea of a person rapidly rising in power as the reincarnation of a previous hero was not unusual in the Greco-Roman world. The Nero-come-back-to-life myth was used to explain the careers of several powerful and violent emperors who followed him. Herod knew God had been at work in John the Baptist's life. **That is why** he concluded that **miraculous powers** were **at work in** Jesus.

The story line of Jesus continues in Matthew 14:13, but verses 3–12 provide a flashback to John the Baptist's death. Verse 3 notes that **Herod had arrested John . . . and put him in prison because of Herodias.** Josephus, the Jewish historian, also states that Herod arrested John the

Baptist and imprisoned him in the palace-fortress called Machaerus above the eastern shore of the Dead Sea. Josephus mentions a political motivation for John's arrest. Herod was afraid John's rising popularity could enable him to spearhead a rebellion. Matthew indicates that Herod arrested John out of a guilty conscience. Herod had fallen in love with his niece

HISTORICAL CONTEXT

HEROD ANTIPAS

Herod Antipas was one of the sons of Herod of the Great who had been made tetrarch of Galilee and Perea after the death of his father in 4 B.C. He was an effective administrator and ruled until his death in A.D. 39. Part of his success lay in the fact that he kept close track of those who influenced the common people in his realm. John the Baptist and Jesus were two such influencers, and Herod kept close track of them.

Herodias, who was married to his brother (also called Herod by Josephus, but Philip by the Gospel writers). Herod and Herodias had divorced their spouses and married. John the Baptist publicly denounced the marriage as sinful (14:4). The marriage also offended Herod's former father-in-law, the king of Nabatea, whose army later attacked Herod, severely damaging both Herod's army and his reputation. Herod was eager **to kill John, but** the Baptist's reputation as a **prophet** forced him to wait. As a shrewd judge of the mood of his **people**, he knew that killing John would cause more opposition to him than it would eliminate (14:5).

The occasion to kill John came soon enough. Though Jews did not celebrate birthdays, Herod had been so influenced by Greek custom that he did celebrate his own **birthday**. Part of the entertainment was a dance performed by Salome, **the daughter of Herodias** (14:6). Herod was so **pleased** by Salome's dance that he offered her **whatever she** might ask (14:7). According to Mark 6:23 the promise was limited to half of Herod's kingdom. Her request, **prompted by her mother**, was **the head of John the Baptist on a platter** (Matt. 14:8). Herod's distress (14:9) was not the gruesome nature of Salome's request but the potential political problem it might cause him with his people. However, he felt pressured by the fact he had given **oaths** and made a promise in front of **his dinner guests** (14:9). As a result, he honored his promise, and **John** was **beheaded in the prison** (14:10). Once John's **head** was delivered to **the girl** and **her mother** (14:11), **John's disciples came and buried his body.**

The final comment that John's disciples came **and told Jesus** (14:12) offers a small clue to why this gruesome story is included in the first Gospel. This story marks the end of John the Baptist's ministry, and thus the ground is cleared for Jesus' ministry. Secondly, the gruesome death of John the Baptist in some measure provides a preview of the coming death of Jesus.

3. FEEDING THE MULTITUDE 14:13–21

The transition from John the Baptist to Jesus occurs quickly in verse 13 with the words, **when Jesus heard . . . , he withdrew by boat privately**. The parallel account in Luke 9:10 states that the withdrawal was to a town called Bethsaida. Bethsaida was east of the Jordan River on the north bank of the Sea of Galilee and thus in the tetrarchy of Herod's brother Philip. This suggests that Jesus may have been fleeing from Herod.

Such a withdrawal was consistent with the view that Jesus was the prophetic successor of John the Baptist. Elijah had been forced to flee into isolated areas several times during his ministry. However, escaping Herod proved easier for Jesus than getting away from the **crowds**. They **followed him on foot** so that when Jesus arrived at his destination, He **saw a large crowd** already assembled waiting for him (14:14). Matthew gives no explanation of the motives of the crowd, but simply notes that Jesus **had compassion on them and healed their sick**. These words express the theme Matthew intends to emphasize about this segment of Jesus' ministry. It makes compassion Jesus' motivation for the feeding of the multitude, which the following verses will narrate.

The feeding miracle is the only miracle story recorded in all four Gospels, and both Matthew and Mark include a second story of the feeding of the four thousand. Thus the theme of multiplying the loaves for a crowd was a very important memory of Jesus' ministry in the early church. Scholarship has offered several explanations for this. The words in verse 19 describing Jesus' blessing and distribution of the loaves are the same words used in the accounts of the Last Supper. As a result, some believe the feeding of the multitude should be understood in terms of the Lord's Supper and, thus, its memory was cherished by early believers.

Others argue that the feedings of the multitudes were messianic signs by which Jesus repeated the miracle of the manna that Israel experienced in the deserted place of the wilderness. Others point to Ezekiel 34:23, where the coming messianic king will shepherd his people, and see the feeding as the fulfillment of that messianic text. Still others argue that the feeding should be understood as an anticipation of the final messianic banquet at the marriage supper of the Lamb. Whether any or all of these explanations are on target, it is clear that the early church loved the story of the feeding of the multitude.

The narrative flow of the text portrays Jesus as so involved in healing the sick among the crowd that He lost track of the time and place. According to Matthew 14:15, His **disciples came to him** and reminded Him of the remoteness of the location. If the people were to eat, they would need to be released to travel **to the villages and buy themselves some food.** Jesus demonstrates no uncertainty according to Matthew. Rather, He contradicts the disciples' suggestion by declaring that the crowds **do not need to go away** (14:16). Jesus himself and His knowledge of the resources available are sufficient to the need. But rather than handing the disciples and the crowds the miracle, the Master commands the disciples to **give** the crowds **something to eat**. This forces the disciples to identify their meager resources: **We have only five loaves of bread and two fish** (14:17). John 6:9 adds the poignant question, "but how far will they go among so many?"

The meager resources of the disciples will only be sufficient when placed in Jesus' hands, and so, in Matthew 14:18, Jesus commands the disciples to **bring** Him the five loaves and two fish. His instruction to seat **the people . . . on the grass** (14:19) portrays Him as the shepherd of Psalm 23 who makes His flock **lie down in green pastures.** The actions of Matthew 14:19—**taking the five loaves**, giving **thanks**, breaking **the loaves**, and giving **them to the disciples and to the people**—are the same actions described in the Last Supper accounts of Matthew 26:26; Mark 14:22; Luke 22:19; and 1 Corinthians 11:23–24. As mentioned earlier, it is possible that Matthew saw a eucharistic overtone in the feeding of the multitude. It is also possible that the fourfold action at the Last Supper is designed to echo the words and actions of

Jesus in the feeding miracle. Perhaps the point is that there is abundant supply of grace for all in the Lord's Supper. Certainly the result of Jesus' words and actions with the five loaves and two fish was an abundant and completely sufficient supply. **All** the crowd **ate and were satisfied,** according to Matthew 14:20.

The Greek word **satisfied** is the same word used in the fourth beatitude—that all who hunger and thirst for righteousness will be satisfied (5:6). Thus the promised blessings of the Kingdom were already coming true in Jesus' ministry. The fact that **twelve basketfuls of broken pieces** were collected indicates enough for all Israel. The point is the abundance of Jesus' supply. Matthew then points out in verse 21, it was not only **five thousand men** but also **women and children** who were fed. Though ancient—and modern—society often neglected the women and children, Jesus supplied their need also.

4. WALKING ON THE WATER 14:22–33

Matthew, Mark, and John all follow the feeding of the multitude with an account of Jesus walking on the water. Matthew's version is the most developed and includes Peter's attempt to walk on the sea. The close connection between the feeding miracle and the miracle of walking on the sea suggests that the early church saw a theological significance to this miracle. The conclusion found in verse 33 suggests the line of understanding we should follow. The confession of the disciples there, "Truly you are the Son of God," and the echoes of Old Testament Scriptures in this passage indicate that the point of the passage is the relationship of Jesus and God the Father. Matthew's point is not that readers should respond in awestruck wonder. Rather, *worship* is the point and the appropriate response to this miracle.

Structurally, verses 22–33 relate a single drama in two scenes. The first scene appears in verses 22–27. The focus is on Jesus coming to his frightened disciples, speaking a word of peace and encouragement. Verses 28–33 comprise the second scene, and the focus is on the dialog between Jesus and Peter. The two scenes intersect in verse 27 with Jesus' statement, **Take courage! It is I. Don't be afraid.** Some interpreters regard Jesus as the central character of the first scene and Peter as the central character of the second. In reality Jesus is the central character of both scenes and of the story as a whole.

Matthew tells the reader that Jesus **made the disciples get into the boat** (14:22). This is the first hint of the unusual picture these verses will paint of Jesus. The word **made** suggests reluctance on the part of the disciples and authority residing in Jesus. The disciples are sent **ahead of** Jesus **to the other side** of the sea. The implied promise is that Jesus will join them there, but He has two things to accomplish first. He would dismiss **the crowd** and go **up on a mountainside by himself to pray** (14:23). Dismissing the crowd brought closure to the feeding incident and shows Jesus in control of the shift in the scene from focus on a multitude to focus on Jesus **alone**. The emphasis on Jesus praying alone shows the Master modeling the life of prayer He had commanded for His disciples in 6:6. The aloneness of Jesus lends an aura of mystery to the scene that is appropriate for the point that will slowly emerge in this text. Verse 24 shows the stark contrast between Jesus' serenity in prayer and the struggle of the disciples in the growing storm on the sea. They are **already a considerable distance from** the security of **land**, and their **boat** is being **buffeted by the waves** and a contrary **wind**.

Then **Jesus** came **to them, walking on the lake** (14:25). Matthew's first readers would have recognized that in the Old Testament it was God, and God alone, who could stride across the sea (Job 9:8; 38:16; Ps. 77:19; Isa. 43:16; Hab. 3:15). When the disciples saw Jesus walking on the water, the correct conclusion they should have drawn is that Jesus is God incarnate. However, their culture, rather than their Scripture, shaped their response, and **they cried out in fear** that they were seeing **a ghost** (14:26). If the reader is as confused about Jesus' identity as the disciples were, His response in verse 27 should bring clarity: **Take courage! It is I. Don't be afraid.** A more literal translation would be: **Take courage! It is I** AM. Fear not. Jesus' identification of himself echoes the divine name given in Exodus 3:14: **I** AM WHO **I** AM. The point of the first scene should be clear. Jesus was not simply a prophet like John the Baptist. He was not simply a miracle worker like Elijah. Jesus was—and is—God present among His disciples. For that reason the appropriate response is to trust and obey rather than fear.

Peter's response attempts to embrace this truth. He addresses Jesus as **Lord** (Matt. 14:28) and comes to a true conclusion. If Jesus is really God, then Jesus could enable Peter **to come to** Him walking **on the water**. Jesus does not flinch from Peter's conclusion but simply invites him: **Come** (14:29). In trusting obedience, Peter stepped **out of the boat** and **walked on the water toward Jesus.** Matthew has no interest in telling how far Peter walked before **he saw the wind,** causing him to fear and **to sink** (14:30). His prayer, **Lord, save me!** echoes the disciples' prayer in 8:25. **Immediately**, Jesus extended

Because Jesus walked on the water, He had the right to ask Peter about his doubt. Perhaps walking on water should be required before a person is permitted to criticize Peter for sinking. Rather than concluding that Peter failed, we should recognize the great act of faith it took for the big disciple to walk on the water in the first place. It should be instructive that his sinking occurred when he turned his attention from Jesus to the storm. It is only as a disciple walks obediently focused on Jesus that the disciple can authentically imitate Him.

a **hand** (14:31) and the same retort found in 8:26: **You of little faith**. Connection with Jesus brought Peter to safety, and **they climbed into the boat** as the storm ceased (14:32). Verse 33 concludes the account by noting the appropriate response of the disciples. They **worshiped** Jesus and confessed that He was **the Son of God**.

5. A SUMMARY OF JESUS' MINISTRY 14:34–36

With the storm stilled, the boat carrying Jesus and the disciples **landed at Gennesaret** (14:34). Gennesaret was a region on the western bank of the Sea of Galilee. It was in the territory of Herod Antipas. It did not take long for the people to recognize Jesus and to spread the news of His arrival. As the word went out, **people brought all their sick to him** (14:35). The people's confidence in Jesus was so great that they did not ask to be healed but only to be allowed to **touch the edge**

of his cloak. The result was the same: **all who touched him were healed** (14:36).

The placement of this paragraph immediately following the walking on the water is significant. The walking on the water portrayed Jesus as God. In verses 34–36, we see this God responsive to the needs of people and caring about everyone, regardless of that person's social status or position.

15

JESUS PROVIDES BREAD FOR ALL

Matthew 15:1–39

The three main sections of Matthew 15 all deal with food in one way or another. The opening section found in Matthew 15:1–20 addresses the question of clean and unclean foods. In 15:21–28, a Canaanite woman boldly asks for the crumbs left from the Jewish table. The chapter concludes with verses 29–39 as Jesus feeds a Gentile multitude.

1. DEBATE OVER EATING WITH UNWASHED HANDS 15:1–20

Matthew returns to the conflict between Jesus and the Pharisees, along with their legal specialists, that he treated in chapter 12. This first section of chapter 15 has three parts. First, verses 1–9 address the Pharisees and condemn their interpretation of the law. Then verses 10–11 address the crowd, challenging them to understand—and follow—Jesus' interpretation of the law. Finally, verses 12–20 address the disciples and explain the meaning of true purity to them.

The detail that **Pharisees . . . came from Jerusalem** (15:1) indicates the heightened conflict between **Jesus** and them. Not only are the Galilean Pharisees attacking Jesus, now the leadership from Jerusalem takes up the attack. Their accusation comes in two parts. First, their general concern is that Jesus' **disciples break the tradition of the elders** (15:2). Second, the specific charge here is that the disciples **don't wash their hands before they eat**. The charge of breaking the tradition of the elders is serious. The Greek verb translated **break** by the New International Version literally means to *transgress*. The charge is that the disciples—and thus Jesus as their teacher—are sinning. The Greek word translated **tradition** here means *that which has been handed down*. The Pharisees believed that, in addition to the written law God revealed to Moses on Mount Sinai, the Lord also revealed commandments orally to Moses, who handed down those laws orally through the centuries to the time of Jesus. That oral law supposedly given to Moses had grown rapidly in content in the century prior to Jesus.

The Pharisees were the largest of the three major religious groups in Palestine at Jesus' time with an estimated membership of about six thousand. As a lay—not priestly—organization, they feared Jewish sins were delaying the coming of the Messiah. They hoped by strict interpretation of the law to prevent such sins. This is why they were so concerned about actions of Jesus' disciples that violated their oral law. For the Pharisees, the consequence would not simply be divine punishment of the disciples but also divine judgment against the whole people of Israel.

Why the Pharisees raised the question of eating with unwashed hands is not clear. Exodus 30:17–21 required the priests to wash their hands and feet before entering the Tabernacle. Leviticus 15:11 implies that washing one's hands after becoming ritually unclean kept that uncleanness from being transmitted to another. But nothing in the Old Testament commands the washing of hands before eating. Despite the hygienic reasons modern people might see for this practice, the evidence suggests the Pharisees were in the process of creating a tradition about hand washing during Jesus' lifetime. Perhaps they wished to give specific application to Exodus 19:6, where God commands all Israel to be a **kingdom of priests** for Him. Perhaps they envisioned one's home as a Temple where all the Old Testament laws regarding sacrifice and worship should be completely observed.

Jesus does not address the benefits of hand washing before eating. He addresses the Pharisees' method of interpreting Scripture, charging them with breaking—literally transgressing—**the command of God for the sake of tradition** (15:3). Jesus does not charge them with posing tradition against tradition or interpretation against interpretation. Rather, He argues that the Pharisees had placed tradition over the command of God. In this, Jesus affirms the priority of the written law over the oral law. He affirms the priority of the actual words of Scripture over any human application of them. This contrast is clear in the opening words of verse 4, **For God said**, and of verse 5, **but you say**.

Perhaps because the Scripture is silent about hand washing, Jesus shifts the argument to relationship with parents. Verse 4 quotes Exodus 20:12, to **honor** one's **father and mother**, and Exodus 21:17, that whoever **curses his father or mother must be put to death**. The absolute command to honor father and mother is applied by the case law example that requires the execution of one who dishonors a parent specifically by cursing him or her.

In a patriarchal society, one might not expect the command to honor one's parents would be abused, but the Pharisees had developed a scheme of interpretation that enabled them to avoid duties to aged parents. Because the law forbids false oaths (Lev. 19:12) and requires keeping of oaths (Num. 30:2; Deut. 23:21), one could swear that all one's resources belonged to God, but keep those resources available for personal use until death. This meant a person could not give money away to support aged parents because that money had been promised to God. The details of this process eventually required a whole chapter in the *Mishnah* when the oral traditions were committed to writing at the end of the second century A.D.

Jesus summarizes the process in Matthew 15:5 and then describes the outcome in verse 6. A person following such a process does **not "honor his father."** Even worse the process and the way it twisted Scripture nullified **the word of God for the sake of tradition.** The tradition itself might be good, neutral, or bad, but when it nullifies the word of God—literally empties or makes void—it must be rejected. In support, Jesus appeals to **Isaiah** (15:7). Verses 8–9 quote almost exactly the Greek translation of Isaiah 29:13. Through the quotation, Jesus accuses the Pharisees of mere lip service to God, scripturally supports His charge—that they substituted human traditions for the word of God—and introduces the central place of one's heart in determining right motivation and right worship.

Verses 10–11 address **the crowd** calling them to **listen and understand.** Numerous Old Testament passages call on people to **listen** or hear. The Hebrew word used in those passages also has the meaning *obey*. The challenge is not simply to hear and mentally process Jesus' words. Rather, this is a call to obedience to God's Word. Jesus declares that uncleanness is not the result of **what goes into a man's mouth**, but the result of **what comes out of his mouth** (15:11). The Pharisees understood **unclean** as a ritual condition prohibiting contact with God and others according to the purity laws of the Pentateuch. Jesus works with the result—loss of contact with God and others—modifying the meaning of **unclean**. What goes into a person's mouth might well render that person ritually unclean, but it does not break contact with God and others. However, what comes out of a person's mouth can indeed break contact with God and others, as the following verses will make clear.

The audience shifts from the crowd to **the disciples** in verse 12. The disciples point out that **the Pharisees were offended** by Jesus' response. Rather than retracting His statement, Jesus pushed the contrast between himself and the Pharisees even further. He describes them as a **plant my heavenly Father has not planted** (15:13) and as **blind guides** (15:14). As blind guides, He predicts the Pharisees **will fall into a pit** along with those who follow them. As a plant not of God's planting, the Pharisees **will be pulled up by the roots.** The passive voice suggests that God himself will uproot the Pharisees and that they will wither away and die.

Peter's request that Jesus **explain the parable** (15:15) might be asking about calling the Pharisees a plant. However, Jesus' frustration is directed to all the disciples—the **you** of verse 16 is plural—calling them **dull.** The Greek word literally means *without understanding*, and so it points back to verse 10. The disciples have failed to obey Jesus' command to understand, so He must further explain His teaching from verse 11.

Beginning with **what goes into a man's mouth** from verse 11, Jesus notes that **whatever . . . goes into the stomach** is eventually eliminated from **the body** (15:17). Thus there is only a temporary relationship between things going into a person's mouth and that person's life. In contrast, **the things that come out of the mouth come from the heart** (15:18). A person's words and actions reveal a person's heart, which is where one's essential being is found. It is at the heart level that the real issue of clean and **unclean** lies. Words and actions, as expressions of one's heart, are what separate a person from God and others. Verse 19 then lists some of the words and actions that separate a person from God and others: **evil thoughts, murder, adultery, sexual immorality, theft, false testimony,** and **slander.** One should recognize the close correspondence of this list and the so-called second table of the Ten Commandments. Interestingly, that second table begins with the command about honoring father and mother.

Jesus concludes that it is these heart issues—words and actions that express one's heart—that **make a** person **unclean**. In contrast, **eating with unwashed hands does not make** a person **unclean.** Thus verse 20 brings the conversation back from the commandment about honoring father and mother to the original discussion about eating with unwashed hands. What Jesus has done in this section is contrast the Pharisees' method of interpreting Scripture, which creates human tradition of interpretation that benefit the interpreters, with His own method of interpretation, which focuses on the actual words of Scripture and how those words reveal the human heart.

Jesus' teaching about ritual purity makes it very clear that holiness is an issue of the heart, not a matter of the strict observance of a legalistic interpretation of the law. Both holiness and unholiness arise from the heart. Both a holy heart and an unholy heart will be expressed in the actions of a person's life. But the question of holiness is not a question of those actions but of the heart revealed by those actions.

2. TABLE SCRAPS FOR A CANAANITE WOMAN 15:21–28

The transition from conflict with the Pharisees over Scripture interpretation to the story of the Canaanite woman is confusing to modern readers. It would have been more meaningful to Matthew's original readers, who were caught in conflict between the Pharisees and the early Jewish Christians over Jewish identity. Jesus' conflict with the Pharisees was not just about Scripture interpretation, but also whether Scripture allowed the Messiah to minister to Gentiles.

The Gentile focus of Matthew 15:21–28 is clear. **Jesus** traveled **to the region of Tyre and Sidon** (15:21) and met **a Canaanite woman from that vicinity** (15:22). The area was north and west of Galilee in the southwestern part of modern Lebanon. Tyre and Sidon were notorious in the Old Testament as centers of Baal worship. Ahab's infamous queen, Jezebel, had come from Tyre. The word **Canaanite** was out of date in Jesus' time but drew attention to the Old Testament use of the word to describe the idolatrous inhabitants of Canaan that the Israelites were commanded to expel. The geographical setting for this passage screams Gentile and thus unclean.

The woman's plea, **Lord, Son of David, have mercy on me!** opens the conversation. The two titles by which she addresses Jesus are instructive. **Son of David** in particular emphasizes the Jewish messianic expectations of the time. One would not expect this title on a Gentile woman's lips. To call Jesus **Lord** was to use the highest confession of faith developed in the earliest Jewish church. The titles reveal that the woman had both listened to the stories about Jesus and understood what they meant (see 15:10). The woman is more perceptive about Jesus' identity than most Jews. Her appeal for mercy echoes that of the two blind men whom Jesus healed, according to 9:27–31. Further, her **daughter** is demon possessed. Jesus has already described His ministry of driving out demons as evidence of the presence of the kingdom of God (12:28). How could He resist the woman's plea? But He does, refusing to even **answer a word** to her (15:23). The **disciples** seem ignorant of the theological issues at stake and want Him to **send her away** because she is a pest.

Jesus' response in verse 24, **I was sent only to the lost sheep of Israel**, echoes His command in 10:6 that disciples limit their mission to **the lost sheep of Israel**. It also articulated the Pharisees' position that the Messiah was only for the Jews. The woman then increased her appeal by kneeling **before** Jesus: **Lord, help me!** (15:25). Not only is her understanding of Jesus correct, so now is her worship. Jesus' response suggests that He is weakening in the face of her appeal. Or perhaps He now has a way by which He can grant her appeal. The statement that **it is not right to take the children's bread and** give **it to their dogs** (15:26) seems quite insulting. Jews often called Gentiles dogs. Dogs were not kept as pets in the ancient world, but were regarded as filthy and vicious scavengers living around the edges of villages making nuisances of themselves. The woman understood the full force of Jesus' insult. But rather than withdrawing in hurt, she retorts to the insults, **Yes, Lord, but even the dogs eat the crumbs that fall from their masters' table** (15:27). Rather than arguing either the justice or the truth of the Jewish insult, she accepts Jesus' terms and points out that some leftovers ought to be available to her.

As quickly as He had been gruff earlier in the story, Jesus now acknowledges her **great faith** and grants her **request** (15:28). As difficult as this passage is for modern readers, Matthew's purpose for including it in his Gospel should be clear. Jesus' reluctance to minister to this Gentile woman and her daughter mirrored the reluctance of the early Jewish church to admit Gentiles into full standing in Christ. But the claim that Jesus excluded Gentiles is undermined by this passage. What is clear is that faith rather than ethnicity determined that Jesus would answer the woman's prayer. The early church eventually concluded that faith in Christ rather than following Jewish traditions should be the basis for every person's entry into relationship with God.

3. FEEDING THE GENTILE MULTITUDE 15:29–39

Matthew 15:29–39 seems to repeat things that have already happened in Jesus' ministry. The journey **up on a mountainside** echoes the setting of the Sermon on the Mount (5:1). The healing of **the blind, the crippled, the mute and many others** described in 15:30–31 recalls the healings of Matthew 8–9. Further, the feeding of the four thousand seems to be a repeat performance of the feeding of the five thousand men plus women and children mentioned in Matthew 14.

One of the important differences between the events described in these verses and those reported earlier in the Gospel is the geographical setting. Matthew is not as clear as the reference to Decapolis in Mark 7:31, but Jesus' journey from the area of Tyre and Sidon toward the **Sea of Galilee** was eastward. To say that Jesus **went along the Sea of Galilee** (Matt. 15:29) implies that He likely moved to the east side of the Sea of

Galilee, which was the Gentile territory of Decapolis. Thus the events of Matthew 15:29–39 are not simply repeating material previously covered. Rather, this passage describes Jesus' ministry to Gentiles in terms identical to His ministry already mentioned among Jews. The point is often missed by modern readers who do not understand the geography, but Matthew clearly indicates that the benefits of the Kingdom are available to Gentiles as well as to Jews.

Jesus clearly states in verse 32 that His motivation for feeding the four thousand is **compassion**, the very motivation 14:14 identifies for His feeding the five thousand. The statement that the Gentile crowd has **been with** Jesus **three days** is the first indication of how extensive that ministry to the Gentiles has been. The reference to **three days** would have also called to early Christian readers' mind the resurrection of Jesus. One of the meanings of the resurrection is that Gentiles must receive the same ministry as the Jews had received. Matthew 28:18–20 will make that clear. Jesus' concern that the **people** might **collapse on the way** home reveals the depth of His compassion.

The feeding narrative proper begins with the helplessness of the **disciples** (15:33). They recognize that they are **in** a **remote place** and that no village or combination of villages would have enough bread on hand to feed the crowd. **Jesus** turns their focus from what they do not have to what they do have by asking **how many loaves** they **have** (15:34). The disciples see no hope in their supplies; they have only **seven** loaves **and a few small fish**. The sequence of Jesus seating **the crowd on the ground** (15:35), giving **thanks**, breaking the loaves, giving the loaves **to the disciples** and the distribution by the disciples **to the people** (15:36) is the same sequence of feeding the five thousand men plus women and children as is found in Matthew 14. That the people **all ate and were satisfied** is the same conclusion as that spelled out in 14:20. The picking up of **basketfuls of broken pieces** described in verse 37 echoes the clean-up found in 14:20. That there are **seven** basketfuls here and twelve basketfuls in chapter 14 is an insignificant detail.

Matthew's description of the crowd as consisting of **four thousand, besides women and children** (15:38) is worded just as 14:21, except that the first group consisted of five thousand men. By including the second feeding of the multitude story, Matthew has not only made clear Jesus' mission to the Gentiles, He has also fulfilled more Old Testament Scripture. Two miracles of manna are described in connection with the ministry of Moses (Ex. 16; Num. 11). Also, two multiplication of food miracles occurred in the ministry of Elisha (see 2 Kings 4:1–7; 4:38–44). In similar fashion, Jesus' ministry fulfilled the Law and the Prophets, as Matthew 5:17 declares.

THE MEANING OF FOLLOWING JESUS

Matthew 16:1–28

M atthew 16 is a transitional chapter. Verses 1–12 bring to a conclusion the questions from the Pharisees regarding food from chapter 15. Verses 13–20 raise one of the central questions of the Christian faith, the identity of Jesus. The final section of chapter 16 contains the first announcement of Jesus' coming suffering and death, as well as the meaning of that death for His disciples.

1. THE REJECTION OF THE PHARISEES AND SADDUCEES 16:1–12

Following Jesus' ministry to Gentiles (15:21–39), Matthew returns to Jesus' relationship with the religious leaders of Judaism. Verses 1–12 of chapter 16 have two sections: verses 1–4 dealing with the request for a sign from the Pharisees and Sadducees, and verses 5–12 dealing with the **yeast** of those religious leaders.

This section is the only place Matthew mentions the **Sadducees** outside of Judea. It would not have been surprising to find **Pharisees** (16:1) investigating Jesus in Galilee because members of their group were scattered throughout Palestine. It is unexpected to find Sadducees outside Jerusalem. The coming together of Pharisees and Sadducees to test Jesus would indicate significant hostility toward Him. Their testing of Jesus anticipates their efforts to trap Him that will be described in chapter 22.

The request for **a sign from heaven** is the second such request. In Matthew 12:38, the Pharisees ask for a miraculous sign from Jesus. As in chapter 12, Jesus disputes the ability of His accusers to correctly understand the sign He is willing to give. He notes that they understand weather events as signs of coming weather changes. They understood that **red sky** at night predicted **fair weather** the following day (16:2). They also knew the **red sky** in the morning was a sign of **stormy** or **overcast** weather (16:3). But their skill at reading signs of changes in the weather exceeded their ability to **interpret** correctly **the signs of the times**.

The demand for signs has always indicated people's unwillingness to trust God with the evidence He has already given. One wonders what kind of sign from heaven would have satisfied the Pharisees and Sadducees. Jesus had twice fed thousands with a few loaves. The mute spoke, the lame walked, and the blind saw as a result of Jesus' ministry. What other sign could the Jewish leaders have wanted? No wonder Jesus describes them as **a wicked and adulterous generation** (16:4). He then promised them the same sign He promised in 12:39–40: the **sign of Jonah**. The **sign of Jonah** points to three days and nights in the tomb and presumably to the resurrection. With this short reply to the demand for sign, **Jesus left.**

As Jesus and the disciples cross **the lake**, Matthew notes that **the disciples forgot to take bread** (15:5). No explanation is given, since Matthew's concern is not the disciples' forgetfulness but the lesson it allowed Jesus to teach. He warns them **against the yeast of the Pharisees and Sadducees** (15:6). The disciples completely misunderstand Jesus' meaning and conclude He was reprimanding them **because** they forgot the **bread** (15:7). Their confusion offers Jesus an opportunity to make His teaching point.

Jesus addresses the disciples as **you of little faith** (15:8). This is one of Matthew's most frequent phrases to describe the disciples when they fail to grasp who Jesus is and what He has done. Jesus reminds them of the feeding of **the five thousand** with **five loaves** (15:9) and the feeding of **the four thousand** with **seven loaves** (15:10). Why should one who feeds the multitude worry whether His disciples brought **bread** on this trip? In retrospect one wonders how the disciples failed to **understand that** Jesus was **not talking about bread** (15:11).

Finally, the disciples realized that when Jesus warned them **against yeast**, He was talking about **the teaching of the Pharisees and Sadducees** (15:12). Both Jesus and Matthew understood very well that the teaching of the Pharisees was very different from the teaching of the Sadducees. What the two groups shared was their rejection of Jesus with their efforts to embarrass and discount Him. Such an attitude is like yeast. It insidiously penetrates until it rises up in every area of life with doubt and cynicism. Followers of Christ must avoid such yeast.

2. THE IDENTITY AND MISSION OF JESUS 16:13–20

The narrative logic of Matthew's transition at this point is not always recognized. The real problem of the Pharisees and Sadducees was their rejection of Jesus' identity and mission. Since Jesus has warned the disciples against the teachings of those groups, He must instruct them on the proper understanding of His identity and mission. Verses 13–16 address Jesus' identity. Verses 17–20 begin the treatment of His mission.

The journey **to the region of Caesarea Philippi** took **Jesus** and **his disciples** north from the Sea of Galilee about twenty-five miles to the foot of Mount Hermon. The area was a beautiful retreat center set on the headwaters of the Jordan River. It was also the center of idolatrous worship. It was an appropriate location to ask **who people say** that Jesus, **the Son of Man is** (16:13).

The disciples' replies focus on the concepts of prophet and forerunner of the Messiah. It should not be surprising that **some say** Jesus is **John the Baptist** (16:14). Herod Antipas had drawn the same conclusion, according to 14:2, but it is doubtful Herod thought of it

Son of Man was Jesus' favorite title for himself. His use of it allowed Him to talk about himself without using the first person singular pronouns. It appears that Jesus derived the title from Daniel 7:13, where the Son of Man is a heavenly figure coming with the clouds of heaven to usher in an eternal kingdom. Thus the popular idea that the Son of Man title points to Jesus' humanity in contrast to His deity is not likely. The title was little known in Judaism and allowed Jesus to develop His own identity through using it.

on his own. Beyond their kinship (Luke 1:36), Jesus and John the Baptist shared a prophetic ministry. Both preached the coming of the kingdom of God (Matt. 3:2; 4:17). The suggestion that Jesus was **Elijah** is also quite understandable. Jesus had identified John the Baptist with Elijah in 11:14. The prophecy of Malachi 4:5 was widely understood to mean that Elijah would return as a forerunner of the Messiah. Jesus' proclamation of the kingdom of God raised hopes that the Messiah would soon come.

The idea that Jesus was **Jeremiah** is more difficult to understand. Matthew is the only Gospel to record this answer to the question of Jesus' identity. Both Jesus and Jeremiah spoke of the coming judgment of God. Both spoke of the Temple in critical ways. Both endured suffering because of their ministry, and both were compared to Moses. Jeremiah announced the new covenant, and Jesus instituted it. The suggestion that Jesus was Jeremiah was a unique and insightful suggestion. **Others** identified Jesus as **one of the prophets.** This suggestion simply recognizes that Jesus' ministry was prophetic in nature.

The purpose of Jesus' questions was not to know the opinion of others. His goal was to establish His identity and mission for the disciples, and so He asks **who** they **say** He is (Matt. 16:15). **Simon Peter** answers (16:16), **You are the Christ, the Son of the living God.** This is the only place where both the names **Simon** and **Peter** are paired this way. Simon was a Hebrew name, while Peter was the Greek form of the name (Cephas) Jesus gave him. The double use gives special attention to Peter's identifying Jesus. The word **Christ** is the Greek translation of the Hebrew word for Messiah. Thus Peter identifies Jesus as the long-awaited Messiah, in contrast to the crowds who only *hoped* He might be the forerunner of the Messiah.

Peter also confessed Jesus to be **the Son of the living God.** This is the only place in the New Testament where this exact phrase is applied to Jesus. The theme of Jesus' divine sonship has been important throughout Matthew. The voice from heaven announced it at Jesus' baptism. Satan tempted Jesus over that point. The disciples had confessed it (14:33) after Jesus and Peter had walked on the water. Now it is combined with the titles Messiah and Son of Man to provide the most complete identification of Jesus in this Gospel.

In response, **Jesus** blesses **Simon** (16:17). The blessing is not a compliment, however, for it was not Peter's wisdom or insight that produced the confession. Peter had not discovered this truth by human teachers or logic. Rather, God the **Father** had **revealed** it to him. The most basic and profound theological truths are the not the products of human ingenuity but are the grace gifts of God. The blessing is also a commission and promise that Christ will make Peter a foundational stone for the building of the church (16:18). Jesus gives Simon the name **Peter**. The Greek form of this name is *petros*, which means rock. Jesus then states that He **will build** His **church on this rock**. This word **rock** is *petra* in Greek. Some see a great significance in the difference between *petros* and *petra*, but both would have translated the same Aramaic word no doubt used by Jesus, *kepha*.

The long-standing debate between Roman Catholic and Protestant interpretations of this passage unfortunately has drawn attention away from Jesus' natural meaning. The traditional Roman Catholic interpretation has seen this text as the authorization of Peter as the first pope and head of the Church. Clearly nothing so institutional appears in these verses. The traditional Protestant interpretation, that the rock upon which Christ builds the Church is Peter's *confession* rather than Peter *himself*, ignores that plain statement of the text. The pun of Peter's name clearly identifies him as a rock, and the New Testament often describes the Church as built with living stones (1 Cor. 3:11; Eph. 2:20–22; 1 Pet. 2:4–7). Jesus identifies Peter as one of the foundation stones upon which He would build His Church. The debate has often forgotten that Jesus is the cornerstone and builder. But He builds the Church using the living stones of obedient human beings.

It is also important to note that *Jesus* builds the Church. It is neither programs nor theologies nor methods that build the Church. It is Jesus. Because Jesus builds the Church, **the gates of Hades will not overcome it**. However precarious the existence of the Church may seem, in the battle with evil there is no doubt about the final outcome. The Church will prevail!

The way Jesus will build the Church using living stones of human beings is illustrated by the leadership role given to Peter in Matthew

16:19. **The keys of the kingdom** do not give Peter the authority to determine who enters the Kingdom and who does not. Rather, the **keys of the kingdom** are given to Peter as a steward or administrator rather than as a gatekeeper. This interpretation is consistent with the responsibility of binding and loosing that is given to him. These words were technical terms for the work of rabbis in forbidding (binding) or permitting (loosing) practices as consistent with the will of God. The role Peter played in the earliest years of the Church in permitting Gentiles into the Church (Acts 10–11; 15:7–11) is a clear example of his use of the keys of the Kingdom.

After such emphasis on Jesus as the Messiah, many find it surprising that He **warned his disciples not to tell anyone that he was the Christ** (16:20). It is likely that His concern was that without the careful instruction He was about to give the disciples, people would misunderstand His messiahship and interpret it in militaristic or self-serving ways. To accomplish His mission of building the Church, it was necessary that His identity be defined by himself and the Father rather than by popular ideas of what the Messiah should do or be.

3. THE COST OF FOLLOWING JESUS 16:21–28

Though some interpreters see a major division between 16:20 and 16:21, the connection and flow of thought is very important. Because the disciples have been shown Jesus' identity and mission, it is essential that they understand the nature of His messiahship and what it will mean for them.

From that time on Jesus began to reshape the disciples' understanding of messiahship (16:21). For the first time—though not the last—Jesus introduces the disciples to His coming suffering and death. The Greek term translated **must** in the New International Version indicates that it would be the will of God for Jesus to make the journey to Jerusalem and to **suffer many things. The elders, chief priests and teachers of the law** are the ones who will cause this suffering. The final blow will be that He will **be killed**. Jesus also mentions that **on the third day** He will **be raised to life**, but Peter seems not to hear that part of His statement.

Peter's **rebuke** of Jesus reveals how completely he rejected Jesus' prediction of His coming death (16:22). The repeated **never** in his response shows that he simply could not comprehend the idea of a suffering and dying Messiah. God's revelation of Jesus' messianic identity to him, and then Jesus' revelation of the meaning of His coming messianic suffering, seemed totally contradictory to Peter. Jesus' rebuke of the disciple He had just blessed is also stunning in its forcefulness. The words addressed to Peter, **Get behind me, Satan!** (16:23) echo His words to Satan in the temptation narrative (4:10). This suggests that Peter's objection to Jesus' mission of becoming a suffering Messiah genuinely tempted Jesus from God's painful will for His life—and death. Like so many disciples after him, Peter wanted to understand Jesus in ways most beneficial to his personal desires and agenda rather than keeping in mind the purpose and will of God.

Perhaps because of Peter's willingness to twist God's will to fit his own agenda for the Messiah, Jesus immediately teaches the disciples the cost for them of His messiahship. **If anyone would come after me** is another way of saying, "If anyone wants to be my disciple." The cost of such discipleship is to **deny** self, **take up** the **cross**, and **follow** Jesus (16:24). These three verbs are all imperatives in the Greek text. The word **deny** meant to disown someone. The cost of discipleship is to break every tie that connects a person to his or her own deepest desires and will. To take up one's cross is to embrace the instrument of suffering and death. To follow Jesus is to align one's life with the one going to Jerusalem to suffer and be killed.

To cling to one's own desires and will is to seek to **save** one's **life**. But the inevitable result of such an attempt will be that one will **lose** his or her **life**. To abandon self and one's deepest desires for Jesus is to lose one's life. But only by such a loss can one find true life (16:25). In fact, gaining **the whole world** is of no value if one loses one's life (16:26). There is nothing in this world worth giving in exchange for one's life. (The words **life** and **soul** in the New International Version of verses 25–26 are translations of the same Greek word.)

The choice to deny self and to surrender all one's desires to follow Jesus in the Kingdom has consequences beyond the immediate present.

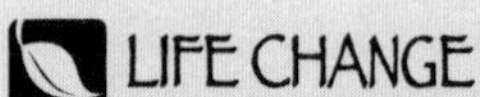

LIFE CHANGE

COMPLETE COMMITMENT

Jesus' commands to deny oneself, to take up one's cross, and to follow Him reveal the costly commitment required of Christian discipleship. He does not paint a picture of partial commitment. Rather, the call to discipleship is a call to radical and complete commitment to the person and mission of Jesus. Our agendas and desires must be nailed to the cross, and our wills must become subordinated to the will of God revealed in the life of Christ.

The Son of Man is going to come in his Father's glory and judge the world. The outcome will be that **each person** will be rewarded **according to what he** or she **has done** (16:27). The choice to follow Jesus has eternal consequences. Jesus emphasized that the time of judgment is not in some far and indefinite future. Accordingly, He states that **some** of those present with Him would **not taste death before they see the . . . coming kingdom** (16:28). As uncertain as the meaning of this verse is, it clearly warns Jesus' followers of the urgency of choosing to follow Him.

17

THE PROMISE OF GLORY AND FRUSTRATION IN DISCIPLESHIP

Matthew 17:1–27

From the demanding challenges of discipleship in chapter 16, Matthew turns for a brief vision of the glory of the coming Kingdom in the account of Jesus' Transfiguration in 17:1–13. The chapter then closes with three brief pictures of the varied experiences of discipleship.

1. THE TRANSFIGURATION OF JESUS 17:1–13

All three Synoptic Gospels link Peter's confession of Jesus as the Messiah; the first prediction of Christ's suffering, death, and resurrection; and the Transfiguration. Many interpreters suggest the Transfiguration provides at least a partial fulfillment of Jesus' strange words in 16:28 that some standing before Him would not die before seeing Him in His coming kingdom.

The precise notice of time in the words **after six days** is rare in Matthew—or any of the Synoptic Gospels. Perhaps Matthew includes this detail with Exodus 24:16 in mind. There, the cloud symbolizing the glory of the Lord covered Mount Sinai before Moses entered the cloud to speak with God on the seventh day. Verse 1 also identifies **Peter, James**

and John as a separate group of the disciples who will be with Jesus at the most significant moments of His life. The initiative for this relationship lies completely with Jesus, who **took** the three **and led them up a high mountain**. The mention of the mountain would have drawn the thoughts of Matthew's first readers to the significant mountains in the Old Testament, especially Mount Sinai.

Three statements in verse 2 describe the unique changes Jesus will experience on the mountain. The summarizing statement is first: **he was transfigured**. The Greek word *metamorpheo* appears four times in the New Testament: in the Transfiguration accounts of Matthew and Mark, and twice in Paul's writings (Rom. 12:2; 2 Cor. 3:18), where it is usually translated *transformed*. The word's root meaning is a change in form. All four instances in the New Testament are in the passive voice indicating that the transformation is accomplished by God rather than by the human subject.

The first specific description of Jesus' transformation is that **his face shone like the sun**. This detail is unique to Matthew's account and is similar to Jewish comments about the radiance of Moses' face when he came down from Mount Sinai (Ex. 34:29–35). The second specific statement is Jesus' **clothes became as white as the light**. Jewish intertestamental literature also describes divine beings appearing on earth as wearing dazzlingly bright clothing. Thus verse 2 suggests both a connection between Jesus and Moses and the divine nature of Jesus. Matthew's common theme of connecting Jesus with the Law and the Prophets appears again in verse 3, when **Moses and Elijah** appear and begin **talking with Jesus** (Matt. 17:3).

In the midst of the divine context, the very human voice of **Peter** speaks. He addresses **Jesus** as **Lord** (17:4). Given the signs of divinity all around, this was an especially appropriate title for Jesus on the Mount of Transfiguration. Peter proposes the building of **three shelters—one** each **for** Jesus, **Moses and Elijah**. Peter's motivation is not mentioned, but one might assume that he wished to prolong the mountaintop experience by providing shelters in which they could stay. If this is the case, Peter is still resisting the suffering mission of Jesus revealed in chapter 16. Regardless, Peter has spoken too soon, because the climax of the Transfiguration is still to come.

As Peter spoke, **a bright cloud enveloped them and a voice** spoke **from the cloud** (17:5). The mention of the cloud echoes the language of Exodus 24:15–18. As at Mount Sinai, the voice of God spoke from the cloud. The words spoken by God here, **This is my Son, whom I love; with him I am well pleased**, are the same words spoken by the voice from heaven at Jesus' baptism (see comments on Matt. 3:17).

At the beginning of Jesus' ministry, the Father had affirmed Jesus' identity as His Son and His mission as suffering Messiah. Now as the journey to the cross draws near, God grants Jesus the gift of reaffirmation. One significant difference between the baptism and the Transfiguration is that Jesus now has enlisted the disciples to follow Him on the road of suffering. They are enamored with the promises of glory but are baffled by the shadow of suffering. To them, God's voice from heaven commands, **Listen to him!** The Aramaic word that was probably used would have also meant *Obey Him.* The purpose of the Transfiguration was both to encourage Jesus and to reinforce the need for the disciples to follow Him obediently even to death.

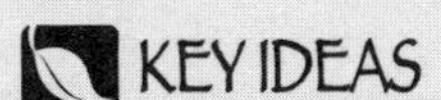

One of Matthew's themes is the similarities and differences between Jesus and Moses. Both receive and teach the Word of God from the mountain. Both are enveloped in a cloud on the mountain while God speaks with them. However, the point of the comparison is not the equality of Jesus and Moses, but Jesus' superiority. As the author to the Hebrews pointed out, Moses was God's servant; Jesus is God's Son (Heb. 3:3–4).

The whole experience **terrified the disciples**, and **they fell facedown to the ground** (17:6). The next thing of which they are aware is Jesus touching them and telling them to **get up** and not **be afraid** (17:7). The instruction to not fear is common in biblical accounts of angelic and divine appearances to humans. **When** the disciples **looked up, they saw no one** but **Jesus** (17:8). The divine encounter had ended, but the teaching continued **as they** went **down the mountain** (17:9). **Jesus** forbids them to **tell anyone what** they had **seen until** after His resurrection.

As with the first prediction of His coming suffering, death, and resurrection, the mention of the resurrection is ignored. Instead **the disciples asked**

why it was necessary for **Elijah** to **come first** (17:10). Their reference to Elijah's coming first suggests they are now thinking of Jesus as the Messiah. Since He, the Messiah, is already present, they wonder how to account for the prophecies of Elijah coming first. **Jesus** affirms the prophecies regarding **Elijah** (17:11) but tells them that the forerunner **has already come** (17:12). This means their confusion is unfounded: Elijah the forerunner has come, and Jesus is indeed the Messiah.

The disciples were not alone in failing to **recognize** Elijah. Jesus accuses another group (**they**) of a similar failure, and that group did **to him everything they wished.** This alludes to the imprisonment and death of John the Baptist described in 14:3–12. But lest the disciples be carried away with the glorious picture of the transfigured Messiah, Jesus reminds them of His coming suffering and death. **In the same way** John the Baptist had suffered and died, Jesus **is going to suffer** also. By then **the disciples** realize Jesus **was talking to them about John the Baptist** in His comments on Elijah and suffering (17:13).

2. THE FRUSTRATIONS AND JOYS OF DISCIPLESHIP 17:14–27

Following the Transfiguration of Jesus, Matthew narrates three brief accounts of life for the disciples as they begin the journey with Jesus to the cross. Verses 14–21 describe the frustrating failure of the disciples to heal a body with seizures. Verses 22–23 present Jesus' second prediction of the suffering, death, and resurrection that await Him in Jerusalem. Finally, Matthew presents the fascinating story of the miraculous resource of money to pay the Temple tax.

As Jesus and the three disciples—Peter, James, and John—return from the mountain they encounter a **crowd** (17:14). **A man** emerged from the crowd **and knelt before** Jesus, begging Him, **Lord, have mercy on my son.** His use of the title **Lord** to address Jesus demonstrates the truth of Jesus' divine identity revealed on the Mount of Transfiguration. The man appeals for his son, since the youngster suffers **seizures and often falls into the fire or into the water** (17:15). The New International Version **seizures** assumes that the Greek word—literally *moonstruck—* refers to epilepsy. The King James translation uses the word *lunatick* (*sic*). Certainly the boy's symptoms are consistent with epilepsy. Verse 18 will attribute his problems to demon possession.

The man's problem was that he had brought his son to the **disciples, but they could not heal him** (17:16). The context implies that the reference to the disciples does not include Peter, James, and John, who had been on the mountain with Jesus. Jesus' reply addresses the disciples rather than the man (**you** is plural): **O unbelieving and perverse generation, how long shall I stay with you?** (17:17). For all of Jesus' teaching and commissioning, the disciples are no more connected to the Kingdom than the crowds. Jesus seems as frustrated with the disciples as they are in their failure to heal the boy. At this stage He will have to deal with the boy himself, and so He asks them to **bring** the boy to Him (the imperative **bring** is plural). **Jesus rebuked the demon, and the boy was healed from that moment** (17:18). Some interpreters see the demon possession as a problem in addition to the epilepsy the boy suffered. More likely verses 15 and 18 describe the same problem from two perspectives—one from the physical symptoms perspective and the other from the perspective of the spiritual world as ultimate cause of all that happens.

The disciples ask why Jesus was able to **drive out** the demon but they were **not** (17:19). The question reveals their frustration that they were not able to fulfill the command Jesus gave them in His instructions on their mission in 10:8. Jesus answers, **Because you have so little faith** (17:20). He then demonstrates how small was their faith. **If** they had **faith as small as a mustard seed,** they could command a **mountain** to **move** and it would. The mustard seed was proverbial for its smallness, as the parable of the mustard seed demonstrates (13:32). If the smallest amount of faith imaginable could move mountains, the

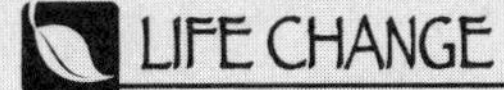

When Jesus speaks of faith, He is not referring to a magical ability to force God to do the things a person wants. Rather, faith is trust in God. What Jesus desired for His disciples—then and now—was sufficient trust in God to become so fully aligned with the will and work of God that whatever God would do, they would do. To say nothing is impossible with faith does not refer to anything a person can imagine, but to anything God would seek to accomplish.

disciples must have had even less faith as they encountered the epileptic boy. Jesus concludes His response to the disciples by telling them that with sufficient faith **nothing** would **be impossible for** them.

The return of Jesus and the disciples to Galilee marks a new scene in verse 22. Matthew uses an unusual word, stating that **they came together in Galilee**. The picture is of Jesus and the disciples coming together to prepare for a journey. Jesus' words reveal that the journey will be to Jerusalem. His message is the same instruction He gave at Caesarea Philippi. This is the second prediction of Jesus' coming passion, death, and resurrection. The details vary from the first prediction in 16:21, but the basic elements are the same. This second prediction states that Jesus will **be betrayed**, but it does not mention the role that the Jewish religious leaders will play.

The unique element of verse 23 is the disciples' response to this second prediction of Jesus' passion. Matthew states that they **were filled with grief**. This brief note makes it clear that the disciples had not yet accepted Jesus' mission as suffering Messiah. They had not yet learned the meaning of faith as trust in God and His agenda. The will of God still frustrated their desires for Jesus.

The final paragraph of chapter 17 moves in a new direction both geographically and emotionally. Verse 24 states that **Jesus and his disciples arrived in Capernaum**. Rather than beginning the journey to Jerusalem—and the suffering and death that awaited Jesus there—they returned to their headquarters, creating a pause in the momentum that has been building toward Jerusalem. It also provides an opportunity for the tax **collectors** to ask **Peter** for Jesus' **temple tax**.

The Temple tax was based on the half-shekel tax instituted in Exodus 30:12–16 for support of the sacrificial system. However, its status in Jesus' time was debated. The Sadducees opposed it, and the members of the Qumran community paid it only once per lifetime. These verses demonstrate that Jesus believed He and His followers should not be required to pay the tax, but it was not an issue over which He wished to create conflict.

The tax collectors appeared to challenge Peter with the question, **Doesn't your teacher pay the temple tax?** Peter's responded that Jesus, indeed, did pay the tax (17:25). But the tax had not yet been paid, and **when Peter** arrived at **the house, Jesus** asked him, **From whom do kings collect taxes—from their own sons or from others?** The question was an obvious set-up for **Peter** to answer, **From others** (17:26). **Jesus** wished to draw the conclusion that **the sons are exempt**. Matthew plays on Jesus' words. Because Jesus and Peter were sons of the Kingdom and thus children of the king, one should conclude that they would be exempt from the tax.

However, Jesus will pay **so that** He might **not offend them** (17:27). To pay the tax was easier than arguing the justice of the tax and perhaps getting out of it. Further, to argue against the tax would break relationships with those who, by conscience, supported it. However, Jesus' method of paying the tax appeals to Jewish humor. He instructs Peter to **go to the lake**—the Sea of Galilee—**and throw out** his **line**. The **first fish** he would **catch** would have a **coin** in its **mouth** sufficient to pay Jesus' and Peter's Temple **tax**.

Many interpreters argue whether this really happened and whether Jesus would resort to such an unfair means of paying the tax. Such arguments miss the teaching point. Jesus was confident that God would supply all His needs—in both amazing and ordinary ways. He also believed some issues are better dealt with by simply submitting to the governing authority rather than entering conflict to prove one is right. Finally, the humorous touch of the story should remind us of the importance of joy on the journey.

Part Five

Grace and Judgment in the Kingdom: Teaching and Examples

MATTHEW 18:1–23:39

The fifth major section of Matthew begins with a collection of Jesus' teachings about life together in the Kingdom. This collection of teachings appears in 18:1–19:1. In this chapter the word *church* will be used to demonstrate that Matthew saw Jesus' kingdom teachings of both grace and judgment being applied in the life of the Church. Following the block of teaching material on the Church is a series of narrative examples of the grace and judgment in the Kingdom in 19:2–23:39 as Jesus makes His final journey to Jerusalem.

JESUS' TEACHING ABOUT LIFE TOGETHER

Matthew 18:1–19:1

Matthew is the only Canonical Gospel to use the word *church* (16:18 and twice in 18:17). Chapter 18 answers questions about the kind of life together one may expect in a community of disciples who followed a soon-to-be-crucified Messiah. Jesus' instructions here are not a manual of procedure or regulations for worship and community life. Rather, they teach His desire for the relationships that exist in the Church. Verses 1–4 raise the question of greatness in the Kingdom. Care for lesser members of the community is the subject of verses 5–9. Verses 10–14 speak of grace in the restoration of the lost sheep of the Church, while verses 15–20 address God's judgment through the community's response to members who sin. Finally, verses 21–35 explore the grace of the extent of forgiveness.

1. GREATNESS IN THE KINGDOM 18:1–4

A question from **the disciples** regarding **who is greatest in the kingdom** introduces this block of Jesus' teaching on the Church (18:1). The question was natural in the honor-shame culture in which Jesus and the disciples lived. But Jesus rejected the pursuit of status in the social order and taught humble service to others. The countercultural impact of

His views was clear when **he called a little child** to serve as the first lesson in His teaching (18:2). Children ranked lowest on the honor-shame scales of personal worth. Though Judaism highly valued the idea of children, their value was more potential than real. It was only when children reached adulthood that their value was realized. Jesus' words were more challenging than His action: **Unless you change and become like little children, you will** have no place in **the kingdom** (18:3).

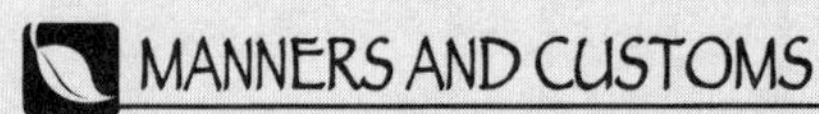

MANNERS AND CUSTOMS

HONOR-SHAME SOCIETY

The biblical world was what anthropologists call an honor-shame society. The social status, and thus the worth of every person in the society, was established through an elaborate system of valuing and devaluing. Every conversation and social interaction was regulated by the relative status of each participant. People often engaged in one-upmanship and other ploys designed to increase their own honor or decrease the honor of another. Jesus persistently rejected both the devaluing of persons and the games played that were part of the honor-shame society.

These words are more powerful in the original language. First, the introductory phrase, **I tell you the truth**, uses the Hebrew word *amen* (often translated *true*) in a way that affirms Jesus' word as a word from God. His teaching was not just His opinion, but expressed the very purpose of God. Second, the word translated **change** literally means *to turn*, but it was used for repentance and conversion. Jesus was telling the disciples in particular, and the ancient world in general, that unless they repented of their cultural assumptions and experienced a conversion to God's value system toward children, they would not **enter the kingdom**. Finally, the Greek construction for the negative (not) is emphatic. They would certainly *not* enter the Kingdom. Jesus placed the greatest possible emphasis on this teaching about the value of children.

However, as important as the teaching about children is, this was not Jesus' primary point. He was teaching greatness **in the kingdom** (18:4). Though verses 2–3 gave children far greater status than they enjoyed in the culture of the time, Jesus assumed the disciples would still hold their cultural view of the low status of children. Though no one in that culture would have wanted to take the status of a child, kingdom greatness consists of humbling oneself **like** a **child**. Kingdom greatness means willingness to embrace low status in the world, to remain at the bottom of the honor-shame ladder, and to humble oneself—to choose lowly status—for the sake of the Kingdom. Persons willing to make such a choice are great in the Kingdom.

2. CARE FOR THE LITTLE ONES IN THE KINGDOM 18:5–9

Verse 5 is a transitional sentence. On the surface, the reference to the **little child** speaks of the child mentioned in verse 2. However, the expression **one of these little ones** in verses 6 and 10 refers to church members. Verse 5 looks back to the child and forward to the members of the Church. To welcome a child is to welcome Jesus *himself*. On the one hand, this articulates the high value Jesus gives to children. On the other hand, it reflects the ways in which Matthew parallels the human responses to disciples with the human responses to Jesus. Thus to welcome another member of the Church is to welcome Jesus.

Another possibility would be to cause **one of these little ones . . . to sin** (18:6). Here Jesus specifically defines **these little ones** as persons **who believe in** Him. This indicates that the subject has shifted from children to members of the Church. The Greek verb could also be translated *cause to stumble*. Such a translation envisions the disciple's life as a journey toward God and His will rather than a state of being righteous or sinful. Jesus considered causing a believer to stumble to be so horrible that the resulting divine judgment would be worse than death by drowning.

Verse 7 addresses **the world** causing the believer to stumble. Jesus acknowledged the inevitability of such spiritual failure but pronounced the **woe** of judgment upon the individual who causes it.

The wording of verses 8–9 is almost identical to that of 5:29–30, and the point is similar. These verses address how serious a matter it is to cause someone to stumble. Instead of another believer or the world being the cause for stumbling, verse 8 envisions one's **hand or foot** being the occasion for **sin**, while verse 9 envisions one's **eye** as the offending party. In either case it would be **better** to remove the offending part of the body than to be sent to **hell.**

Two observations are in order. First, the assumption of these verses is that causing a believer to sin makes one subject to eternal judgment. The words **eternal fire** in verse 8 and **the fire of hell** in verse 9 make it clear that Jesus saw severe judgment as the consequence of causing one of the little ones to sin. Second, this divine judgment will be far worse than losing an eye or having hands or feet cut off.

3. RESTORING THE LOST SHEEP 18:10–14

To further illustrate the importance of these little ones who believe, Matthew turns to Jesus' parable of the lost sheep. This parable also appears in Luke 15:3–7, but the teaching function for the parable differs in the two Gospels. The parable in Luke clearly envisions an evangelistic effort by believers to seek and save lost sinners. Matthew uses the parable to teach the critical importance of pastoral care and preserving members who have wandered away from the church.

Jesus introduces the parable with a warning: **See that you do not look down on** another believer (Matt. 18:10). Looking down on another believer in the honor-shame society of Jesus' world was a way of lowering the person's honor and sense of worth. The concern was not the actual worth of the other, because Jesus had already established the great worth of every believer in the preceding verses. He was not concerned about the actual honor of the person; the culture would establish that. His concern was the attitude of one believer toward another believer that disdained and devalued one whom Jesus had called into discipleship.

The reason He gives for not devaluing the other believer is that **their angels in heaven always see the face of** the **Father** (18:11). The text clearly assumes that believers have angels assigned to them. The angels' assignment may have been intercession and protection. Judaism taught that only select angels had the privilege of seeing God face to face. Obviously, in a status-conscious world, these angels were the most important of all angels. Jesus points out that the angels assigned to the humble little ones who believe are the most important angels. If the most important angels care for the insignificant little ones, then so should their fellow believers.

Jesus then asks the disciples to consider the significance of these little ones. The words **What do you think** (18:12) invite the listeners (the you is plural) into conversation. Jesus begins with a hypothetical but typical scenario. **A hundred sheep** was an average-sized flock. That **one of them** would wander away was quite common. The listeners might have wryly thought that the shepherd was fortunate if only one **wandered away**. While the shepherd would **leave the ninety-nine**, he would not leave them untended. Flocks grazed in close proximity to each other, so the shepherd whose sheep had wandered away would leave the ninety-nine under the watchful eye of the other shepherds in the area.

Matthew emphasizes that the one sheep **wandered** away. The verb appears twice in verse 12 and once in verse 13. The similar parable in Luke 15:3–7 describes the sheep as lost rather than as one who had wandered away. This emphasis on wandering in Matthew places a greater emphasis on the pastoral responsibility of the shepherd and the community. Here Jesus did not envision the sheep as lost, at least not yet. One wandering sheep can be found alive and restored to the flock without serious consequences.

The finding and restoration of the wandering sheep is not guaranteed. Matthew 18:13 is a true conditional sentence. **If** the man **finds** the sheep, then **he is happier** for the **one** found **than** for **the ninety-nine that did not wander off.** The details of the restoration of the sheep are not told in the parable. They will be presented in verses 15–18. Verse 14 states Jesus' conclusion: It is not God's will **that any of these little ones should be lost.** The wanderer must not be left wandering but must be found. If left too long, that wandering believer would be lost. God's desire is that the church value its members so much that when even one wanders away, the others spring into action to find that wanderer and to restore him or her to the flock.

4. RESTORING THE SINNING CHURCH MEMBER 18:15–20

Through the parable of the lost sheep, Jesus clearly envisioned a difference between a sheep—or believer—wandering and being lost. He then prescribed a process of church discipline to show the way a wanderer can be restored rather than lost. The language shifts from one of **these little**

ones to **brother** in verse 15. This is clear indication that the primary subject of chapter 18 is relationship with brothers and sisters in the church, not simply small children. The audience also shifts in verse 15 from the you plural to a you singular form.

The scenario is of a brother committing a sin. The sin terminology of verse 15 is different from that of verses 6–9, where the word translated *sin* in the New International Version properly refers to a stumbling block or the cause of possible sin. Verse 15 uses the common Greek verb *hamartano*, to sin. This change of words demonstrates that verses 15–18 address the situation in which the wandering church member is in danger of being lost. The words **against you** are not present in the oldest and best Greek manuscripts of this text. Thus Jesus' instructions for restoration were intended for every believer, not just one who had been sinned against.

The procedure for restoring the wanderer is simple, though not easy. If one sins, another believer is to **go and show him his fault**. The Greek word translated **show his fault** could be translated simply *rebuke*. However, a stronger translation such as *try to convince of sin* appears to be Jesus' intention. This attempt to bring awareness of the sin is to be done privately, **just between the two**. If the sinning member **listens**, he or she will be **won over**. Further, the brother or sister will be given opportunity to confess and make any restitution necessary without public disgrace. The Hebrew and Aramaic word behind **listens** could also mean to obey. The private exposure of sin is an act on behalf of God, and so the offender's response becomes a matter of obedience or disobedience to God.

If the private meeting is unsuccessful, **one or two others** should be taken **along** so that the confrontation is limited to a few, presumably more mature, members of the community (18:16). Jesus appealed to the Old Testament principle that issues of conflict could only **be established by the testimony of two or three witnesses** (Deut. 19:15). The pastoral care concern is to protect the reputation of the sinning member. If he or she will respond to the persuasion of the two or three, the matter may remain private and the offender will not be shamed in the community.

Refusal to respond to the small group requires that the two or three witnesses **tell the church**. At this point, privacy and concern for the honor or shame of the offender can no longer be preserved. The sinning member has chosen to make the matter public by refusing to respond to the previous entreaties. Presumably Jesus hoped that when the matter went before the church, the offender would confess and be restored. However, only the negative possibility is described in the text. If the sinning member **refuses to listen to the** counsel of the **church,** he must be treated as **a pagan or a tax collector** (Matt. 18:17).

Jesus' intention here appears to be twofold. First, treating the offender as a pagan or tax collector included withdrawal from fellowship with the person. The privileges of community participation and membership are removed from the offender. This step reflects the Old Testament pattern of cutting off people who violated the community standards of Israel (Ex. 12:15). Any good Jew would understand ostracizing to be the appropriate response to a pagan.

Second, however, Jesus' own attitude toward tax collectors, pagans, and other sinners makes it clear that He envisioned a continued ministry of inviting the offender to repentance. One might say that a sinning member of the church who refused to repent, when confronted by the united counsel of the church, should be removed from the membership list and placed on the prospect list.

Matthew 18:18 is almost identical to 16:19, except that it is addressed to the whole church (you plural) rather than to Peter. In this context, the binding and loosing describe the church's responsibility to interpret the meaning and consequences of a sinning member's behavior. The Greek grammar suggests that Jesus believed the real decision regarding the offender's sin and consequences of that sin had already been made in heaven. When united in prayer and obedience, the church will affirm **on earth** what God had already decided **in heaven.** This can happen **if two on earth agree about** something they might **ask** God because **it will be done for** them **by** the **Father in heaven** (18:19).

This is not a legalistic proposition by which any two people can force God into a line of action. Rather, **where two or three** people who trust God **come together** in Jesus' **name,** He will be present **there with them** (18:20). In the biblical world, to do something in a person's name meant more than simply pronouncing that name over the event. It meant to carry out the action in accordance with the purpose and character of the one whose name they invoked. That Jesus envisioned himself to be present with them indicated that He supported the proposed course of action.

5. THE EXTENT OF FORGIVENESS 18:21–19:1

The subject of restoring a sinning brother triggered another theological issue for Peter. His question in verse 21 provides a brief narrative interlude in the teaching material. **Peter asked, Lord, how many times shall I forgive my brother when he sins against me?** The question of how often a person could sin, repent, and be forgiven of the same sin was debated by Jewish rabbis. They were concerned with the genuineness of the repentance. Peter narrows the question to the specific response of one believer to another who has sinned against him or her. Thus the issue here is not the general subject of what constitutes authentic repentance, but how believers live together in Christian community. That Peter addressed his question to Jesus as **Lord** is also important. As Lord of the Church, Jesus' answer is authoritative and binding on believers.

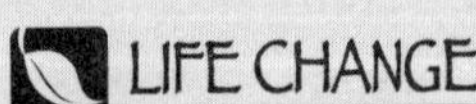

The Greek word consistently used in the Gospels for forgiveness literally means to let go of. While this provides a beautiful picture of what must happen in forgiveness, it also teaches that forgiveness is an action one can—and must—choose to do rather than being simply a feeling that one tries to create. The apostle Paul commonly used another Greek word for forgiveness. It meant to be gracious or to extend grace. Forgiveness is not about what the other deserves; it is about the grace that God would give.

The rabbis generally agreed that three times was the maximum number of times a person could sin, repent, and be forgiven of the same offense. Thus Peter's suggested answer to his own question, up to seven times, must have seemed very generous. Jesus' reply (18:22) puts an end to all limits on forgiveness and all calculations about how much His followers are to forgive. He replied to Peter, **not seven times, but seventy-seven times.** Interpreters have disagreed whether His answer should be translated seventy-seven times or seventy times seven times. To debate the question is to fall into the trap of doing what Jesus was trying to stop—keeping track of forgiveness. The point of His answer—whether seventy-seven times or 490 times—is that one cannot place limits on forgiveness. To place limits means that forgiveness has become a bargaining chip in the relationship rather than an act of grace. Jesus probably intended His answer of forgiving seventy-seven times to provide a positive counterpart of the boast of Lamech in Genesis 4:24 that he had avenged himself seventy-seven times.

Jesus then told the parable of the unforgiving servant in Matthew 18:23–35 to explain why His disciples were to forgive without limits.

This parable deserves a reputation like that of the good Samaritan and the prodigal son. Jesus introduced the parable as a story about **a king who wanted to settle accounts with his servants** (18:23). Early in the process, the king encountered **a man who owed him ten thousand talents** (verse 24). If the servant worked 365 days per year, he would need at least one hundred fifty thousand

A talent was the highest denomination of currency used in the Roman world. Estimates of its value range from six thousand to ten thousand denarii. A denarius was the standard day's wage of the time. Thus a debt of ten thousand talents would be the equivalent of between sixty million and one hundred million days' wages. Clearly a debt of such magnitude would be impossible to repay. This would have been Jesus' point.

years to earn enough money to pay the debt—assuming he had no expenses! It is no wonder that **he was not able to pay** (18:25); one wonders how he could ever have amassed such an incredible debt.

The king's decision to sell the servant, **his wife, his children,** and **all** his possessions would have been standard procedure in the ancient world despite the fact that the price would have been a mere drop in the bucket compared to **the debt.** The servant's plea that if the king would **be patient,** he would **pay back everything** is clearly ludicrous (18:26). The surprising development of the story is the **pity** of the king, canceling **the debt,** and letting the servant **go** (18:27). Surely such a king must have incredible wealth if he can afford to cancel such a debt.

In contrast, **that** forgiven **servant went out** from the king's presence, **found one of his fellow servants who owed him a hundred denarii,** and demanded immediate payment (18:28). A hundred denarii represented a little more than three months wages. It is doubtful that the debt could have been paid back that quickly, but repayment was possible. The second servant then **begged** for time, using the exact plea spoken by the first servant (18:29). However, the first servant **refused** and threw his fellow servant **into prison until he could pay the debt** (18:30). **Other servants** who observed this **were greatly distressed** and reported to the king the actions of the servant he had forgiven (18:31). The king **called** in the first **servant** and pointed that he had graciously **canceled** that servant's incredibly huge **debt** that could never have been paid (18:32). Surely, if he had any remote concept of the grace that had been shown him, he should **have had mercy on** his **fellow servant** (18:33). Obviously the first servant had no sense at all of the grace that had been extended to him. In frustration, the king canceled the forgiveness he had given the first servant and **turned him over to the jailers** (18:34).

Jesus concluded the parable by declaring that God would so **treat each of** His listeners **unless** they would **forgive** their **brother from** their **heart** (18:35). The point of the parable is painfully clear. The debt believers owe God for their sin is incredible large, far too great to ever repay. But God graciously forgives that debt. For believers to refuse to forgive someone else who has offended them reveals a failure to understand and receive God's forgiveness. Even if the offense is great, it pales in comparison to the debt owed God. To complain about Jesus' demand that His followers forgive without limits or conditions shows that they are still keeping track of wrongs. To truly understand and receive God's forgiveness means a heart that forgives others without conditions or limits.

The words **when Jesus had finished saying these things** (19:1) mark the end of the teaching block in chapter 18.

19

THE DEMANDS OF THE KINGDOM

Matthew 19:2-30

In chapter 19 Matthew returns to narrative form after the teaching material he has collected in chapter 18. However, this narrative contains significant teaching material. Chapter 19 begins with Jesus' teaching on divorce in verses 1–12. His blessing of children follows in verses 13–15. The encounter with the rich young man in verses 16–30 concludes the chapter.

1. JESUS' TEACHING ON DIVORCE 19:2-12

After the teachings about life together in the Kingdom, Jesus began the journey to Jerusalem that would culminate in His death and resurrection as predicted in 16:21 and 17:22–23. Jesus **left Galilee and went into Judea** (19:1), where He had been baptized and begun His ministry. The popularity of His Galilean ministry continued. Matthew reports **large crowds followed him, and he healed them** (19:2). The healing ministry would continue, but Jesus would focus on teaching.

Jesus' teaching on divorce is a response to a provocative question posed by **some Pharisees** (19:3): **Is it lawful for a man to divorce his wife for any and every reason?** The question of divorce was a topic of public discussion during Jesus' life. John the Baptist had been killed because of his statements about the divorce of Herod Antipas (14:1–12). The Pharisees were divided by the issue. The followers of the rabbi Shammai argued that divorce was only permissible in the case of adultery. Followers of Hillel permitted divorce for causes as insignificant as a wife burning the food she was cooking or the husband seeing a woman more attractive than his wife. The Pharisees wanted to clarify Jesus' teaching on this subject.

When they asked about the lawfulness of divorce, Jesus responded by quoting from the first book of the Law. His first words, **Haven't you read?** (19:4), were often used in rabbinic arguments to imply that the other in the debate did not really understand the Scripture. Jesus' choice of where to begin the debate reveals an important element in His understanding of how Scripture should be interpreted. Before answering the divorce question, Jesus chose to describe the purpose of marriage. He started **at the beginning** with **the Creator** and the creation of **male and female,** alluding to Genesis 1:1, 27. He then quoted Genesis 2:24 almost verbatim: **For this reason a man will leave his father and mother and be united to his wife, and the two will become one flesh** (Matt. 19:5). One of the reasons for marriage is God's creation design of males and females. One of the requirements for marriage is separating from one's birth home to be united with one's spouse.

The most important phrase from Genesis 2:24 is that the two **become one flesh**. One could develop a comprehensive theology of Christian marriage from this text. However, Jesus simply concludes that the man and woman **are no longer two, but one** (19:6). If this is true, then this change in status has priority over the personal desires and agendas of the two individuals. Jesus' conclusion was that God created the marriage union—divorce is not the reversal of human choices but breaking the bond created by God—and, therefore, people must **not separate what God has joined together**. There is no exact way to translate the Greek construction, which uses a third-person imperative. Jesus' point is that it is imperative that human beings not separate through divorce what God has joined through marriage.

The Pharisees countered with their scriptural proof text, asking why **Moses commanded that a man give his wife a certificate of divorce and send her away** (19:7). Their citation is Deuteronomy 24:1. (See comments on Matt. 5:31–32.) The Pharisees were at a disadvantage in the argument. By their own rules of interpretation, the older a scripture the more weight it carried. Since Jesus quoted from Genesis—the very beginning—His arguments would be considered more significant than their arguments deriving from the time of Moses and Deuteronomy. Further, they had misinterpreted Deuteronomy 24.

There is no command to divorce in Deuteronomy 24:1–4. The command forbids remarriage to the original spouse after a second marriage is terminated. Jesus corrected the Pharisees: **Moses permitted you to divorce your wives** (Matt. 19:8). The distinction between divine purpose (marriage) and divine permission (divorce) is important. Jesus further declared the reason that God granted such permission had nothing to do with His purposes but only with the fact that human **hearts were hard.** Thus divorce was God's concession to human sinfulness.

Jesus then made it clear that there is no divorce without consequences. Verse 9 is a close paraphrase of 5:32. The simple sentence reads, **anyone who divorces his wife and marries another woman commits adultery.** This assumes that a man who divorces his wife will remarry, but Jesus identified the remarriage as sin. This text does not envision the various modern options such as abandonment of spouse, legal separation, and divorce without remarrying. That the question is more complicated today is evidence of the hardness of human hearts, but Jesus took no delight in describing divorce and remarriage as sin.

Jesus did include an exception clause in verse 9. Divorce **except for marital unfaithfulness** and remarriage is sin. The Greek term translated **marital unfaithfulness** is *porneia*, a general word for any and every kind of sexual misconduct. Its most common uses in Scripture are to describe fornication (premarital sexual activity), incest, and adultery. While it is true that any of the wide range of sexually immoral behaviors damage the marriage relationship, Jesus' point seems to be to narrow the list to that which

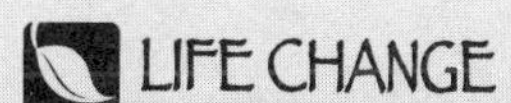

Marital Failure

The failure of marriage is a tragedy to be lamented, not the occasion for condemning people. One should consider the significance of the fact that Matthew placed Jesus' teaching on divorce immediately following His teaching on forgiveness in the church (18:21–35). Jesus' gift to us is that while He upheld the holiness of marriage, He recognized that human sin may cause divorce. He never regarded that sin as unforgivable. May His followers be as gracious in this arena as He was.

most completely undermines marriage. For that reason it is most likely He referred to adultery in the exception clause.

The disciples' response is a sad commentary on their understanding of marriage. They concluded that if Jesus was right about divorce and remarriage being a sin, then **it is better not to marry** (19:10). They obviously considered marriage with no consideration of divorce something impossible. Jesus' answer acknowledges the difficulty of His vision for marriage in a world full of hard-hearted people. He admitted that **not everyone can accept this word** (19:11). Embracing such a commitment to marriage would be possible **only** for **those to whom it has been given.** This awkward expression indicates that the kind of marriage Jesus envisioned is indeed a gift from God.

Jesus then pointed out that celibacy and singleness come into people's lives for different reasons. For some, birth gives them characteristics that lead to singleness and celibacy. Some are forced into such a life by others, and some choose the single, celibate life for the sake **of the kingdom** (19:12). His final comment that those **who can accept this should accept it** can be understood as referring to His whole teaching on marriage and divorce. However, it is better to understand it as referring to His teaching on celibacy. Thus Jesus taught that the ability to be successfully married and the ability to be successfully celibate are both grace gifts from God.

2. JESUS' BLESSING OF THE CHILDREN 19:13–15

To bring children to the elders on the evening of the Day of Atonement for a blessing and prayer was a Jewish custom. Though there is no indication of when the events of 19:13–15 took place, it is possible that this custom lay behind the request that Jesus bless the children. Certainly the desire that Jesus **place his hands on** the children **and pray for them** fits the Day of Atonement practices. If that was the case, perhaps **the disciples rebuked those who brought** the children because they felt the title elder was inappropriate for Jesus. Given the other titles Jesus bore—Prophet, Son of Man, Son of God, Messiah, and Lord—the disciples may have believed Him to be too busy to do things assigned to elders.

Jesus' response includes two commands, one positive and one negative. Permit **and do not hinder** the **children** to **come to** Him (19:14). As He had done in 18:2–3, Jesus affirmed the value of children and committed His time and energy to spending time with them as well as with the adults. In the same spirit as 18:2–3, He then declared that **the kingdom belongs to such as these** children. Part of Jesus' kingdom work was to elevate those considered worthless in society and restore everyone to the place God designed for those persons in creation. Because children were devalued in Jesus' world, His ministry included them in redemptive work of the Kingdom.

The act of laying **hands on** another's head was a common gesture in praying a blessing in the ancient world (19:15). Matthew's brief comment illustrates that not only did Jesus teach the value of children, He spent the time necessary to touch them and bless them. The importance of children to Him can be seen by the fact that it was only after blessing them that **he went on from there** on His journey to Jerusalem.

3. THE COST OF PERFECTION IN THE KINGDOM 19:16–30

Jesus' teaching on marriage and divorce provides one example of His understanding of the demands of the Kingdom and of how Scripture should be interpreted. His encounter with the rich young ruler in 19:16–30 provides another. The final words of verse 15 remind the reader that Jesus and His disciples were on their final journey to Jerusalem. In that context, **a man** approached **Jesus and asked, Teacher, what good thing must I do to get eternal life?** (19:16). Though it is possible the man was asking about everlasting life in heaven someday, it is more likely he wanted to know about life in the kingdom age. Since Jesus was the Messiah, the man wanted to know what he could do to become an insider in the Kingdom.

Jesus used the man's word, **good**, to turn the question around on him (19:17). The focus of the Kingdom is not on good things people do but on the **One who is good**, the one whose reign is the Kingdom. If the Kingdom consists of the sovereign rule of God in people's lives, then the man's interest in the Kingdom should be evidenced by obeying **the commandments.** This basic truth has often been forgotten in the history of both the Jewish and Christian communities.

The rabbis had identified 613 commandments in the Old Testament, and their content and application were widely discussed in Jesus' time. Many rabbis looked for a single commandment that would sum up all the others and provide the general principle by which one might please God. Thus the young man's question, **Which ones?** (19:18), arose from the way the commandments were talked about in his world. Jesus did not rebuke him for the question but gave him a representative list. The commands prohibiting **murder, adultery,** stealing, and **false testimony** all came from the so-called second table of the Ten Commandments. The command to **honor** one's **father and mother** (19:19) was the first command on the second table. Jesus had already mentioned these commandments in 15:4, and 19 during His conflict with the Pharisees. To give the principle that tied all these and many more commandments together, Jesus concluded with the command from Leviticus 19:18 to **love** one's **neighbor as** oneself.

The young man confidently affirmed that he had **kept all these** commandments (Matt. 19:20). One might assume that he had successfully kept the commandments to honor his parents, to not murder, commit adultery, steal, or give false testimony. It is more difficult to believe that he enjoyed perfect success at loving his neighbor as himself. However, Jesus did not need to challenge him on the accuracy of his testimony, for the man himself asked, **What do I still lack?**

On the surface, Jesus' answer seems to concede that the young man had kept all the commandments just mentioned. However, Jesus' answer can also be understood as an application of the commandment to love one's neighbor as oneself. Jesus' words are as startling today as they were to the young man: **If you want to be perfect** (19:21). This is the second time the word **perfect** appears in Matthew. The first appearance was in 5:48, where Jesus' listeners are commanded to be perfect as their Heavenly Father is perfect. The context implies a perfection in love for others. The context here defines perfection in terms of love for one's neighbor.

The way perfect love for neighbor would be demonstrated would be to **go, sell** his **possessions and give to the poor.** If he would do this, Jesus promised, he would **have treasure in heaven.** The ultimate expression of love for others is to share everything one has with them. The ultimate Kingdom value is love for the poor and marginalized. If the young man could venture to that level of love and Kingdom commitment, he would be ready to **follow** Jesus.

Matthew tells us the young man **went away sad, because he had great wealth** (19:22). The young man was not the only one who was sad. So was Jesus. For if the Kingdom is to truly come—as Jesus taught His disciples to pray in 6:10—people must step forward, embrace its values, and begin to live them out in the real world.

The following verses point out that Jesus perceived wealth as an obstacle to entry into the Kingdom. His introductory words, **I tell you the truth**, indicate that His teaching had the status of Scripture. The statement that **it is hard for a rich man to enter the kingdom** was not simply His opinion; it was a word from God (19:23). His comment that **it is easier for a camel to go through the eye of a needle than for a rich man to enter the kingdom** demonstrates how great an impediment wealth is to the Kingdom (19:24). Interpretations that try to explain how a camel could pass through the eye of a needle are misguided. Jesus' point is the human impossibility of wealthy people submitting to Kingdom values, as verse 26 makes clear.

The disciples understood Jesus' words to be impossible. Matthew describes the men as **greatly astonished** and won-

RICH YOUNG RULER

He who reads the heart saw his bosom sin was love of the world; and knew he could not be saved from this, but by literally renouncing it. To him therefore he gave this particular direction, which he never designed for a general rule. For him that was necessary to salvation: to us it is not. To sell all was an absolute duty to him; to many of us it would be an absolute sin.

—John Wesley, commenting on the rich young ruler

dering **who can be saved** if their Master's words were accepted (19:25). The statement **Jesus looked at them** indicates a sustained gaze, perhaps with a mixture of love and frustration. Leaving the figure of speech about the camel behind, He stated His point plainly, that from a human perspective **this is impossible** (19:26). However, the good news is that **with God all things are possible.** God is able to win such trust even from the wealthy that they abandon their reliance on their wealth and put all their trust in Him.

As was often the case, **Peter** did not understand all that Jesus was saying. He bragged that he and the other disciples had **left everything to follow** Jesus (19:27). Peter overstated the degree of sacrifice he had made, since he returned to his home and wife following the resurrection. But it is his question **What will there be for us?** that most clearly indicates his failure to understand. The point of the Kingdom is not following Jesus to get something in return, even though there will be a reward for discipleship. **Jesus** promised that **at the renewal of all things,** His followers **will sit on twelve thrones, judging the twelve tribes of Israel** (19:28). The language completely reflects the terminology of the Jewish apocalyptic eschatology that arose between the testaments. Jesus' disciples will participate in God's glorious restoration of all things.

Whatever sacrifice a disciple might have made to follow Jesus will be compensated. Whether **houses** or family or **fields** were sacrificed, the disciple will be compensated a hundred times and **will inherit eternal life** (19:29). Whether **eternal life** refers to life in the Kingdom or everlasting life in heaven or both, Jesus' teaching comes back finally to the subject about which the young man asked in 19:16. The concluding comment (19:30) that **the first will be last** and the **last will be first** illustrates the way Jesus' teaching about the Kingdom and obedience completely reverses the typical cultural values of society.

GRACE FOR THE JOURNEY

Matthew 20:1–34

Matthew 20 narrates the final events and teachings of Jesus before He arrived in Jerusalem for the final week of His life. Verses 1–16 present the parable of the workers in the vineyard. Another prediction and application of Jesus' coming suffering, death, and resurrection in Jerusalem appears in verses 17–28. The chapter concludes in verses 29–34 with two blind men receiving their sight. In each segment of the chapter, grace is a central theme.

1. THE PARABLE OF THE WORKERS IN THE VINEYARD 20:1–16

There is no transitional phrase introducing the parable of the workers in the vineyard. This indicates that Matthew saw it flowing directly from Jesus' concluding words in chapter 19 that addressed the difficulty wealth created for people's entry into the Kingdom. The parable describes itself as a story about **the kingdom** (20:1). The Kingdom **is like a landowner who went out to hire** workers for **his vineyard.** Strictly speaking the King (God) of the Kingdom is like the landowner. By comparing the Kingdom to a vineyard, Jesus connected His audience to a well-known song about a vineyard from Isaiah 5. There the prophet compared Israel to a vineyard. So Jesus' listeners would immediately look for how they, as members of Israel, fit in this parable.

The parable reflects the economic practices of small rural villages in Galilee at the time of Jesus. The unemployed and tenant farmers who had already brought in their small harvest would gather **early in the morning** at the village marketplace, hoping the landowners would hire them as extra workers for the harvest. The standard day's wage was **a denarius**, so when the landowner offered that wage **for the day**, the workers were happy to go to the landowner's **vineyard** (Matt. 20:2).

Those who were not hired early in the day often went to another village to see if landowners there were hiring. As a result, at various hours of the day, the landowner could expect to find additional workers available **in the marketplace** (20:3). It was customary for such workers to be hired and paid proportionally for the amount of daylight left in which they could work. Thus the landowner's promise to pay workers hired at the later hours of the day **whatever is right** was a normal practice (20:4). Landowners hiring workers at the third, **sixth,** and even **the ninth hour** (20:5) was also a common practice.

LABORS AND DEMANDS

Most property in Galilee was owned by wealthy landowners who leased land to tenants to farm. The landowner would keep a large section of the best land for himself. Though he would have servants, the labor demands were seasonal. Only during planting and harvest would he need to hire additional workers. During those seasons the landowner would go to the marketplaces of the surrounding villages, looking for workers he could hire for the day.

The landowner's desire for workers becomes very clear when he returned to the market place at the **eleventh hour** and again found workers seeking employment (20:6). A coin valued at one-twelfth of a *denarius* existed so there was no problem in hiring workers that late in the day. Before hiring them the landowner asked, **why have you been standing here all day doing nothing?** Their answer in verse 7, **Because no one has hired us**, implies that they had been seeking work in several village marketplaces through the day. They were desperate enough to still be looking for work at 5:00 p.m. The landowner felt it was worth the investment of one-twelfth a day's wage to hire them and sent them to **work in** his **vineyard**.

It was customary to pay the workers **when evening came** (20:8). Many workers were so poor that the denarius enabled them to buy flour on their way home to bake the bread they would eat the next day. Leviticus 19:13 and Deuteronomy 24:14–15 specifically commanded payment of workers at the end of the day for this very reason. When the landowner was wealthy enough to have a **foreman** or steward, the actual payment was delegated to him. Jesus' literary skill as a parable teller is evident throughout this parable. The way in which all the details so thoroughly reflected typical Galilean practice would have drawn His listeners into the story. But the teaching point of Jesus' parables usually occurred at a point where the parable departed from reality. The first clue of the surprise ending comes in Matthew 20:8, when the foreman is ordered to pay the workers **beginning with the last ones hired and going on to the first.** The normal order of payment would have been the order in which the workers were hired, so that each group was paid less than the previous group. This unusual feature in the parable alerted Jesus' listeners for something unusual.

The surprise is quickly revealed. **The workers hired about the eleventh hour each received a denarius** (20:9). Such payment was an unexpected bonanza. **So when** the other workers came **they expected to receive more** (20:10). Perhaps they assumed the landowner would pay proportionally, and those who worked all day would receive twelve denarii, but they **received** only one denarius. Now it is clear why the landowner instructed the foreman to begin paying by those who had worked the least. In this way the people who worked the longest got to see what everyone who worked less was paid.

It is no surprise that the workers who worked all day **began to grumble** (20:11). The injustice was clear to all, but especially to them because they had carried the main load **of the work** and had suffered **the heat of the day** (20:12). It did not seem fair to them, but the landowner disputed their accusation, **Friend, I am not being unfair to you** (20:13). The word **friend** spoke of a cordial relationship, but in all three uses in the New Testament the word was used by a superior to address a subordinate. By its use here the landowner gently reminds the worker of their relative status and who is in charge. The reason he was not unfair is that the worker and he had agreed that a denarius would be the pay. The point is not injustice to the person who worked all day but the goodness the landowner wanted to extend to the worker hired last. Both verses 14 and

15 emphasize that the landowner wanted to give every worker the same. The problem was that the worker was **envious because** the landowner was **generous** (20:15).

Jesus' parable speaks specifically of the generosity of God's grace. He may have first spoken this parable in response to Pharisees who objected to His invitation to sinners and tax collectors to enter the Kingdom. That context teaches a very important lesson: No one deserves the benefits of the Kingdom. Some have worked longer and harder than others, but the reward of the messianic banquet is offered to all without regard to the work they have done.

The parable also answers Peter's question in 19:27: "What will there be for us?" The question assumed that he and the other disciples deserved a greater reward because of their greater sacrifice and commitment. The parable tells us—and Peter—that God does not judge on the basis of what is earned but on the basis of grace. Peter's question shows that he had not understood the parable of the unforgiving servant. The parable of the workers in the vineyard gave him another chance to comprehend the incredible grace that characterizes God himself. The fact that the parable is bound at its beginning (19:30) and its end (20:16) by the saying that the **last will be first, and the first will be last** shows the mind-boggling reversal of values that the kingdom of God brings.

2. JESUS' COMING DEATH AND RESURRECTION 20:17–28

Turning from the amazing picture of God's grace revealed in the parable of the workers in the vineyard, Matthew brings the journey **to Jerusalem** back into focus (20:17). Jesus' concern is with **the twelve disciples**, whom He **took aside** to tell them once again of His coming suffering, death, and resurrection. Jesus first predicted His death in 16:21. A second prediction came in 17:22–23. This is now the third time in Matthew's gospel that the prediction of His death appears.

Most of the information given in verse 18 appeared in the first two predictions. The location in **Jerusalem** and the role of the **chief priests and teachers of the law** had been revealed in the first prediction in 16:21. The word **betrayed** was part of the second prediction (17:22). A new term here is the word **condemn** to describe Jesus' fate. The details of Jesus being **mocked and flogged and crucified** (20:19) appear here for the first time. Though the promise of His being **raised to life** appears again, this third prediction paints the most horrible picture yet of the fate awaiting Jesus in Jerusalem.

As was the case in the two previous passion predictions, the disciples fail to respond appropriately. Here, the incongruous response comes from **the mother of Zebedee's sons**—James and John—who **asked a favor** from Jesus immediately after His passion prediction (20:20). She wished Jesus to **grant** her sons positions of honor **at His right and left** when the **kingdom** arrived in its fullness (20:21).

The disconnect between Jesus' passion prediction and this request was mind-boggling, and Jesus responded directly to James and John, who had apparently put their mother up to making the request. Jesus' response is they **don't know what** they **are asking** (20:22). In a kingdom where the first are last and the last are first, the very idea of positions of honor is meaningless. James and John have apparently not understood any of Jesus' teaching about the Kingdom. He then asked them if they were able to **drink the cup** He was **going to drink.** The Old Testament contains many references to the **cup** as a metaphor for a destiny of suffering (see Isa. 51:17, 22; Jer. 25:17–29; Ezek. 23:31–34). The way the cup metaphor will apply to Jesus' death will become clear in Gethsemane (Matt. 26:39).

Apparently oblivious to the painful suffering implied by the word **cup**, the sons of Zebedee confidently affirmed, **We can** drink your cup. Jesus solemnly responded, **You will drink from my cup** (20:23). Indeed, they did drink Jesus' cup. Acts 12:2 relates James' death at the hands of another Herod, while John's suffering took him to Patmos. However, the privilege of assigning seats at the messianic banquet does not belong to Jesus. As He consistently did throughout the Gospels, Jesus subordinated himself to His **Father**. The eschatological honors are God's to give, and He will give them to the ones **for whom they have been prepared**. In affirmation of God's omniscience, Jesus declared that God has already prepared these positions of honor for their rightful recipients.

When the other **ten** disciples became aware of the requested favor, they **were indignant with** James and John (Matt. 20:24). One must wonder whether their indignation was over the lack of Kingdom understanding demonstrated by the two or over the fact that James and John had gotten to Jesus first with their request. Regardless, the moment became a teaching opportunity for Jesus. He pointed out something the disciples knew very well: **Gentile rulers lord it over** their subjects, **and their high officials** exert **authority over them** (20:25). Though the ideal king envisioned in the Old Testament was different, the reality of Israel's history was that her rulers were equally oppressive. However, in Judea and Galilee during Jesus' time, the most notable example of such oppression was found in the Roman occupiers, who brutalized the Jews as part of imperial policy.

But the pattern the disciples saw all around them must not be the case among them (20:26). **Instead, to become great** in the Kingdom, a disciple **must** become a **servant** of the others. To become **first**, a follower of Jesus **must** become a **slave** for the others (20:27). Clearly the pattern of relationship in the Kingdom reverses the values to which people are accustomed in the world. These statements of Jesus build on the saying that the "first will be last" and the "last will be first" found in 19:30 and 20:16. To be a follower of Jesus is to renounce the schemes of self-advancement, status, and power that were and are so common in society and to take the role of a servant to others.

Lest there be any question, Jesus reminded the disciples that what He asked of them was the very same as what He was giving to them of His own life. He had **not come to be served, but to serve** (20:28). Jesus' life demonstrated the reversal of values He taught. As the Son of Man, who Daniel 7:13 said is coming with the clouds of heaven and great glory, Jesus could have

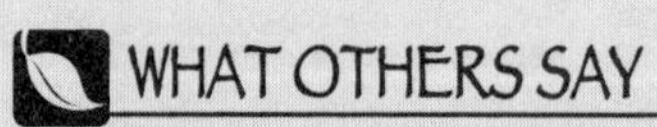

THE CHURCH

The *government* of the *Church* of Christ is widely different from secular governments. It is founded in humility and brotherly love: it is derived from Christ, the great Head of the Church, and is ever conducted by his maxims and spirit. When *political* matters are brought into the Church of Christ, both are ruined. The *Church* has more than once *ruined* the *State*; the *State* has often *corrupted* the *Church*: it is certainly for the interests of both to be kept *separate*.

—Adam Clarke

rightfully demanded honor and status. Instead, He took the role of a servant. His mission was **to give his life as a ransom for many.** Though these exact words do not appear in Isaiah 53, they paraphrase concepts from Isaiah 53:10–12. Jesus understood His coming death in terms of the vicarious suffering of the servant of Isaiah 53.

3. TWO BLIND MEN RECEIVE THEIR SIGHT 20:29–34

As a further expression of the grace of God at work through Jesus, Matthew narrates the final miracle story of his Gospel: the healing of two blind men. The relationship of this account to other Gospel narratives of the healing of the blind is problematic. Most of the details of this passage are parallel to the healing of blind Bartimaeus found in Mark 10:46–52, except that this passage describes two blind men receiving their sight, while in Mark only Bartimeaus is healed. Also, Matthew 9:27–31 tells of two blind men receiving their sight. Many, but not all, of the details are similar in the two stories. Focusing primarily on such literary and historical problems can cause the interpreter to miss the truths Matthew wished to communicate.

Matthew describes this miracle taking place **as Jesus and his disciples were leaving Jericho** (20:29). This means the journey to Jerusalem was almost complete. The healing of these two blind men will be the final event narrated on the journey. The fact that **a large crowd followed** historically fits with the throng of pilgrims that would be making their Passover journey to Jerusalem. However, from a literary standpoint, the presence of a large crowd tells us that the ministry of Jesus was not diminishing in effectiveness as He drew near Jerusalem.

One would expect that the **two blind men** would be **sitting by the** road to most effectively beg for alms from the crowds traveling to Jerusalem for Passover. The word that **Jesus was going by** stirred the blind men to appeal to Him for help: **Lord, Son of David, have mercy on us!** (20:30). (See comments on the title **Son of David** at 9:27.) The title **Lord** is occurring more often as the Gospel reaches its climax. The appeal for mercy would include both an appeal for alms and a prayer for God's grace to be given to them.

Healing miracles often involve a person overcoming obstacles to the healing. The obstacle here is **the crowd** rebuking and trying to silence the blind men. But they overcame the obstacle by shouting **all the louder** (20:31) until **Jesus stopped and called them** (20:32). By asking them **what** they **want** Him **to do for** them, He required them to publicly confess their need. Jesus asked the mother of James and John the same question, but here the question led to a positive outcome. For the third time, the blind men address Jesus as **Lord** (20:33). The threefold repetition gives emphasis to the title and suggests that part of Matthew's goal is for his readers to understand the lordship of Jesus as He enters Jerusalem.

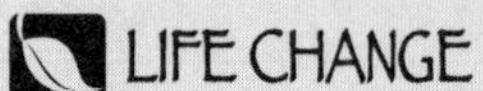

> **LIFE CHANGE**
>
> **THE LORDSHIP OF CHRIST**
>
> It is easy to affirm the lordship of Christ when things are going well. It is more difficult to live the lordship when He invites us to follow Him to the cross. The cruciform life is stronger evidence that He is Lord than any song or affirmation we might make during the good times of our lives. That blind men, who had finally received their sight after a lifetime of hoping, would then follow Jesus to the cross, should instruct us in the life of discipleship.

The blind men request their **sight.** Matthew notes that **Jesus had compassion on them and touched their eyes** (20:34). The immediate result was that **they received their sight**. In response to the gracious healing, they **followed him**. After several chapters in which the disciples seem to not understand anything of Jesus' self-giving mission, He finally has two disciples with clear vision and gratitude who will follow Him to Jerusalem and the cross.

21

JESUS' PROPHETIC AUTHORITY IN JERUSALEM

Matthew 21:1–46

Jesus' triumphal entry into Jerusalem provides a major turning point in Matthew's gospel. Matthew 21:1–11 uses the entry to focus attention on Jesus' identity. Verses 12–17 describe the question of His authority that arises with the cleansing of the Temple. The story of the withering fig tree in verses 18–22 also reinforces Jesus' authority. Then, as He returns to the Temple the next day, verses 23–27 describe more questions from religious leaders concerning His authority. The parable of the two sons told in verses 28–32 and the parable of the tenants presented in verses 33–46 deal with the question of Jesus' authority as the Jewish Messiah.

1. JESUS' ROYAL ENTRY INTO JERUSALEM 21:1–11

The entry into Jerusalem is very important from almost every perspective. Historically, it marked a very significant point in Jesus' life and ministry. From that point on there was no turning back from the destiny God had prepared for Him in Jerusalem. From a literary standpoint the entry represents a key point in Matthew's gospel. After chapters depicting Him on a journey to Jerusalem, Jesus now has arrived. All the themes Matthew has been developing can be brought to conclusion. Theologically the entry enables Matthew to proclaim truth about Jesus that could not be as effectively communicated in any other way.

Matthew's account focuses on the question of Jesus' identity. The issue will be most directly raised by the city's question in verse 10: **Who is this?** Though the crowd will answer that it is **Jesus, the prophet from Nazareth in Galilee**, the reader has already learned much more about Jesus from Matthew's account of the entry.

As Jesus and the disciples came near to **Jerusalem**, they entered **Bethphage on the Mount of Olives** (21:1). The Mount of Olives stood on the east side of Jerusalem overlooking the city as a whole and especially the Temple courtyard. Bethphage was either on the top or slightly down the eastern slope of the mountain. It marked the end of the road from Jericho and entry into the environs of Jerusalem. Upon arrival at Bethphage, **Jesus sent two disciples** to begin preparation for the entry into the city.

Though mid-twentieth-century commentators argued that Jesus had made prior arrangements for the donkey He would ride into the city, the natural narrative logic implies divine foreknowledge on His part. The disciples were to **go to the village ahead** and **find a donkey** (21:2). The village may have been Bethany, but Matthew saw no value in naming it. They would not need to search, but **at once** they would encounter the donkey **with her colt**. Matthew is the only Gospel to mention both the donkey and the colt. Perhaps he considered both to be part of the Scripture fulfillment that he will mention in verse 5.

Jesus instructed the disciples to **untie** the animals and **bring them to** Him. While some might regard this appropriation of the animals as stealing, ancient culture assumed that a king could requisition any possession of one of his subjects. Some rabbis also claimed the right to requisition resources from the common people. Thus the instructions to the disciples presupposed Jesus' identity either as rabbi or, more likely for Matthew, as king. Verse 3 provides further explanation of taking the animals. **If anyone says anything**, Jesus instructed the disciples to reply, **The Lord needs them**. The play on words is clearer in Greek than in English. The word **Lord** in Greek is *kyrios*, which was used both of a property owner or master as well as the primary name for God in the Old Testament. Thus the disciples are to tell any who object that the owner—God himself—needs the animals.

Then, in 21:4, Matthew comments that **this took place to fulfill** the Scripture found in Zechariah 9:9, which he quotes in Matthew 21:5. This pattern of introducing Scripture quotations was common in the early chapters of the Gospel but has not been used since chapter 13. The Scripture provided another reason for the disciples to say that the **Lord needs** the animals. The prophecy spoke of Israel's **king** coming to the people. The use of the Zechariah passage enabled Matthew to claim the title **king** as part of Jesus' identity. The text then described the king as **gentle and riding on a donkey, on a colt, the foal of a donkey.** Most interpreters agree that the reference to the colt in Zechariah is an example of Hebrew parallelism, so both lines refer to a single animal. The second line, referring to the colt as the foal of a donkey, would be another way of saying that the donkey was young and unbroken. For reasons, perhaps known only to Matthew, he read the text to refer to two animals.

The frequent assertion is that Jesus rode a donkey to symbolize His message of peace rather than riding a horse, which would have symbolized a militant view of the Messiah. This is based on practices later than the biblical period. The Old Testament suggests that the heir of David would ride a donkey to his coronation. Solomon did, according to 1 Kings 1:32–40. Absalom (2 Sam. 18:9) and Mephibosheth (2 Sam. 19:26) were both claimants to David's throne, and both rode donkeys. Thus the symbolism, most likely intended by Matthew and understood by the crowds in Jerusalem that day, was that by riding on the donkey Jesus laid claim to the title Son of David, King of Israel.

Verse 6 states that **the disciples went and did as Jesus had instructed.** Is their obedience an indication that they were finally beginning to understand Jesus' identity? The disciples **placed their cloaks on** the animals, and **Jesus sat on** the cloaks riding into Jerusalem (Matt. 21:7). Matthew's choice of words, saying that Jesus **sat** on the donkey rather than riding it, reflects his intention to portray Jesus as king. Sitting was the normal posture associated with kings.

Matthew understood Jesus' royal entry into Jerusalem as a huge public event. **A very large crowd** (21:8) participated by spreading **their cloaks on the road** and by cutting **branches from the trees** to **spread** before the entering king. These acts also signify Jesus' kingly role. People

MANNERS AND CUSTOMS

ENTERING THE CITY

The accepted way pilgrims entered Jerusalem for religious festivals was to walk. Even persons with mounts to ride to the city would dismount and walk the final steps into Jerusalem to show their humble gratitude at coming to the house of the Lord. That Jesus, who had no animal to ride, sought out the donkey and rode into the city made a strong statement that He was no ordinary pilgrim but God himself coming to His own house.

spread their cloaks before Jehu, proclaiming him king (2 Kings 9:13). Cutting the branches from trees would have been part of the way the road was prepared for royalty (Isa. 40:3–4). The crowds were so large that some **went ahead of** Jesus and some **followed**, but all **shouted** praises to Him (Matt. 21:9).

The shouts of the crowd were interwoven with phrases from Psalm 118:25–26. This was one of the psalms frequently sung by pilgrims entering Jerusalem during the great festivals like Passover and Tabernacles. **Hosanna** is the actual Hebrew word used in Psalm 118:25 and usually translated *save us* or *save us, now*. While such a plea was often directed to the king, evidence suggests that by the time of Matthew the word **hosanna** had acquired the meaning of praise. This acclamation is directed to Jesus as **Son of David. Blessed is he who comes in the name of the Lord** is the first line of Psalm 118:26. As Matthew 11:3 showed, *he who comes* was understood as a messianic title in Jesus' time. Thus the crowd praised Jesus as the Son of David, the long-expected messianic king.

Matthew notes that **the whole city** of Jerusalem **was stirred** by Jesus' royal entry (21:10). However, emotion is no substitute for knowledge, and the city had to ask, **Who is this?** The answer should have been clear from the acclamations of the crowd recorded in verse 9. However, **the crowds answered** with a surprisingly low-key response: **This is Jesus, the prophet from Nazareth in Galilee** (21:11). While modern Christians might have thought the crowds would have proclaimed Jesus as Messiah, or king of Israel, or Son of God, or Lord, the answer that He was a prophet was also true. That answer rounded out the prophetic identity of Jesus that Matthew was building through these verses, and it prepared for Jesus' ministry that will be described in the following verses.

2. THE CLEANSING OF THE TEMPLE 21:12–17

The entry into Jerusalem was also an entry into **the temple area** (21:12). The road from the Mount of Olives would have come down the western slope of the mountain, through the Kidron Valley, and up into the eastern gate of Jerusalem, which opened into the Temple courtyard. In a single verse (21:12), Matthew summarizes Jesus' prophetic act of cleansing the Temple. He **drove out all who were buying and selling there** and **overturned . . . the benches of those selling doves**. The sale of sacrificial animals was an important part of Temple worship. Many of the worshippers came from hundreds and even thousands of miles away. It was not practical for them to bring their sacrificial animals to Jerusalem. Rather, they sold the animals in their hometowns and brought the money to Jerusalem, where animals were available to be purchased. Rabbinic evidence indicates that the Sanhedrin provided for the sale of these animals in four markets located on the Mount of Olives. However, other rabbinic evidence suggests that Caiaphas, the high priest, set up a market in the Temple courtyard in the year A.D. 30 to compete with the markets of the Sanhedrin on the Mount of Olives. Caiaphas's new market in the Temple courtyard did not become an established institution.[1] The Gospel accounts suggest that the market in the Temple courtyard may have lasted only one year.

Jesus also **overturned the tables of the money changers**.

Greek authors used two words often translated *temple* to distinguish between the whole Temple area or courtyard and the actual sanctuary containing the Holy Place and the Most Holy Place. It is the Temple courtyard, not the sanctuary, that is in view in the cleansing of the Temple account. The courtyard would have included the Court of the Gentiles, the Court of the Women, and the Court of the Men before reaching the Court of the Priests and the sanctuary itself.

The Sadducees required the Temple tax to be paid with Tyrian coins rather than Greek or Romans coins, which had pagan images or mottoes on them. Thus money changing was also needed for many worshippers. The *Mishnah* indicates that the money changers were set up three weeks prior to Passover each year. Jesus' motivation in ridding the Temple courtyard of the animals, sellers, and money changers is not clear. It may have been that He wished to perform a symbolic action that would mark the end of the sacrificial system. It may have been that He believed all the stuff in the court of the Gentiles blocked their access to God. It may have been that He was offended by the mixture of business and worship in space dedicated to worship. All of these possibilities are legitimate readings of evidence found in at least one of the Gospel accounts of the cleansing.

The justification in Matthew appears in verse 13 through a mixed quotation from Scripture. **My house will be called a house of prayer** quotes the final line of Isaiah 56:7. As important as these actual words are, the larger context of Isaiah 56:3–8 speaks of God creating a welcome space in the Temple area for eunuchs, foreigners, and exiles. It is hard to imagine Matthew's readers hearing the words **My house will be called a house of prayer** without their minds supplying the final words of the line: for all nations.

Jesus also quotes from Jeremiah 7:11: **but you are making it a "den of robbers."** The Jeremiah passage speaks judgment against Jerusalem for trusting in the Temple and ritual worship while neglecting the commandments that require love for one's neighbor.

Matthew 21:14 is unique to the first Gospel's account of the cleansing of the Temple: **The blind and the lame came to him at the temple, and he healed them.** This fits with the quotation from Isaiah 56 and the eunuchs. According to Leviticus 21:18–20 and Deuteronomy 23:1, both the disabled—such as the blind and the lame—and the disfigured—such as eunuchs—were forbidden entry into the worship space of Israel. Isaiah 56 looked forward to a day when God would invite such disabled and disfigured people into His presence. By His actions in Matthew 21:14, Jesus declared that the day envisioned by Isaiah had come.

The chief priests and the teachers of the law were not happy with these developments (21:15). If Matthew's expression **the wonderful things he did** refers to the healings of verse 14, it is amazing that the Temple officials were angry at those healings rather than the disruption of the sellers and money changers. They seemed most angry that **the children** were **shouting in the temple area**. This was consistent with the low value given children in that society. Their **indignant** question asked whether Jesus had heard what the **children** were **saying** (21:16). His answer, **have you never read**, chided their lack of biblical understanding. He then quoted Psalm 8:2 to them: **From the lips of children and infants you have ordained praise!** The acclamation of the children had been ordained by God centuries earlier. Jesus would not—and the Temple official should not—interfere with what God has ordained. With that comment the cleansing of the Temple account concludes, and Jesus **left** the Temple area to spend **the night** in **Bethany** (Matt. 21:17).

3. THE WITHERING FIG TREE 21:18–22

Both Jesus' royal entry into Jerusalem and the cleansing of the Temple were symbolic actions. A third symbolic action is the withering of the fig tree. Though it was not nearly as public an event as the preceding two, it reveals the authority of Jesus. Verse 18 sets the context **early in the morning** of the following day. Jesus was returning to Jerusalem and **was hungry.** When He saw **a fig tree by the road, he went up to it**, presumably to pluck some figs to satisfy His hunger. However, He **found nothing except leaves** on the fig tree (21:19). In response He said to the fig tree, **May you never bear fruit again!** Amazingly, Matthew narrates, **Immediately the tree withered.**

This verse has created a number of problems for Christian readers. Some wonder how Jesus could be so petulant and self-centered as the text appears to make Him. Others note that it wasn't even the season for figs to be ripe, as Mark 11:13 also mentions. Beyond the motivation, others see the action as destructive and out of character for Jesus. What are we to make of Jesus effectively cursing a fig tree and causing it to wither up and die?

First, the temptation story (Matt. 4:1–4) makes it clear that hunger did not drive Jesus' decisions. Second, though it was not the season for ripe figs, if there were leaves there should have also been fruit buds that would eventually ripen. The contrast was between reality (no fruit buds) and expectation (if there were leaves there should be fruit buds).

The severity of Jesus' response indicates this was another prophetic, symbolic act. The barrenness of the fig tree symbolized the spiritual barrenness of the Jewish leaders. They were indignant about the children singing in the Temple when the messianic King came to take possession of His capital city. They complained when the Son of God came to take possession of His Temple. The religious leaders showed a tragic gap between reality and what God should have been able to expect from them. Jesus' words announce the end of the spiritual leadership of those Temple officials. Forty years later, the Temple and the Sadducees who managed it were destroyed.

It is no wonder **the disciples were amazed when they saw** the withered fig tree (21:20). Their question, though, is not why, but **how did the fig tree wither so quickly?** No doubt the correct answer would have been that Jesus accomplished it by His divine power. However, He chose to answer in a way that instructed the disciples in their spiritual lives. **Jesus** declared that **if** a person has **faith and** does **not doubt,** fig trees can wither and mountains can be thrown **into the sea** (21:21). If the disciples would just **believe** they could **receive whatever** they **ask for in prayer** (21:22).

Once again Jesus' point is not that faith is a handle by which people can force God to do their bidding. Rather, the verb **believe** in verse 22 could best be translated *trust.* When people learn to trust God and to enter into intimate relationship with Him, there comes a joining of their human wills to the divine will, and God delights to grant them whatever they ask for in prayer.

4. THE AUTHORITY OF JOHN THE BAPTIST AND JESUS 21:23–27

From the three symbolic actions demonstrating Jesus' authority, Matthew turns to describe a series of conflicts between Jesus and the Jewish leaders. These conflict stories begin in 21:23 and continue through the end of chapter 23.

The narrative flow suggests that after cursing the fig tree Jesus continued into the city, **entered the temple courts,** and began **teaching** (21:23). In the very act of teaching, He was challenged by **the chief priests and the elders of the people,** who asked, **By what authority are you doing these things?** The context makes it clear that the Temple officials were not challenging Jesus' authority to teach as much as the royal entry, the cleansing of the Temple, and the cursing of the fig tree. Their question might be paraphrased, "What right do you have to come into our Temple and pronounce God's judgment against us?" They seemed to think that simply by territorial principles—Jesus was a Galilean, not from Jerusalem as they were—He had no authority to interfere with their system.

These Temple officials did not expect Jesus to have an answer to their authority question. But He did, responding to their question with His own, promising if they could answer His question, He would answer theirs (21:24). Without waiting for their agreement, Jesus asked, **John's baptism—where did it come from? Was it from heaven, or from men?** (21:25). Some have objected that Jesus was evading the question and playing coy with the chief priests by refusing to answer them. However, His question was very much to the point, because the source of John the Baptist's ministry was the same as the source of Jesus' authority.

The chief priests immediately knew that they were caught on the horns of a dilemma. If they were to acknowledge that John's baptism was authorized **from heaven**, Jesus could fairly ask **why** they **didn't believe him.** The verb **believe** points not simply to intellectual assent but to a life of trust that leads to obedience. Regardless of what the chief priests thought about John the Baptist, they had clearly refused to open their hearts to his message and to respond obediently. Further, if they acknowledged that John's baptism was **from heaven** they would also have to acknowledge that Jesus' authority was too.

On the other hand, if the chief priests would answer that John's baptism was merely **from men**, they were in danger of inciting a riot among **the people** who were convinced **that John was a prophet** (21:26). Beside that, Jesus' credentials as a prophet were even stronger than John's. So when the chief priests responded, **We don't know**, they did not mean they did not know the answer to the question (21:27). They meant they didn't know what to say without conceding that Jesus had the authority to do the things that had made them so angry. Jesus did not directly answer their question either. When **he said, "Neither will I tell you by what authority I am doing these things,"** He really meant, "Obviously you know the answer. You are just refusing to accept My authority."

5. THE PARABLE OF THE TWO SONS 21:28–32

With no transition, Jesus began telling the parable of the two sons. Thus Matthew understands this parable as part of Jesus' response to the question of His authority. The opening words, **What do you think?** (21:28), are addressed to the chief priests and elders of the people. The parable contrasts **two sons**. Their father **went to the first and** asked him to **go and work today in the vineyard**. Though the opening sentence does not provide sufficient information to know already the purpose and meaning of the parable, critical elements are already obvious. The reference to the vineyard would have brought the song of the vineyard in Isaiah 5 to Jesus' listeners' minds. The vineyard represented Israel there. Further, the Old Testament often represented the relationship of God and Israel as a Father-son relationship. So already the possibility exists that this parable is about God and Israel.

The first son refused the Father's command: **I will not** go and work in the vineyard (Matt. 21:29). This immediately marked the son as a sinner and thus to be rejected by God. However, **later** this sinful son **changed his mind and went** to the vineyard. The New International Version **changed his mind** accurately reflects the roots of the Greek word. It does not make clear to English readers, however, that this word was commonly used for repentance. Thus the parable suggests the repentance of the sinful son.

Then the father went to the other son with the same request to go and work in the vineyard (21:30). The second son **answered, 'I will, sir,' but he did not go.** The picture is clear: The second son honored the father with his lips, but his heart and thus his actions were completely disobedient. The answer to Jesus' question in verse 31—**Which of the two did the Father's will?**—was obvious.

With their agreement established, Jesus turned to the interpretation of the parable: **tax collectors and prostitutes are entering the kingdom of God ahead of** the Temple officials. In general terms, the Temple officials were the second son, who gave lip service but not obedience to the Father. Tax collectors and prostitutes represent the first son, whose first word to God was no, but who later repented and became a part of the vineyard, Israel.

However, Jesus gave a more particular interpretation connecting the parable to the questions of His authority and the source of John's baptism in verse 32. **John came** and showed the chief priests **the way of righteousness**, but they **did not believe**. The word **believe** here is the same word used in verse 25 to describe the Temple officials'

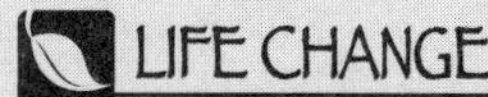

The parable of the two sons is a sobering reminder to religious people of God's expectations of us. It is easy to fall into a pattern of saying the right words and living our lives by our own agendas rather than by God's agenda. Of course, God would prefer children who both say and do the right things. However, if He has to choose, He always prefers children who obey rather than those who just say the right words.

refusal to believe John the Baptist. In contrast, like the first son of the parable, **the tax collectors and the prostitutes did** believe John. One could add the **blind**, and **lame**, and **children** mentioned in verses 14–15, **did** believe Jesus and His message of the arriving Kingdom.

Jesus' final word interpreting the parable appeals to the chief priests. He pointed out that **even after** they **saw** John's ministry, they **did not repent and believe him.** They missed their first opportunity. Their second opportunity was speaking to them and had cleansed their Temple. Jesus' words were an implicit invitation to the Temple officials to repent and believe Him. Of course, to do so they would have to accept His authority.

6. THE PARABLE OF THE TENANTS 21:33–46

Without waiting for a reply, Jesus moved immediately into another parable. It also involved a vineyard, but is a more extended parable or story. There is considerable scholarly discussion as to whether this story should be understood as a parable proper or as an allegory. There are clearly allegorical elements to the story, and Matthew appears to have allegorized the story beyond the parallel parable we find in Mark 12:1–12.

This **parable** also concerns **a vineyard**, and so, once again, it would bring the song of the vineyard in Isaiah 5 to the listeners' minds. But this parable strengthens that connection by repeating several of the details of the prophet. For example the **landowner** of Jesus' parable **dug a winepress in**

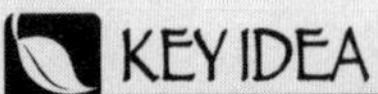

KEY IDEA

ALLEGORY

Both a proper parable and an allegory have a story form. The distinction has to do with how the details of the story function.

Normally in a parable the details are present to make the story make sense. The parable usually has *one major point*, and the details contribute to that point.

In an allegory the details are important for themselves. An allegory is a story in code, so many details must have meaning both in the story being told *and* in the other story that is the real message of the allegory.

his vineyard (Matt. 21:33). So did the loved one of Isaiah 5:2. The landowner **built a watchtower** in both Matthew and Isaiah 5:2. These details clearly indicate the vineyard of Jesus' parable is to be understood as Israel, the vineyard of Isaiah 5.

The landowner then **rented the vineyard to some farmers** and departed the scene. But **when the harvest time** came, the owner **sent servants to collect his fruit** (Matt. 21:34). This would have been standard procedure for landowners in the ancient Near East. But **the tenants seized** the **servants**, beating, killing, and stoning them (21:35). Such disrespect for the landowner would have been shocking to Jesus' audience. They would have anticipated swift and brutal retribution. Instead, the landowner **sent other servants**, who were **treated the same way** (21:36). The references to servants, beating, stoning, and killing suggest an allegorical interpretation. The servants would have represented the prophets, and the violent rejection of them was a matter of Old Testament history.

Last of all the landowner **sent his son**, hoping the tenants would **respect** him (21:37). No Christian reader who had understood the allegory to this point could fail to see the reference to Jesus here. Verse 37 is almost a Matthean form of John 3:16. **But the tenants** chose to **kill** the son in order to **take** the **inheritance** (Matt. 21:38). The clearest allegorical element comes in verse 39, which states that the tenants **took** the son, **threw him out of the vineyard and killed him.** Jesus was taken outside the city and then crucified. But staying within the story, Jesus concluded with the question, **what will the owner do to those tenants** when he **comes?** (21:40).

The Temple leaders were forced to pronounce their own judgment. They knew the landowner would have to destroy **those wretches** and

rent the vineyard to other tenants who would respond appropriately (21:41). **Jesus** then quoted Psalm 118:22–23. He was **the stone the builders rejected**, and the builders were the Jewish religious leaders. But God has made Him **the capstone** (Matt. 21:42). Truly, this **is marvelous in our eyes**.

Verse 43 responds most directly to the Temple leaders' declaration in verse 41 that the landowner would destroy the first tenants and give the vineyard to others. Jesus plainly stated, **The kingdom will be taken away from you and given to a people who will produce its fruit**. Though Jesus does not clearly indicate that the Kingdom will be given to the Gentiles, much of Christian interpretation has assumed that to be His meaning. Returning to the **stone** metaphor in verse 44, He points out the crushing judgment that will come upon those who reject Him.

The meaning of the parable had become clear to the Temple officials, and **they knew he was talking about them** (21:45). For the first time Matthew tells us they began looking for an opportunity **to arrest** Jesus but were **afraid** to proceed because the **crowd** knew that **he was a prophet** (21:46). Jesus' prophetic character demonstrated at the beginning of chapter 21 is the reason He is not arrested at the end of the chapter.

ENDNOTES

1. William L. Lane, *The Gospel According to Mark*, The New International Commentary on the New Testament (Grand Rapids, Mich.: Eerdmans, 1974), 403–404.

22

CONFLICT WITH JEWISH RELIGIOUS LEADERS IN JERUSALEM

Matthew 22:1–46

The stories of Jesus' conflict with Jewish religious leaders that began in 21:23 continue throughout chapters 22 and 23. Chapter 22 begins with the parable of a wedding feast in verses 1–14. A discussion over paying taxes to Caesar follows in verses 15–22. A question about Jesus' understanding of resurrection occupies verses 23–33 and is followed by the question of the greatest commandment in verses 34–40. The final section of the chapter consists of verses 41–46, which present Jesus' question about David's son.

1. THE PARABLE OF A WEDDING FEAST 22:1–14

The parable of a wedding feast is the third consecutive parable included by Matthew in this section of Jesus' conflict with various Jewish leaders in the Temple courtyard. The two preceding parables (the two sons in 21:28–32 and the tenants in 21:33–46) had no introductions. The introduction here is quite brief, simply indicating that **Jesus spoke again in parables** to the same audience (22:1). As with the parable of the tenants, scholars debate whether the parable of the wedding feast should be understood as a parable or as an allegory. The question of whether Matthew (or Jesus) has combined two parables that were once separate also arises in technical discussions of this passage. Verses 1–10 are similar to a parable related in Luke 14:15–24 and in the gospel of Thomas, a gnostic gospel discovered in the mid-twentieth century. However, the relation of Matthew 22:11–14 to verses 2–10 is difficult to determine.

The parable begins by comparing **the kingdom** to **a king who prepared a wedding banquet for his son** (22:2). In the ancient Near Eastern culture, the king, as a person of wealth, would have been expected to provide a public banquet on various occasions. Certainly the marriage of his son would have been one such occasion. As the parallel text in Luke 14:16 makes clear, invitations would have gone out to the community several days or even weeks in advance of the wedding. This detail is implied in Matthew 22:3, when the king **sent his servants to those who had been invited** to tell them the banquet was ready. This was a common custom in the biblical world, where there were no clocks and time was often a matter of personal interpretation. When the meal was about ready, the servants would be sent to tell the guests that it was time to come.

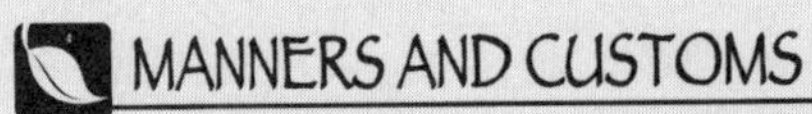

INVITATIONS

In the honor-shame society of Jesus' world, the king would have been the most honored person in the region. For him to invite guests to the wedding banquet of his son would have been an act of bestowing honor or status upon those guests. For the guests to refuse to come not only rejected the offered honor, it also would have brought shame and dishonor both to the guests and to the king. The guests' refusal of the king's invitation was culturally incomprehensible.

Most parables reflect normal life in Jesus' culture until near the end, when the parable takes a surprising turn that will reveal the teaching point. The proper response to the announcement of the king's servants that the banquet was ready would be to drop whatever one was doing and come to the banquet. Instead, Jesus said, the invited guests **refused to come.**

The king seemed confused by the news of their refusal. He responded as if they had misunderstood the message, by sending **more servants** and repeating the message in greater detail (22:4). The message concluded with the emphatic command: **Come to the wedding banquet.** But the guests **paid no attention** and continued with their own agendas, **one** going **to his field, another to his business** (22:5). This was shocking behavior. One can almost see Jesus' audience looking at each other with worried and questioning glances. They have no idea where this story is going, but the worst is yet to come. Other persons who had been invited **seized his servants, mistreated them and killed them** (22:6). Such behavior was absolutely unacceptable in the ancient world, and **the king was enraged** (22:7). His honor has been flagrantly impugned. In the cultural context in which Jesus and His audience lived, the king had no choice; **he sent his army and destroyed those murderers**. Finally, he **burned their city.**

The artificial nature of this story is very clear at this point. The parable assumes that the sending of the army, destruction of the invited guests, and the burning of their city all takes place in no more time than it takes to tell it. In verse 8 the king announces to **his servants** that **the wedding banquet is ready**. The meat didn't even get cold while the army was out burning the city. But since the guests the king had invited **did not deserve to come**, the servants are sent **to the street corners** to **invite to the banquet anyone** they can **find** (22:9). **So the servants went out and gathered all the people they could find.** It didn't matter whether the people were **good** or **bad**; the goal was for the **wedding hall** to be **filled with guests** (22:10).

This strange story immediately invites allegorical interpretation. God is the king inviting the selected guests—the elect Jewish people—to the messianic banquet, the wedding supper of the Son. The servants sent out to summon the guests were the prophets of the Old Testament who were mistreated and killed. The invited guests pursuing their own agendas represent the Jewish religious leaders to whom Jesus was speaking. God would have no choice but to destroy the Jewish people and burn their city. This detail reflects a perspective from after A.D. 70, when Jerusalem was burned and the Sadducees were destroyed. But God still had a banquet, and so He sent out His servants, the apostles, to bring people (Gentiles) from everywhere to fill the banquet hall.

The parable takes another strange turn at verse 11. As **the king** strolled through the banquet hall, **he noticed a man not wearing wedding clothes.** It is not clear how Jesus' first listeners would have understood this detail, except that they would have been horrified. To attend a wedding feast without proper wedding attire was unthinkable in ancient Palestine. It is not clear whether the wedding clothes were simply regular clothes specially washed and bleached for the banquet or if the king supplied the wedding clothes. In either case, appropriate wedding clothes were available, but the guest had refused to take advantage of that availability.

When the king confronted him, **Friend, how did you get in here without wedding clothes? The man was speechless** (22:12). His silence was tacit admission that he had chosen to crash the wedding banquet without wedding clothes. Most guests came to the banquet to honor the king and his son. Perhaps some came just to eat. This guest obviously thought he would get the benefits of the wedding banquet without honoring the king by wearing the required apparel. Again the king had no choice but to **throw** this guest **outside**, bound **hand and foot** (22:13).

If the allegory is extended, verses 11–14 describe the messianic banquet with all people as the guests. Perhaps the one without the wedding garment was a Gentile who thought he could sneak into the Kingdom without honoring God the King. Though the Gentiles have been invited late to the messianic feast, there will be no crashing of God's party. Gentiles must also honor God by obediently clothing themselves with the garment of purity. The message of this parable again confronts the Jewish religious leaders with the truth that their time for salvation will soon be past. They need to repent and embrace Jesus as their Messiah. It is true that God has **invited many, but few** actually make it to the messianic banquet (21:14).

2. PAYING TAXES TO CAESAR 22:15–22

After the three parables Jesus told in response to the question of the chief priests and elders of the people (21:23) about His authority, Matthew tells of another attempt to **trap** Jesus **in his words** (22:15). This trap is baited by the **Pharisees** through their **disciples**, who are accompanied by **the Herodians** (22:16). The views and activities of the Pharisees are fairly well known; in contrast, nothing is known of the Herodians. The only mention of such a group in all of ancient literature is this passage, its parallel in Mark 12:13, and in Mark 3:6. In all three passages the Herodians are associated with the Pharisees. Many scholars confidently describe the Herodians as a Jewish party supporting the rule of the Herod family and particularly the rule of Herod Antipas during Jesus' time. A few scholars note that the Herodians are never mentioned outside the Gospels and the Essenes are never mentioned in the gospel and wonder if the Herodians were actually the Essenes. There is not sufficient evidence to describe the Herodians as a Jewish party. They may have been no more than agents employed by Herod Antipas who worked with certain Pharisees.

Those wanting to trap Jesus began with a long list of compliments apparently designed to impress Him. They addressed Him as **Teacher**, the original Aramaic word was probably *Rabbi,* and described Him as **a man of integrity** (Matt. 22:16) who wasn't **swayed by** others. Though the compliments may have been true, they sound more like bait for the trap than the sincere view of Jesus by the Pharisees. Verse 17 then springs the trap, asking Jesus' **opinion: Is it right to pay taxes to Caesar or not?**

The question was widely discussed in Jesus' time. The word translated *taxes* was not the general word for taxes but a specific property tax imposed by the Romans since they had conquered Jerusalem in 63 B.C. It symbolized their power over the Jews and was deeply resented. Already one rebellion had broken out in A.D. 6, primarily over the tax. Some evidence suggests the tax pressure was gradually increasing. The question to Jesus was not a philosophical question about how to support a just government. It was a politically loaded question of whether Jesus supported the right of Rome to subjugate Jews through oppression and military force. If Jesus answered affirmatively, the Pharisees and most of the crowd supporting Him would angrily reject the answer. If He answered negatively, the Sadducees, perhaps the Herodians, and certainly any Roman secret service spies in the crowd would label Him as a revolutionary. He would be liable to surveillance at the least and arrest with possible execution at the worst.

Matthew notes Jesus' wisdom in recognizing **their evil intent** (22:18). His response was also profoundly wise. He asked for **the coin used for paying the tax,** and someone in the crowd produced **a denarius** (22:19).

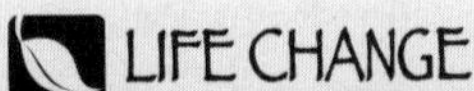

LIFE CHANGE

STEWARDSHIP

If all things belong to God, then the follower of Jesus cannot segregate life into spiritual and material, Christian and secular, or any of the other dualisms we often use. These dualisms, often unintentionally, remove areas of our lives from the scrutiny and control of God. When all things belong to God, then we are responsible to deal with every area of our lives and our world as part of our stewardship offered to God. No portion of life can be excluded and treated as a separate matter.

Looking at the coin, **he asked, "Whose portrait is this? And whose inscription?"** (22:20). The answer was obviously **Caesar's**. Jesus then told them to **give to Caesar what is Caesar's, and to God what is God's** (22:21). Modern Western adherents to the separation of church and state have made Jesus' answer the foundation for their political philosophy. However, it is doubtful that Jesus' answer was so simplistic.

The real question Jesus' answer raises is what belongs to Caesar and what belongs to God. Or, are there things that do not belong to God? Jesus' answer forces people to identify the ultimate commitment or commitments of their lives. It is no wonder His questioners **were amazed** and **left him** (22:22).

3. A QUESTION ABOUT RESURRECTION AND MARRIAGE 22:23–33

Since Jesus had silenced the Pharisees regarding the Roman property tax, **the Sadducees . . . came to him with a question** (22:23). Matthew notes that the Sadducees did not believe in **resurrection**. This group consisted of the leading priestly families in Jerusalem and was the smallest of the major Jewish sects. They had made power-sharing deals with the Romans and, though they controlled the Temple, in many ways they were the most secular of the Jewish religious groups. They only accepted the authority of the Mosaic Pentateuch, denied the immortality of the soul and the hope of resurrection, and did not believe in predestination, fate, or any involvement by God in human affairs. It is possible they rejected belief in angels also.

Their question for Jesus reflects their commitment to the Mosaic Pentateuch and the lack of resurrection hope. They granted Jesus the same title used by the Pharisees, **Teacher**. They then refer to what is often called the levirate marriage law. **If a man dies without having children, his brother must marry the widow and have children for him** (22:24). This instruction came from **Moses** in Deuteronomy 25:5–10. In the hypothetical case they created, **there were seven brothers** (22:25). The **first married and died** childless, so the second **brother** took the widow as his wife. Tragically, **the same thing happened to the second and third brother, right on down to the seventh** (22:26). **Finally, the woman died** (22:27). The question they posed was **whose wife** the woman would be **at the resurrection** (22:28).

The Sadducees may have drawn their story from the apocryphal book of Tobit, in which the heroine, Sarah, married seven men, each of whom died before consummating the marriage. The Sadducees' skepticism was transparent because of the unbelievable series of coincidences they constructed. Their view of resurrection was crudely literalistic, as if resurrection life would be an exact replica of the present. Jesus declared that they understood neither **the Scriptures** nor **the power of God** (22:29).

He rejected their caricature of resurrection replicating earthly life, saying, **At the resurrection people will neither marry nor be given in marriage** (22:30). Jesus' statement that people **will be like the angels in heaven** at the resurrection suggested similarities and differences between resurrection and earthly existence. The example of the angels suggests a corporeal but spiritual existence—what Paul called a **spiritual body** in 1 Corinthians 15:44. But angels were generally not understood by Jews to marry or engage in sexual activity. However, debunking the Sadducees' story was not sufficient for Jesus; He wanted to affirm **the resurrection of the dead** to them (22:31).

His argument for the resurrection was built on Jewish methods of scriptural interpretation and Jewish theology. Its logic does not always persuade modern logicians. He quoted Exodus 3:6: **I am the God of Abraham, the God of Isaac, and the God of Jacob** (Matt. 22:32). The operative word in His argument was the present tense verb **I am**. This implied that God and Abraham, Isaac, and Jacob are **not dead but living**. Since the deaths of the three patriarchs are noted in the Pentateuch, and they are now in living relationship with the living God, they must have been raised from the dead. If the Sadducees were not convinced, **the crowds** were. Matthew states that **they were astonished at his teaching** (22:33).

4. THE GREATEST COMMANDMENT 22:34-40

The response of the Sadducees to Jesus' teaching on resurrection is not mentioned until verse 34, which states that they were **silenced** by what He said. The Pharisees, who had been bested by Jesus in addressing the tax question, were interested in Jesus' answer. The Pharisees believed in the resurrection and so had argued with the Sadducees over that issue in the past. Apparently Jesus' answer to the Sadducees caused the Pharisees to come **together** to find another **question** by which they could test **him** (22:35). They sent **one** of their best debaters **with this question: "Teacher, which is the greatest commandment in the Law?"** (22:36).

This was not a trick question in the way the two previous questions had been. Both the Jewish religious leaders and many of the common people discussed the relative weight of the various commandments and which was the greatest. Perhaps the Pharisee believed his question would force Jesus to take a position for or against one of the common answers to this question. That would enable the Pharisees to identify Him as a follower of someone whose position on the greatest commandment question He supported. This would allow them to return to their question about His authority asked in 21:23. Unfortunately, the question was based on a wrong understanding of the Law. Both Sadducees and Pharisees saw the Law as an arena for debate in such a way that the victorious debater finds the will of God by virtue of being humanly right. Jesus' reply moves the question of the Law and its commandments out of the arena of human argument and power back to the Old Testament concept of covenantal relationship with God and others.

Jesus answered by first quoting the second line of the *Shema*, beginning with Deuteronomy 6:5: **Love the Lord your God with all your heart and with all your soul and with all your mind** (Matt. 22:37). **This** He then identified as **the first and greatest commandment** (22:38). Every Jew recited the *Shema* every day. It appears in Deuteronomy as explanation of the first commandment of the Ten Commandments, to have no other gods. The way to monotheism was not by intellectual argument but by covenant relationship. The faithful God of covenant had brought Israel out of bondage in Egypt. The only appropriate response for Israel—and for us—was to love God completely.

Such complete love implied a commitment to covenant loyalty that would guard God's unique status and place.

Without pausing Jesus continued. **And the second is like it: "Love your neighbor as yourself"** (Matt. 22:39). This quotes Leviticus 19:18, which He had already quoted in Matthew 19:19 as the summation of the second table of the Ten Commandments. Jesus' appeal to the love of neighbor as the second commandment demonstrated the importance of relationship with others in His understanding of the will of God. The importance of these two commandments is

GREAT THEMES

CHRISTIAN HOLINESS

Jesus was not the last to identify love of God and love of neighbor as the two greatest commandments. Two of His very influential followers, St. Augustine and John Wesley, also placed major emphasis on these two love commands. Wesley defined the holiness he preached as nothing more and nothing less than loving God with one's whole heart, soul, mind, and strength, and one's neighbor as oneself. He understood that everything essential about the doctrines of entire sanctification and Christian perfection could be summed up in these two commandments.

clear from His concluding comment: **All the Law and the Prophets hang on these two commandments** (Matt. 22:40). In this way Jesus declared that the totality of the Old Testament could be summarized by these two great commandments.

5. JESUS' QUESTION ABOUT DAVID'S SON 22:41–46

Matthew records no answer from the Pharisees, but while they **were gathered together, Jesus asked them** a question (22:41). He asked their opinion about the Messiah (**Christ** could be best translated Messiah here). Specifically, He wanted to know **whose son** they thought the Messiah to be (22:42). Naturally they answered, **The son of David**. Matthew and Jesus would have agreed with them. However, that answer was insufficient by itself for Jesus, so He pressed the question further.

He asked why **David** called the Messiah **Lord** (22:43) and quoted Psalm 110:1: **The Lord said to my Lord: "Sit at my right hand until I put your enemies under your feet"** (Matt. 22:44). Though the psalm text itself does not identify David as author, it was attributed to him by later editors, and the Pharisees accepted that attribution without question. The psalm is generally understood to have been a coronation psalm sung at the installation of a new king. If the psalm addressed a new king, it would certainly apply to the coming Messiah as the one who would renew the Davidic kingdom. So, if **David** wrote the psalm, in essence, he called the Messiah **Lord** (22:45). Given that the Messiah was David's **Lord**, how could he also be David's **son**?

The Pharisees were unable to answer Jesus' question. In that context it meant that Jesus' interpretation of the Scriptures was superior to that of the Pharisees. Because of His superior interpretation of Scripture, **no one dared to ask him any more questions** (22:46). In every instance of conflict described in chapter 22, Jesus had answered best. The natural conclusion should be that His interpretation should be followed.

JESUS' DENUNCIATION OF THE PHARISEES

Matthew 23:1–39

Jesus' teaching in the Temple courtyard continues from 21:23 through chapter 23. However, the material in chapters 21 and 22 is composed of questions or attempts to trap Jesus by Jewish religious leaders and of His responses. The rhetorical form is dialogue. In chapter 23, the form shifts to monologue as Jesus mounts a sustained attack on the Pharisees and teachers of the law. Verses 1–12 are directed to the crowds and His disciples, warning them to not fall into the patterns of behavior demonstrated by the Pharisees. Verses 13–32 address the Pharisees and teachers of the law directly through a series of seven condemnations. The final warning, summing up the condemnation of these Jewish leaders, appears in verses 33–39.

The language of chapter 23 is harsh and seems unlike Jesus to many readers. Those sensitive to anti-Semitism find this chapter difficult. The words of Matthew 23 became part of the basis for hundreds of years of official condemnation

HISTORICAL CONTEXT

ZEALOTS

The Zealots were the "fourth sect of Jewish philosophy," according to Josephus. Their zeal for freedom led to the name Zealots as well as to violent actions against Romans or Roman sympathizers. Their fierce independence made it difficult for them to cooperate with other Jewish groups or even with others sharing most of their resentment against foreign occupation. A rebellion in A.D. 6 led by Judas the Galilean drew the Zealots together and eventually, in A.D. 66, they instigated the revolution known as the First Jewish War.

and rejection of the Jewish people by Christians. How can a Christian reader understand this chapter?

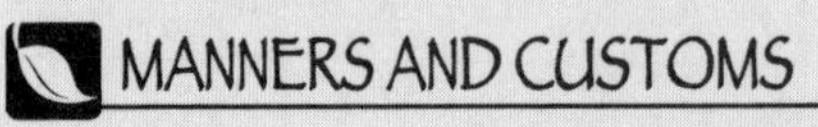

MANNERS AND CUSTOMS

HARSH LANGUAGE

Harsh-sounding language was not unusual in religious debates in first-century Judaism. Words and phrases like *blind guides, twice the sons of hell, hypocrites,* and *brood of vipers* were typical expressions in such debates between Jewish religious groups at Jesus' time. This kind of language was the way a person or a group staked out territory. Ancient listeners would not have heard these words and thought how much the speaker hated the other people. Rather, ancient listeners would have concluded that the speaker firmly believed the other party was wrong, and his or her party was right.

One should note that the words of Jesus in chapter 23 were not any stronger than the words of the prophets of the Old Testament as they denounced both the nations surrounding them and Israel herself. The problem arises when these words are transported from first-century Jewish culture, where they were common parlance, to other cultures where such language is understood very differently. It is also important to remember that Jesus was speaking to His own followers as much as He was speaking to the leaders of Jewish parties. Properly understood, Matthew 23 is as much a warning to believers to avoid the errors of the Pharisees as it is a frontal attack on those Jewish leaders. The sensitive Christian will find more reason to grieve over the practices of the Christian Church through the centuries while reading this chapter than to gloat about how bad the Pharisees were.

1. A WARNING ABOUT THE PHARISEES' HARMFUL PRACTICES 23:1–12

The opening verses of Matthew 23 are directed to **the crowds and** Jesus' **disciples** (23:1). One might envision the various Jewish groups who had attacked Him in the Temple courtyard withdrawing to lick their wounds while Jesus turns to the crowds and His disciples to give the closing lesson about these religious groups. The first thing He said was that **the teachers of the law and the Pharisees sit in Moses' seat** (23:2). In later Judaism, Moses' seat was a chair at the front of the synagogue in which the official teacher of the synagogue sat to deliver the official interpretation of the Law. Scholars debate whether such a chair was used in first-century synagogues or whether the words simply described the official teaching role of the rabbi. In either case, the statement of verse 2 attributes authority to the teachers of the law and the Pharisees.

The consequence of that authority is that the crowds and Jesus' disciples **must obey them and do everything they** say (23:3). These words are surprising to many people who do not realize the way in which Jesus participated in the Jewish culture of His time. For all His criticism of the Pharisees that will follow, there were many points of similarity between the theology of Jesus and the theology of the Pharisees. **But** Jesus' followers were **not** to **do what they do.** Jesus' problem with the Pharisees was less with their theology and more with the practices of their lives. He summarized their problem: **They do not practice what they preach.** Verse 4 focuses His critique: **They tie up heavy loads and put them on men's shoulders.** This is usually thought to mean that the Pharisees created burdensome requirements through their oral traditions and tried to force all Jews to follow those rigorous practices. In contrast, Jesus' yoke is easy and His burden is light.

Another problematic practice of the Pharisees is that **everything they do is done for men to see** (23:5). Jesus had already addressed this problem of doing religious practices to be seen by people in 6:1–18, though He did not call the Pharisees by name there. The practices mentioned in chapter 6 were giving to the needy, praying, and fasting. Here, the practices include wearing **wide phylacteries and long tassels.** The phylacteries were small boxes containing small scripts from the Law tied to their foreheads and arms in literal fulfillment of Deuteronomy 6:8. They also **love the place of honor at banquets and in the synagogues** (Matt. 23:6). Once they occupy those positions of honor they demand that people address them using the title **Rabbi** to show their importance (23:7). The meaning of *Rabbi* in Hebrew is *my great one.*

The comment that the Pharisees require people to call them Rabbi caused Jesus to give a series of commands directly to His disciples. They are not to let people call them **Rabbi** because **all** followers of Jesus **are brothers** and sisters, and thus no one is more valuable or more honored than another (23:8). Further, all believers have **only one Master** and that is Jesus, not a fellow believer. Extending this thought, Jesus forbade the disciples to use the title **father** for **anyone on earth** because there is **one Father, and he is in heaven** (23:9). Continuing in this vein, Jesus declared that believers are not to call each other **"teacher."** For the followers of Jesus, He will always be the **one** and only **Teacher** (23:10).

The reason Jesus forbade the use of these titles of earthly honor was that **the greatest among** His followers **will be** their **servant** (23:11). Verse 11 echoes and summarizes what Jesus taught as He and the disciples had traveled toward Jerusalem on reversing human systems of honor and value described in 20:25–28. In the value system of the Kingdom, the person who seeks honor for himself or herself **will be humbled** (23:12). The passive voice of this verb suggests that God will be the one who humbles the status-seeking believer. Likewise, **whoever humbles himself** or herself **will be exalted.** The passive voice again suggests God will be the one exalting the truly humble follower of Jesus. His followers must avoid the status-seeking practices of the Pharisees because in the Kingdom, God is reversing the symbols and meaning of status.

2. SEVEN CONDEMNATIONS OF THE PHARISEES 23:13–32

Turning from the crowd and His disciples, Jesus addressed the Pharisees and teachers of the law with seven condemnations introduced by the word woe. The word woe was the cry of lament of ancient Israelites when overwhelmed by tragedy and grief. It was a cry of pain. The prophets introduced the word as an expression of judgment when they sang funeral dirges over the coming judgment of God upon Jerusalem. The context of Matthew 23 shows that these seven woes are words of effective judgment spoken by Jesus on behalf of God against the Pharisees and teachers of the law.

The first woe condemns the Jewish religious leaders for shutting **the kingdom in** people's **faces** (23:13). By multiplying required rituals and their stuffy demand for titles, they blocked the door of the Kingdom with their religious clutter. The result was that not only did they **not enter**, they prevented **those who are trying to enter.** The words found in verse 14 in certain translations were not part of the original manuscripts of Matthew. They appear in the authentic texts of Mark 12:40 and Luke 20:47.

The second woe also addresses the question of how converts were gained. Jesus accused the Jewish leaders of traveling **over land and sea to win a single convert** (Matt. 23:15). The Greek word translated **convert** here is *proselytos* from which we get the English word *proselyte.* The word meant *one who has come over* from one faith to another. This comment by Jesus is historically interesting because it supplies evidence that Judaism was involved in some form of missionary or evangelistic outreach in Jesus' time. The words **over land and sea** suggest a missionary process that was widespread in the ancient world. The problem with such missionary outreach was not that it brought Gentiles into relationship with God through the covenant, but that it made that convert **twice as much a child of hell as** the Pharisees were. These words are similar to Jesus' accusation in John 8:44 that the Jewish religious leaders were children of their father the devil.

The third woe addresses the religious leaders as **blind guides** (Matt. 23:16). Jesus had already used this label in 15:14 to describe the Pharisees. The term in verse 16 assumes the comment made in 15:14: the Pharisees are **blind guides** leading blind people until both fall into the pit. Jesus' concern in this third condemnation is the strange rules on oaths that the Pharisees had devised. His general teaching on oaths was given in the Sermon on the Mount in 5:33–37. The Pharisees had ruled that **if anyone swears by the temple** the oath is not binding, **but if** the oath is sworn **by the gold of the temple** it is a binding **oath.** Such an interpretation gave priority to the gold of the Temple over the Temple itself. Jesus pointed out that the **temple makes the gold sacred**, and thus they have inverted the real priorities (23:17).

Likewise the teachers of the law had ruled that **if anyone swears by the altar** that oath was not binding, **but if** they swore **by the gift on** the altar the oath would be binding (23:18). This is simply another illustration of the previous point: It is **the altar that makes the gift sacred** (23:19). Jesus rejected these fine distinctions regarding oaths. He concluded that if a person swore **by the altar**, then he or she had sworn by **everything on it** (23:20). Likewise, to swear **by the temple** is the same as swearing **by the one who dwells in it** (23:21). Since the one who dwells in the Temple is God, He claimed that any oath by anything associated with God was the same as swearing by God himself, a practice avoided by the Pharisees. Verse 22 equates swearing **by heaven** with swearing **by God's throne**, and that is the same as swearing **by the one who sits on** that throne, namely God himself. As 5:34 demonstrates, the Pharisees wanted to distinguish the basis for oaths. Jesus' point here is the same as it was in 5:33–37: Oaths are unnecessary if one will simply tell the truth as God desires.

The fourth woe begins with the teaching on tithing by the Pharisees and teachers of the law and concludes by criticizing their neglect of the important matters of relationship with God. The Pharisees taught that one could not lawfully eat food that had not been tithed. Thus one-**tenth** of all their foods would have been given to God, presumably through bringing it to the synagogue. Jesus accused them of even requiring a tithe of the **spices—mint, dill and cumin** (23:23). The demands to tithe the dill and cumin still survive in the written record of the oral tradition, though no mention of dill is found in those records such as the *Mishnah*.

Many interpreters apparently fail to notice that Jesus did not object to tithing these spices. In fact, He stated that the Jewish leaders **should have practiced** these things. What He objected to was their neglect of **the more important matters of the law—justice, mercy and faithfulness.**

Perhaps Jesus was thinking in terms like those of Micah 6:8: **What does the LORD require of you? To act justly and to love mercy and to walk humbly with your God.** Certainly the prophets gave far more emphasis

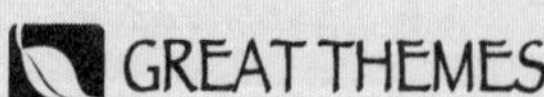

JUSTICE, MERCY, AND LOVE

Twice in Matthew (9:13; 12:7) Jesus quoted Hosea 6:6: **I desire mercy, not sacrifice.** While it is wrong to conclude, as some do, that the prophets saw no value in sacrifice, they clearly rejected the idea that the right sacrifices appeased God. A consistent theme in the prophets is that God desires righteousness and mercy, faithfulness and love. It is from the Old Testament that we first learn that God values right relationships among His worshippers and between His worshippers and himself. No amount of sacrifice or ritual can compensate for a heart that does not treat people as God would treat them.

to justice, mercy, and covenant faithfulness than they did to the laws of tithing or the sacrificial system. In this condemnation Jesus echoed the prophetic demand that the relational and ethical heart of God was more important than the religious practices that served to remind people of God's call on their lives.

Jesus did not pose the relational against the external symbols of relationship with God in an either/or way. Rather, He called for both when He said, **You should have practiced the latter, without neglecting the former.** Then in another vivid word picture, He accused the Pharisees of straining **out a gnat but** swallowing **a camel** (Matt. 23:24). This is sarcastic Jewish humor at its best. It would be difficult to contrast reversed priorities more succinctly than that.

The fifth woe addresses a similar misplacing of priorities in the pharisaic practices of purity. Jesus accused the religious leaders of cleaning **the outside of the cup and dish** and neglecting the **inside** (23:25). Though the ancient world had not discovered germs and microbes, they were astute enough to recognize that if the inside of a **cup** or **dish** was filthy, the purity of the outside was of little worth. However, Jesus mixed the metaphor of the cup or dish being clean on the outside. By implication the contrast was with the inside of the vessel. What Jesus actually contrasted was an **inside full of greed and self-indulgence.** The **outside** He spoke of was a cup. The inside He spoke of was the human heart. The contrast He drew in verse 25 is similar to His teachings in 15:16–20.

The remedy Jesus commanded is intriguing: **First clean the inside of the cup and dish, and then the outside also will be clean** (23:26). In washing dishes, if one cleans the inside of the cup the outside will usually be taken care of also. So Jesus commanded the Pharisees to clean the inside of the cup. However, the **inside** He spoke of in verse 25 was the heart. By implication His command suggests they should deal with the matters of the heart, and when that has been taken care of, the ritual purity issues that are external will have been addressed.

The sixth woe continues to address the contrast between externals and the heart. Jesus compared the Pharisees to **whitewashed tombs** (23:27). Even though such tombs appear **beautiful on the outside,** they **are full of dead bones** so that **everything** that comes in contact with such a tomb will be **unclean.** The Pharisees strictly observed the laws regarding ritual purity and refused to come into contact with anything unclean, especially corpses and tombs. The problem with the Pharisees was that they were just like such whitewashed tombs. **On the outside** they appeared attractive and **righteous but on the inside** they were **full of hypocrisy and wickedness** (23:28). Jesus' argument is from lesser to greater. As much as the Pharisees abhorred tombs because of the uncleanness within them, so the Pharisees ought to be abhorred

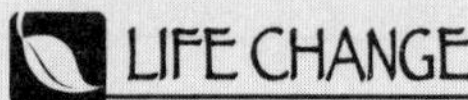

INTEGRITY

Integrity demands that we deal honestly with the significant religious leaders of the past. It is easy to praise the well-known and popular leaders of generations gone by without coming to terms with the fact that they may have strongly opposed positions or activities that characterize our lives. It is easy to grumble about the leaders of the present or the generation just older than we are because we are keenly aware of their weaknesses and fail to recognize their strengths.

for their internal ugliness that no amount of whitewash could overcome.

The final woe accused the Pharisees and teachers of the law of building **tombs for the prophets** and decorating **the graves of the righteous** (23:29). The problem is that such acts of pious remembrance give the impression that the religious leaders **would not have taken part in shedding the blood of the prophets** (23:30). Unfortunately, Jesus declared, they **are the descendants of those who murdered the prophets** (23:31). Their pious observances do not whitewash the reality of their rejection of those who brought the word of God to them. Jesus' final words in the woe bitterly challenge them to **fill up the measure of the sin of** their **forefathers** (23:32). They would accomplish that by putting Jesus to death.

3. A FINAL WARNING TO JERUSALEM 23:33–39

Jesus' final words of warning to the Jewish religious leaders are some of the strongest words of condemnation yet to appear in this chapter. Given the list of accusations, Jesus wondered **how** they would **escape being condemned to hell** (23:33). Suddenly speaking as God, Jesus declared that He was **sending prophets and wise men and teachers** to the Jewish leaders (23:34). These words look back to the Old Testament messengers of God; they also look forward to the Christian witnesses who would bring the Word of God in obedience to Christ's command. But the response of the Jewish religious leaders in either case was to **kill and crucify; to flog** them **in** the **synagogues and pursue** them **from town to town**.

As a result, Jesus declared that **all the righteous blood** that had been shed in the whole course of human history would **come upon** them (23:35). **Righteous Abel** was the first human recorded to have been murdered (Gen. 4:1–14). The identity of **Zechariah son of Berekiah** is unclear. Perhaps the best suggestion is that he was killed at the end of the biblical period, so that the murders from the first to the last of Scripture are on the heads of the Jewish religious leaders. Matthew 23:36 then issues a sobering statement from Jesus: **All this will come upon this generation.** The generation of Jewish religious leadership whom Jesus addressed would bear the judgment of God for the whole biblical history of disobedience and murder.

Lest one think Jesus spoke these words of judgment with any satisfaction or joy, He broke into lament: **O Jerusalem, Jerusalem, you who kill the prophets and stone those sent to you, how often I have longed to gather your children together, as a hen gathers her chicks . . . , but you were not willing** (23:37). The tragedy was twofold: first, the pain of Jesus' desire to save His people and second, their unwillingness to receive the grace of God. As a result **your house is left to you desolate** (23:38). The period of grace would soon be over, and God's judgment that had been delayed so long would no longer be postponed. In verse 39 Jesus quotes Psalm 118:26: **Blessed is he who comes in the name of the Lord.** These were the words of messianic acclamation sung by the crowds during His royal entry into Jerusalem (21:9). The Messiah who entered the city to shouts of praise will return in judgment.

Part Six

The End of the Age and the End of Jesus' Earthly Ministry

MATTHEW 24:1–28:20

The sixth and final section of Matthew's gospel begins with the final block of teaching material collected by Matthew in 24:1–26:1. These chapters contain Jesus' teachings on the end of the age. The following narrative portion of this section describes the final events leading to Jesus' death and resurrection in 26:2–28:20. The final section of Matthew begins with Jesus' teaching on the end of the age. The final words of Matthew 28:20 contain Jesus' promise to be with His followers to the end of the age.

TEACHINGS ON THE END OF THE AGE

Matthew 24:1–51

Jesus' closing comments in Matthew 23 regarding the coming divine judgment lead naturally to the final block of teaching in Matthew, chapters 24–25. This is Matthew's version of what is often called the Synoptic Apocalypse and is also found in Mark 13:1–37 and Luke 21:5–36. This material is also called the Olivet Discourse, since Matthew 24:3 notes that it was spoken while Jesus and the disciples sat on the Mount of Olives. The organization of this material appears to answer two questions that 24:1–3 asks: one regarding when the destruction of the Temple would take place, and the other regarding the sign of the Messiah's coming and the end of the age. Most of 24:4–35 answers the first question, while most of 24:36–25:46 answers the second. Matthew 24:4–14 forms the first section of the material responding to the first question, while verses 15–35 present the heart of the argument. Verses 36–51 provide the main teaching responding to the second question. These verses will be followed by a series of parables illustrating the point in chapter 25.

1. THE SETTING OF JESUS' FINAL TEACHINGS 24:1–3

The announcement in 23:37–39 of Jerusalem's impending judgment is followed immediately in 24:1 by the notice of **Jesus** leaving **the temple and walking away**. The Gospels provide no record that He ever again returned to the Temple. For Matthew, Jesus' exit from the Temple symbolized God's abandoning the holy place. As was the case in Ezekiel 11:23, where the glory of the Lord departed from Jerusalem and withdrew to the Mount of Olives, Jesus left the Holy City and went to the Mount of Olives. As they were leaving, **his disciples** drew **his attention to** the **buildings**. During Jesus' lifetime the Temple compound was undergoing a major renovation and beautification process begun by Herod the Great. Several more years would be required to complete the process.

It is likely the disciples were commenting on how impressive the buildings of the Temple compound were. Jesus' response must have been shocking to them: **Not one stone here will be left on another; every one will be thrown down** (Matt. 24:2). This prophecy was fulfilled literally when the Romans destroyed Jerusalem and the Temple in A.D. 70. It is likely that Matthew and his first readers knew Jesus' prophecy had been fulfilled.

The scene shifts to the **Mount of Olives** with **Jesus sitting** there overlooking the city (24:3). The mountain stood several hundred feet above the Temple area so that anywhere on the upper third of the mountain would have afforded a beautiful panoramic view of the Temple and its surroundings. The emphatic note in the Greek construction that Jesus was sitting means that Matthew regarded the words on the mountain as authoritative and official teaching by the Master. Matthew makes the unusual comment that **the disciples** questioned Jesus **privately**. This suggests that Matthew regarded the material in the Olivet Discourse as insider information rather than the common public teaching of Jesus.

The disciples had two basic questions. The first was **when this will happen**. The **this** must refer to Jesus' prophecy of the destruction of Jerusalem. They wanted to know how imminent the destruction of the Holy City was. Jesus' prophecy was a sobering one. Their second question asked about **the sign of** His **coming and of the end of the age**. The fact that they connected the coming of the Messiah and the end of the age reflected their acceptance of the general Jewish understandings of eschatology. Most Jews believed human history was divided into two great ages: the present, evil age and the glorious age to come. The end of the present, evil age would occur when the Messiah came, and the Messiah would usher in the beginning of the glorious age to come. The ages overlapped during the lifetime of the Messiah. The present, evil age would experience its death throes and the age to come would experience its birth pangs through a series of cataclysmic events coinciding with the Messiah's ministry.

These general Jewish assumptions regarding the Messiah and the end of the present age with the beginning of the coming age provide the context of the disciples' questions and of Jesus' answers. The disciples believed Jesus was the Messiah as Peter's confession at Caesarea Philippi shows (16:16). As a result, they believed they were living in the last days of the present, evil age. That faith brought them as much anxiety as it did hope.

2. INDICATIONS ANTICIPATING THE END 24:4–14

Jesus' first response to the disciples' questions was His concern that **no one** deceive them on this subject (24:4). Speculation about the end of time, as well as apocalyptic warnings and visions, were rampant in first-century Judaism. Jesus refused to abandon the subject to the extremists. He carefully answered the disciples' questions, but He first downplayed the sensational claims that circulated in His time and that have continued to circulate in our time. The key word in verses 4–14 is **deceive**, which appears in verses 4–5 and 11.

The most common deception would be the false claim of being the Messiah. In fact, Jesus warned there would be **many** making the claim using the very words, **I am the Christ,** which in Greek is *Messiah* (24:5). His warning showed that wild, emotional apocalyptic preaching of the

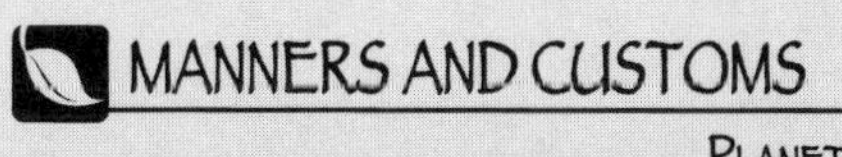

The Greek word for deceive is *planao*, from which we derive our English word planets. To the ancient Greek, the planets were deceitful because they looked like stars but did not follow a consistent pattern of movement through the sky like the true stars did. The word was sometimes translated *wanderers*. The wandering, inconsistent pattern of the planets earned them the name of deceivers. That name was then applied to people who were inconsistent.

time produced messianic claimants. This phenomenon moved into mainstream Judaism in the second century A.D. when Bar Cochba was acclaimed messiah by a leading rabbi, Rabbi Akiba. The result was the outbreak of the Second Jewish War in A.D. 132, which culminated in the horrible destruction in A.D. 135 of Judea and the Jerusalem that was just being rebuilt. Jesus' concern was that such false messiahs would **deceive many.** He did not want His followers to be among the deceived.

The popular preachers of the false messiahs would point to a series of signs that they saw validating their claims. These signs would include **wars and rumors of wars** (24:6); **nation** rising **against nation, and kingdom against kingdom; famines and earthquakes in various places** (24:7). Such signs were noted in the apocalyptic sections of the Old Testament, such as Daniel 9:26; 11:44, and various apocalyptic writings of the time. Thus such events were attributed with end-time significance before Jesus spoke these words. His response was to tell His disciples to **not** be **alarmed. Such** events would **happen, but the end** would **still** be in the future. In Matthew 24:8, He identified these events as **the beginning of birth pains.** Thus, while such signs should be taken seriously, they call for repentance and preparation rather than panic.

More directly pertinent to the disciples were the specific difficulties Jesus' followers would face. The word **then** (24:9) indicates that Jesus regarded the persecution of the Church as an end-time birth pang. The Greek word used for persecution in verse 9 has often been translated *tribulation.* The word spoke of pressure, and the early church used it for all kinds of pressures, persecutions, and difficulties that led people to abandon their faith in Christ. Jesus also mentioned **death and** being **hated by all nations because of** faith in Him as beginning evidences His followers were living in the transition of the ages.

The somber result would be **many** believers turning **away from the faith and** hating **each other** (24:10). That Jesus could imagine His followers hating each other shows that He had a more realistic picture of the pain of persecution than many of His modern followers. When some church members betrayed others to save their own lives, the emotional responses of surviving family members of those killed often included hatred. The pattern of turning away, betrayal, and hatred has played out over and over through periods of persecution in all of Church history. Such circumstances provide fertile fields for **false prophets** to **appear and deceive many people** (24:11).

The picture continues in verse 12. As **wickedness** would **increase, the love of most will grow cold.** The Greek word translated **wickedness** literally speaks of lawlessness. As the order and safe structures of Christian society disappear, Christian love will wane away as well. This is the converse of the comment in 1 John 4:18, that **perfect love drives out fear.** Increasing fear undermines love. A Church fearfully obsessed with survival loses its ability to love every neighbor.

But Jesus did not see this persecution destroying the Church. Rather, the one **who stands firm to the end will be saved** (Matt. 24:13). But before that end comes, the **gospel of the kingdom will be preached in the whole world as a testimony to all nations** (24:14). The end-time visions of Isaiah portrayed a worldwide impact even on the Gentiles (Isa. 2:2–4; 11:1–16; 42:1–9; 49:1–7; 66:18 23). Jesus' vision of reaching the whole world in the end times had long been anticipated by Isaiah. Only after the mission of the Church has been accomplished **will the end come.**

3. SIGNS OF THE IMPENDING CRISIS 24:15–35

Verses 4–14 respond to the question posed in verse 3 about **the end of the age,** but they point to signs of the beginning of **birth pangs.** Beginning in verse 15, Jesus will address the question more directly. The focus of these verses seems to be Jerusalem and Judea. They address the coming judgment against Jerusalem that will result in not one stone of the Temple building being left on top of another.

Some argue that the details of this section are such accurate descriptions of the events of the First Jewish War from A.D. 66–70 that Jesus could not have predicted them forty years in advance. They argue that Matthew wrote his gospel after A.D. 70 and placed these words on Jesus' lips. However, this view fails to provide an adequate motivation for Jesus prophesying about an event long after His time, but fresh in the memories of Matthew's readers. If Matthew's purpose was to portray Jesus with divine foreknowledge, it is not likely his purpose was accomplished. Much more specific prophecies would have been necessary to make that point. Compared with other Jewish apocalyptic literature, Jesus' predictions here are not very detailed. What He says in Matthew 24 following verse 2 would have been fulfilled in any war with Rome.

Verse 15 points to the appearance of **"the abomination that causes desolation" standing in the holy place** as the sign of impending doom. **Daniel** 11:31 and 12:11 had **spoken** of this desolating **abomination**. In the Old Testament, the word **abomination** usually referred to any idolatrous affront to the true worship of God. Most scholars agree that the references in Daniel point to the actions of Antiochus Epiphanes who, in 167 B.C., erected an altar to and a statue of Zeus in the Holy of Holies in the Temple and sacrificed pigs. First Maccabees 1:54 called this abomination of Antiochus a desolating sacrilege. Jesus' point was that something as outrageous as Antiochus' sacrilege would occur again before the end of time.

ABOMINATION AND DESECRATION

Some believe that Jesus' reference to the abomination that causes desolation was fulfilled by the attempt of Emperor Gaius to set up a statue of himself in the Temple in A.D. 40–41. However, that event was not directly connected to the destruction of Jerusalem in A.D. 70. Josephus, the first-century Jewish historian, stated that the Zealots desecrated the Temple in the winter of A.D. 67–68, but he made no mention of an idolatrous statue. In A.D. 70, the Romans planted their standards with images of Caesar over the ruins of the destroyed Temple, but that was after the fact, not a sign of the coming destruction of the Temple.

Jesus pointed out that when such attacks against the Temple began, His followers **who** were **in Judea** should **flee to the mountains** (Matt. 24:16). The danger would be so imminent that persons **on the roof of** the **house** should not **go down to take anything out of the house** (24:17). Most peasant homes in Judea at that time had a flat roof that served as additional work area at the home, and it was accessed by stairs on the outside. Jesus urged the disciple to run down the stairs and into the mountains, leaving everything inside the house. In times of trouble from the time of David (1 Sam. 24:3) to the intertestamental period (1 Macc. 2:28–36) Judeans had fled to the mountains to hide in the caves and rocky crevices. Immediate flight was urgent. In a similar fashion, if a man was working **in the field** when the attacks began, he should flee directly to mountains without taking time to return to his house to **go get his cloak** (Matt. 24:18). A person's cloak was the bed and blanket by which he or she kept warm at night and an overcoat during the winter. It was one of the most valued possessions necessary for survival, but the time was so urgent that it would have to be left behind.

Jesus envisioned throngs of people rushing into the mountains and hills to hide. **Pregnant women and nursing mothers** would find it hard to keep up and cope with the physical demands of their pregnancy or children (24:19). Slow moving women such as these would not survive. The disciples should **pray that** their **flight not** be **in** the **winter or on the Sabbath** (24:20). The limitations of Sabbath travel would not allow them to escape. The cold of winter would make conditions unbearable for those caught outside without shelter during the night.

Jesus described these circumstances as a time of **great distress**—tribulation—**unequaled** in human history, either past or future (24:21). If such distress was unequaled, then one would wonder how many might **survive.** Jesus anticipated that question and declared that by the grace of God such **days** would be **cut short for the sake of** the survival of **the elect** (24:22). Such times bring imposters out of the woodwork. As a result Jesus warned **if anyone** should say, **"here is the Christ!" or, "There he is!"** His followers should **not believe** such a person (24:23). **False Christs**—persons claiming to be the Messiah—**and false prophets will appear** in the midst of such terrible times **to deceive even the elect** (24:24). Such persons might even **perform great signs and miracles**, which superficially would appear very persuasive. But Jesus' followers should not be deceived because, through this teaching, He has **told** them **ahead of time** what to expect and how to keep faith in such a time (24:25).

As a result, **if anyone** were to tell a disciple, **"There he is, out in the desert,"** Christ's follower should **not** be misled into going **out** to meet him. If someone should say that the Messiah **is here, in the inner rooms,** Jesus' followers should **not believe it** (24:26). Disciples do not need to worry about missing the time of His coming. **As the lightning is visible, so the coming of the Son of Man** will be visible and easily recognized by all (24:27). The point is that until one sees the clear and visible coming of Christ, there is no need to heed the false prophets and religious profiteers who take advantage of the signs of the beginning of the birth pangs of the end of time. Jesus then gave a gruesome image of **the vultures** gathering **wherever there is a carcass** (24:28). The point of this image is that one can infer an outcome, such as the final coming of the Messiah, from certain signs like those He has just described.

Jesus continued the sequential unfolding of signs in verse 29. The words **immediately after** indicate that He was describing the signs in a chronological order. Following **the distress**—again tribulation—**of those days**, cosmic signs will occur. These signs—in which **the sun will be darkened and the moon will** fail to **give its light; the stars will fall from the sky, and the heavenly bodies will be shaken**—were common themes in Old Testament eschatology. Isaiah 13:10; 34:4; Ezekiel 32:7; Joel 2:10, 31; 3:15; and Haggai 2:6 all associate such heavenly signs with the end-time judgment or salvation of God.

At that time the sign of the Son of Man will appear in the sky (Matt. 24:30). It is likely that this sign is the picture from Daniel 7:13 that Jesus then mentioned: one like **the Son of Man** would appear **coming on the clouds with power and great glory.** This final coming of the Son of Man will have two consequences. First, **all the nations of the earth** that are unrepentant and thus unprepared **will mourn.** For them the sign of the **Son of Man** is the terrifying sign of final divine judgment. Second, for **his elect**, the coming of the **Son of Man** will be marvelous news. **He will send his angels with a loud trumpet call** to gather the elect **from the four winds, from one end of the heavens to the other** (Matt. 24:31). The time of distress will be over—forever.

Verses 30–31, dealing with the coming of the **Son of Man**, seem to have moved beyond the question of the timing of the destruction of Jerusalem to respond to the question of the final coming of the Messiah and the end of the present, evil age. However, verses 32–35 turn back to events that seem much closer at hand and thus perhaps to the disciples' question about the destruction of Jerusalem. The illustration Jesus used was a **lesson from the fig tree** (24:32). One cannot but wonder if the disciples' minds went back to the fig tree Jesus cursed on the way into Jerusalem the morning after the royal entry (21:18–20). The point of the fig tree here is that it follows a predictable sequence: **Its twigs get tender and its leaves come out,** and then one knows **that summer is near**. The lesson of the fig tree teaches that **when** Jesus' followers **see all these things**, they can **know that it is near** (24:33). The interpretation of **these things** and of **it** divides the various eschatological perspectives in Christian theology.

Some interpret **all these things** as referring to all the signs described in Matthew 24:1–26. They see the Rapture and tribulation leading to the end of time clearly described in these verses. Others interpret **all these things** as referring only to events that took place in Palestine in the first century. Some interpret the **it** of verse 33 as referring to Jesus' second coming. Others see the **it** referring to the sequence of events described in the preceding verses. In the context of Matthew 24, a logical meaning of **these things** would be the distress and persecution coming on Jesus' followers. The **it** would be the destruction of Jerusalem. When persecution would begin to intensify, Jesus' followers would know that the destruction of Jerusalem was near.

Jesus' next statement supports the interpretation of **it** being the destruction of Jerusalem and the Temple. He declared, **This generation will certainly not pass away until all these things have happened** (24:34). Persons of the Bible generally understood a generation to be forty years. On the most common dating of Jesus' death in A.D. 30, it was almost exactly 40 years, a generation, from Jesus' prophecy to

The early church historian Eusebius, writing in the fourth century, stated that in response to these instructions of Jesus, disciples in Jerusalem fled the city and surrounding villages at the beginning of the First Jewish War in A.D. 66. Persecution had been increasing, and James, Jesus' own brother, had apparently suffered martyrdom. These Jewish believers fled to Pella, east of the Jordan River between the Sea of Galilee and the Dead Sea. There they established a Jewish Christian church that flourished for several centuries.

the destruction of Jerusalem and the Temple in A.D. 70. Jesus paraphrased what He had said in the Sermon on the Mount (5:18): **Heaven and earth will pass away, but my words will never pass away** (24:35). When the heavens and earth are shaken with the cosmic signs of the end of times, Jesus' followers are to remember that His words are more secure than the seemingly everlasting **heavens and earth.**

4. THE UNEXPECTEDNESS OF THE MESSIAH'S COMING 24:36–51

Most interpreters believe that a significant change takes place in verse 36 or 37. From the confident prediction of verse 34 that all these things will take place before the present generation passes away, Jesus moved on to declare that no one except God knows the exact time of the coming of the Son of Man. The following verses seem to repeat certain concepts that have already been treated in verses 4–35. The best way to understand these shifts is to assume that the subject being discussed after verse 35 is different from the subject under consideration before the verse. In general, from verse 36 on Jesus deals with His final coming and the end of time more consistently, whereas prior to verse 36 He had mostly dealt with the timing of the destruction of Jerusalem.

Jesus states that **no one knows about** the timing of His final coming except **the Father** (24:36). The perspective is quite different from verses 30–31, where there is no mention of the Father, and the Son of Man appears in complete control of the chronology. However, with regard to the **day or hour, not even** Jesus **knows** the timing. The implication of this statement is particularly important in this context. If Jesus does not know the time of His final coming, then His followers should not seek to determine it. Such human efforts attempt to acquire knowledge not even given to the divine Teacher. The disciples are not to be above the Teacher. For Jesus it would be enough if His followers would be ready for His final coming regardless of its timing.

The apparent normalcy of life is not evidence that one does not need to be ready. Jesus compared the time

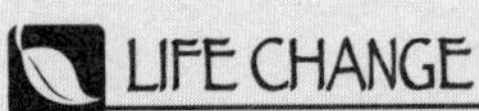

READINESS FOR THE SECOND COMING

Many evangelical believers have only heard preaching about the second coming of Christ that used fear as the motivation for readiness. As a result many people live with a certain resentment toward God and the idea of the second coming. But the dominant pattern of New Testament teaching is that Christ's return will be a time of great joy for those who are prepared to meet Him. For those who are ready, that day will be a day of celebration and joy as Jesus' followers enter His presence for unbroken fellowship with Him. Such a joyful possibility should also be a major motivation to be ready for that day.

leading up to **the coming of the Son of Man** with **the days of Noah** (24:37). **In** those **days** prior to **the flood, people were eating and drinking, marrying and giving in marriage** (24:38). The point is that people were involved in the normal processes of life right **up to the day Noah entered the ark. They** seemed to have no idea of the impending **flood until** it **came and took them all away** (24:39). The point of comparison was that the suddenness and unexpectedness of the Flood provide an analogy for **the coming of the Son of Man.** Had people then been ready, they might have averted judgment. Christ's final coming will be as unexpected as the Flood was to them.

Jesus then gave two illustrations of the difference repentance and readiness could make. **Two men will be in the field; one will be taken and the other left** (24:40). Taken out of context, one might conclude that this verse demonstrates the arbitrariness of salvation. But in this context—dealing with being prepared for the unexpected timing of the Messiah's final coming—one must conclude that one man in the field was prepared and the other was not. One experienced the salvation of the end of the age, and the other experienced the divine judgment of the end of time. Verse 41 makes the same point using the illustration of **two women grinding with a hand mill.**

Jesus' listeners were to conclude that they should **keep watch.** That is the point of the **therefore** that begins this verse (24:42). The Greek word for **keep watch** often simply meant to stay awake. This wakefulness is necessary **because** Jesus' followers **do not know on what day** their **Lord will come.** To illustrate this needed watchfulness, Jesus told two stories. The first described an **owner of** a **house** who was robbed (24:43). **If** he **had known** when **the thief was coming, he would have kept watch** and prevented the robbery. The point is that he should have been watching, but because he was not, he suffered loss. In like manner, Jesus' followers **must be ready, because the Son of Man will come at an** unexpected **hour** (24:44).

The second story is a parable of a **faithful and wise servant, whom the master has put in charge of the servants** while the master goes away on a journey (24:45). **It will be good for that servant** if his master returns and **finds him doing** what he had been told to do (24:46). Should that happen, the master **will put** that servant **in charge of all his possessions** (24:47). The reward for being ready for the master's return would be a promotion to the highest possible level of service in the master's household. **But** if **that servant** becomes lax and concludes that his **master is staying away a long time** (24:48), and so begins to mistreat **his fellow servants** (24:49), a disastrous outcome will occur when his master returns. That **master will come on a day** the servant **does not expect him** (24:50), and the master **will cut him into pieces and assign him a place with the hypocrites** (24:51). Jesus mixed together phrases of divine judgment in the culture of the time: **cut him in pieces** and **assign him with the hypocrites**. The point, however, is that just as the servant should have been prepared for the coming of his master, so Jesus' followers should be prepared for His final coming.

PARABLES TEACHING READINESS FOR THE END OF THE AGE

Matthew 25:1–26:1

The final collection of Jesus' teaching material in Matthew's gospel began in chapter 24 and continues through all of chapter 25. The disciples had asked Jesus what would be the sign of His coming and the end of the age. Matthew 24:36–25:46 responds to that question. However, the main thrust of Jesus' response is that His followers should not worry about a sign but be concerned about being ready for His coming. Four parables make that point and suggest ways believers should live while they wait. Matthew 24:45–51 presented the first parable, that of a slave caring for his master's servants. Chapter 25 consists of three parables dealing with the importance of being ready for Christ's coming: Verses 1–13 relate the parable of the virgins; 14–30 present the parable of the talents; and verses 31–46 conclude Jesus' teaching with the parable of the sheep and the goats.

1. THE PARABLE OF THE TEN VIRGINS 25:1–13

The parable of the five wise and five foolish virgins continues the theme of the importance of being ready for the unexpected coming of the Messiah. The parable begins by stating that **the kingdom** can be compared to **ten virgins who took their lamps and went out to meet the bridegroom**

(25:1). If this parable were Jesus' only teaching about the Kingdom, it would imply that the Kingdom was still in the future at the time He spoke. However, other teachings about the Kingdom earlier in this Gospel (4:17; 13:24, 31, 33, 44, 45, 47) imply that the Kingdom was already present in Jesus' ministry.

Several solutions have been proposed to this apparent contradiction. Some scholars believe that Jesus always thought the Kingdom was in the future, and the passages that imply that it was a present reality are either misunderstood or fabrications of the Gospel writers. Others believe that Jesus always thought of the Kingdom as present, and the passages that imply a future Kingdom are either misunderstood or additions of early Christians. A compromise view embraced by the majority of New Testament scholarship now suggests that Jesus believed that the Kingdom was present and had come into reality through His own ministry, but that a consummation of the Kingdom would come in the future. The early church quickly identified that future consummation with a second coming of Christ, but the disciples apparently had no conception of Jesus' ascension and absence on earth in the future. As Jesus spoke these words they were looking toward His coming in great glory to usher in all the implications of God's sovereign rule on earth.

MANNERS AND CUSTOMS

BRIDAL PROCESSION

In ancient Palestine young, unmarried girls of the village who were of marriageable age waited with the bride at her home until the bridegroom arrived. These virgins would then accompany the couple as the bridegroom took the bride to his home, where the final wedding ceremony and celebration would take place. If the procession took place after dark, they would carry torches to light the way. These torches consisted of oil-soaked rags wrapped at the top end of a stick.

Some modern translations use the word *bridesmaids* in this parable rather than the more literal translation **virgins**. In the culture of Jesus' time, these women would not have been bridesmaids in the modern sense of those who stand up with the bride during the wedding ceremony. Rather, such **virgins** normally accompanied the bride before the wedding. Most of the details of the story fit with the wedding customs of an ancient Palestinian village.

Scholars debate whether details are designed to allegorically provide specific meaning in the parable or are simply details to make an interesting parable with a single point.

In a way characteristic of Jewish moral literature, **five of the** virgins are identified as **foolish** while **five** are identified as **wise** (25:2). Jesus had already made a similar distinction in 7:24–27 in the parable of the wise and foolish builders. As far back as Proverbs, Jewish sages divided the world into the wise and the foolish. Though there have been periods of Christian history when interpreters saw the foolish virgins as a symbol of the Jews and the wise virgins as symbolic of Christians, it should be clear that the parable addresses followers of Jesus and is designed to urge them to be wise rather than foolish.

In the parable, the **foolish** are foolish because they **did not take any oil** along to soak more rags to replenish the fuel of the torches (Matt. 25:3). However, the **wise took oil in jars along with** them in order to replenish the torches (25:4). Wisdom is clearly identified with being ready with oil for when the bridegroom might come. Perhaps the most unusual feature of the parable, from the standpoint of ancient culture, was the delay of the bridegroom. In a culture that did not give major emphasis to time, one's wedding was still an event to which the bridegroom would not be late. In that culture, he had money as well as anticipation invested in the bride. So when Jesus stated that **the bridegroom was a long time in coming**, so much so that those waiting for him **became drowsy and fell asleep** (25:5), the listeners would have looked at each other in wonderment and known that this strange development pointed toward the teaching point.

Then **at midnight**, long after one would have expected, **the cry** announcing the arrival of the **bridegroom rang out** (25:6). The crier summoned the wedding party to **come out to meet** the bridegroom. **All the virgins all woke up and trimmed their lamps** (25:7). This means they scraped off the burned rags, wrapped the torches with new rags, and soaked them with oil. By then, everyone's original oil-soaked rags were gone, and the torches needed to be put together again. At this point, the **foolish** virgins discovered they were out of oil and could not replenish their torches. They begged the **wise** virgins to **give** them **some oil** since their torches were **going out** (25:8).

But the wise virgins refused to give away their oil because there would not be enough for **both** them and the foolish virgins (25:9). The point of the parable here is not to justify selfishness by the example of the wise virgins. Rather, the point is that being prepared is an individual responsibility. One cannot be prepared for someone else, only for oneself. The wise virgins suggested that the foolish **go to those who sell oil and buy some for** themselves. Jesus' listeners would know what a precarious task that would be. The oil sellers would be asleep in bed; it would take quite awhile for the foolish virgins to buy more oil.

It is not surprising then that **while** the foolish virgins **were on their way to buy the oil, the bridegroom arrived** (25:10). Those who **were ready went in with him to the wedding banquet.** The word **in** suggests the parable is being adjusted from the cultural realities to the point Jesus wished to make. The next phrase completes that process: **the door was shut.** Wedding banquets in the ancient Near East did not occur in banquet halls that could be locked shut. Rather they occurred in the public space of the village. Even for the wedding of a wealthy person who had a big home with a large courtyard, the courtyard gate would remain open and the whole village would be the guests. The allegory of Christ's second coming and the end of the age drives these details and creates a picture by which the wise are inside and the foolish are locked out.

The foolish did come **later** and begged for the bridegroom to **open the door for** them also (25:11). The bridegroom's response from inside was, **I don't know you** (25:12). This reply echoes the Lord's response to the people who wanted entry into the Kingdom because they prophesied, drove out demons, and performed miracles (7:23). These words are not a statement of fact but a formula of rejection. Such rejection makes no sense in the context of an ancient Near Eastern wedding; rather the allegory of Christ's return required that there be no secondary way into the Kingdom for those not prepared.

Verse 13 provides the application to the allegorical parable. The imperative for Jesus' followers is to **keep watch**. This is the identical command given in 24:42. Alertness, rather than drowsiness, is the requirement for Christ's followers as they await His return. The reason given for the command is that the disciples **do not know the day or the**

hour. The parable of the ten virgins provides a most interesting lesson in readiness for the second coming. The problem of the five foolish virgins was not that the bridegroom came quickly; their problem was that he delayed and they became lackadaisical. Readiness for Christ's return cannot be based on the nearness of that return. Disciples must be ready because they do not know and cannot know when the Messiah will come again.

2. THE PARABLE OF THE TALENTS 25:14–30

The theme of being ready is also an important element in the parable of the talents. However, this parable begins to address more specifically the question of what readiness means. The wise and foolish virgins were mostly passive in the preceding parable, doing nothing but waiting for the coming bridegroom. Lest anyone think that doing nothing is an appropriate way to await the coming Kingdom, Jesus told the parable of the talents.

There are a number of similarities between the parable of the talents and the parable of the pounds found in Luke 19:12–27. As a result some scholars argue that Jesus told only a single parable and that one, in the process of interpretation, should seek the single original parable rather than either its Matthean or Lucan form. However, there are a number of significant differences between the two parables, and there is no reason to assume that a Gospel writer was more capable than Jesus of modifying a parable for a different context. It is best to consider this parable as it stands rather than as it might have been used in another context.

Like the parable of the faithful servant found in Matthew 24:45–51, the parable of the talents begins with **a man going on a journey** (25:14). However, instead of a single servant being entrusted with responsibility by the master, three **servants** were **entrusted** with the master's **property**. He gave one servant **five talents of money, another two talents, and another one talent**. Jesus stated that **each** servant received the number of talents that corresponded **to his ability** (25:15).

When a landowner went away on a journey in the ancient Near East, it was customary to spread management responsibility for his property out over several servants. Often these servants were described as stewards or managers. The advantage of using several slaves is that the mutual accountability would make embezzlement more difficult. The landowner's expectation was that the slave put in charge would carry on in the same way that the landowners would have functioned himself. Upon return, the landowner would summon the managing slaves for an accounting of their stewardship. In all these details, the parable is quite real to ancient eastern Mediterranean life.

Some have questioned whether Jesus exaggerated the amount of money given to each servant. The total of all the talents would represent something over two million dollars in contemporary currency. Such a large amount was not inconsistent with the immense wealth accumulated by some ancient rulers. However, it is also possible that Jesus chose larger than normal figures to show the priceless nature of the privileges that are at stake in serving God. The large numbers show that the stewardship given to us by God is no trivial matter.

As would have been expected in that culture, the servant **who received five talents at once put his money to work and gained five more** (25:16). The servant who received **two talents** gained the same rate of return on his investment of the two talents (25:17). Though there was no stock market in which the servants could invest, significant investments in real estate, livestock, and international commerce were available in the world of Jesus' time. However, the servant **who had received the one talent** did not invest it. Rather, he **dug a hole in the ground and hid his master's money** (25:18). Because there were no banks in the ancient world, the most secure way to protect money was to bury it. Stories of people who hid money in the ground and went off and either forgot where it was or never returned for some other reason were common. Jesus could tell the parable of the hidden treasure (13:44–45) assuming such an event. Rabbis taught that hiding money in the ground protected a person from liability if it were stolen. At this point of the story there is no reason to question the behavior of the third servant.

As Jesus' listeners would have anticipated, **after a long time the master returned and settled accounts with** the servants (25:19). In the flow of the narrative, the master's delay in returning was not seen as a bad thing. Rather, the longer the master stayed away, the more time the servants had to increase the return on their investments. The statement that the master **settled accounts with** the servants makes it clear that talents were not given to them for safekeeping but for investment. The servant **who had received the five talents brought** the return on his investment, the additional **five** talents (25:20). As would be expected, the **master** was delighted. He affirmed the slave: **Well done, good and faithful servant! You have been faithful with a few things; I will put you in charge of many things. Come and share your master's happiness!** (25:21).

In similar fashion, the servant who had received **the two talents also** brought the **two**-talent return on his investment (25:22). The master affirmed the second slave with the identical words used to praise the first slave (25:23). The fact the master used the same words of praise reinforces the statement in verse 15, that each servant was given money in accordance with his own ability. The 100 percent increase was the same for both the five-talent and the two-talent slaves. The repeated—and thus emphasized — word in the master's affirmation of both is **faithful**. Faithfulness in investment is why the master also called each servant **good**.

The exact repetition of the words of affirmation for both servants emphasized two other facets: (1) that faithfulness in **a few things** is the basis for further future responsibility, and (2) the reward for faithfulness was sharing in the joy of the master. While listeners might suppose that the master's happiness represents a party or some physical celebration, the natural meaning is that the servants have come to value what the master valued, and so part of their reward is sharing the satisfaction of the master of good investments.

When the servant **who had received the one talent came**, his first word addressing the master is the same as the other two servants (25:24), but his report quickly deteriorated.

Some teaching on the second coming of Christ emphasizes knowledge of the signs of the times. However, the parable of the talents promises no reward for knowing when the Lord might return. What that parable affirms is faithfulness in pursuing the Lord's work until He comes. The faithfulness required is not consistency of one's private devotional life but the practice of investing in people's lives like Jesus invested in people's lives.

His description of the master as **a hard man** is unexpected. The other two servants gave no such impression. The third servant then defined a **hard man** as one who harvests **where** he has **not sown and** one who gathers **where** he has **not scattered seed.** This description actually provides the listener a clue to what made the master happy with the first two servants. But the third servant **was afraid** of such demands, and so he reports his action of burying the master's one **talent** (25:25).

The **master** responded, naming the third servant as a **wicked, lazy servant** (25:26). If the listener has not realized it before, it is clear now that the purpose of the master's giving money to the servants was not to save it but to invest it. The servant was both **wicked** and **lazy** because he knew the master's desires but did not act on them. The least he could have done would have been to have **put** the one talent **on deposit with the bankers, so that** it could have gained **interest** (25:27).

The punishment for the **lazy** servant was that first his **talent** was taken **from him** and given **to the one who** had received **ten talents** (25:28). The principle at work is that one **who has will be given more,** and the one who **does not have** will lose even the little that he or she was thought to have (25:29). Verse 29 repeats 13:12. The master then commanded other servants to **throw that worthless servant outside, into the darkness** (25:30). This outside darkness and the accompanying **weeping and gnashing of teeth** are common expressions in Matthew (see 8:12; 13:42, 50; 22:13; 24:51) and symbolized the horror of divine judgment.

The parable of the talents continues the theme of readiness for Christ's coming that began in chapter 24. However, this parable provides definition to the meaning of readiness. Believers who are ready for the coming of the Kingdom—and the coming of Christ—will not be passively waiting for that moment. Rather, they will faithfully invest in the Kingdom according to their abilities. The nature of the investment requires that the believer understand the mind of Christ, because the investment is to be done as the Master, Jesus, would do if He were present. Failure to involve oneself in Christlike ministry invites terrible judgment when Christ returns.

3. THE PARABLE OF THE SHEEP AND THE GOATS 25:31–46

The final teaching material of Jesus presented in Matthew's gospel brings the Olivet Discourse to a powerful climax in 25:31–46. The series of parables that began in 24:46 has increasingly raised the question of what it means to be ready for Christ's coming again. The parable of the sheep and the goats will advance further the disciples' understanding of readiness.

Jesus did not begin with a statement of comparison to the Kingdom as was common in His parables. Rather, the introduction immediately points to the time **when the Son of Man comes in his glory** (25:31). This phrase connects this parable to 24:27, 30, 39, and 44. Though it does not answer the disciples' question in 24:3 of what sign will accompany Jesus' coming, it does describe what will happen when the Son of Man comes and the basis upon which God's judgment will be meted out. For that reason it deals with the theme of readiness. Jesus stated that **all the nations will be gathered before him** (25:32). The wording echoes Isaiah 66:18, and it is most likely that **all the nations** means all humanity at this point. Jesus was describing the final judgment of humankind.

In that judgment, the Son of Man **will separate the people one from another as a shepherd separates the sheep from the goats. He will put the sheep on his right and the goats on his left** (Matt. 25:33). Sheep and goats were normally herded together during the day but separated by the shepherd at night. Perhaps because of their wool, sheep were better able to withstand the cold temperatures of the night. The goats had to be separated for special protection from the weather. Though the sheep were more valuable, it was often difficult for the casual observer to distinguish between the sheep and the goats. Perhaps Jesus' point is that only the Son of Man will be able to distinguish between the righteous or more valued people and the unrighteous.

In verse 34 the subject shifts from the Son of Man to **the King**. This is another example of the application beginning to shape the parable rather than the historical circumstances upon which it is built. It is the King of the kingdom of God who will speak in verse 34 **to those on his right** and invite them to receive their **inheritance, the kingdom prepared for** them from the beginning. The reason they are so **blessed by** the **Father** is that when the King **was hungry**, they **gave** Him **something to eat**. When He was **thirsty**, they **gave** Him **something to drink**. When He **was a stranger**, they **invited** Him **in** (25:35). When He **needed clothes**, they **clothed** Him. When He was **sick**, they **looked after** Him. When He was **in prison**, they **visited** Him (25:36).

At this point, the sheep on the right, **the righteous, will answer** (25:37). The title of their address to the King will be **Lord**. But in verses 37–39, they will ask **when** they did any of the things the King attributed to them in verses 34–36. They seem unaware of the virtuous deeds the King saw them perform. **The King will reply** to them, **whatever you did for one of the least of these brothers of mine, you did for me** (25:40).

Turning **to those on his left**, the King will command, **Depart from me, you who are cursed, into the eternal fire prepared for the devil and his angels** (25:41). The reason for this terrible sentence of judgment is that the King had been **hungry, thirsty** (25:42), **a stranger**, needing **clothes, sick and in prison** (25:43). But despite these terrible needs of the King, those on the left **did not look after** Him. Those on the left **also** answered, asking **when** they had seen the King in any such need and **did not help** Him (25:44). The King's response condemns those on the left: Because they **did not do** these things **for one of the least of these**, they **did not do** them **for** Him (25:45). The end result **will** be **eternal punishment** for those on the left, and **eternal life** for the **righteous** (25:46).

For a number of years, especially in the mid-twentieth century, scholars have interpreted this passage as if it were appealing to a general kind of humanitarian kindness to people in need. They argued there is no specific Christian content in the parable. Such an interpretation expresses the love of God for all humankind and rightly calls the Church to compassionate ministry and to support social justice. Further, such an interpretation promised salvation on the basis of kind treatment of needy people.

In recent years, a more careful reading of the text has renewed the historic Christian interpretation that the compassion Jesus desired is compassion to believers in need. The criterion of judgment is the treatment of disciples by the nations rather the treatment of the nations by the disciples. The parable provides an extension of the teaching in 10:40–42, which commended those who give a cup of cold water in Christ's name.

Though this parable does not reject general humanitarian concern for the needy, that is not its point. The point is that all the peoples of the earth will be judged on the basis of their response to the message of the Kingdom. That message is always brought to them by brothers or little ones or disciples. Readiness for Christ's coming does not happen simply by being kind to everybody. Such readiness occurs when we join our lives and fortunes with those who carry the gospel message. When we feed one of Christ's brothers who is about the work of the Kingdom, when we visit one of Christ's sisters who is proclaiming the gospel message, it is the same as if we had done that act of identification with Christ himself. Readiness for Christ's return is not passive; it is not just investing. Rather it is investing in the ministry of Christ through His followers.

The words of Matthew 26:1, **When Jesus had finished saying all these things**, mark the end of Matthew's final collection of Jesus' teachings.

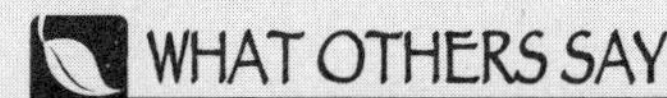

WHAT OTHERS SAY

BEFRIENDING AN ENEMY

For even though you should meet your enemy, is not his suffering enough to overcome and subdue your resistance to being merciful? And what about his hunger, cold, chains, nakedness and sickness? What about his homelessness? Are not these sufferings sufficient to overcome even your alienation? But you did not do these things for a friend, much less a foe. You could have at once befriended and done good. Even when you see a dog hungry you feel sympathy.

—John Chrysostom

26

THE UNFOLDING PLOT TO KILL JESUS

Matthew 26:2–75

Following the conclusion of the final block of teaching material in Matthew, the narrative turns to the final events of Jesus' life. Chapters 26 and 27 will narrate those events and Jesus' crucifixion and burial. Chapter 26 begins in verses 2–16 with the plot to kill Jesus. Verses 17–35 describe Jesus' last Passover. After the account of Jesus' Last Supper, verses 36–56 narrate the arrest of Jesus. The chapter closes with the account of the so-called Jewish trial and Peter's denial of Jesus in verses 57–75.

1. THE PLOT TO KILL JESUS 26:2–16

Matthew artistically develops the account of the plot to kill Jesus in three sections. In verses 2–6, he introduces the idea of a plot, but circumstances seem to stymie it. He then narrates in verses 7–13 the anointing of Jesus in which very expensive perfume is poured out upon Him. Finally, in verses 14–16, he returns to the plot to kill Jesus, with Judas agreeing with the chief priests on a price for betrayal.

The shadow of the impending death of Jesus has been hanging over the gospel of Matthew since Jesus first predicted it in 16:21. Now Jesus connects His coming death to **the Passover** (26:2). English is unable to capture the possible double meaning present in the Greek text of verse 2. The grammatical form of the verb **know** may be either indicative or imperative. The New International Version, and virtually every modern English version, translates it as indicative, **as you know**. It could also be translated as an imperative: Know that the Passover is **two days away**. The advantage of the imperative translation is that it makes it clearer that Jesus wanted His disciples to recognize the connection between the Passover and His death.

As a chronological statement, Jesus' words indicate that the events at the beginning of chapter 26 occurred on Wednesday or possibly Thursday of Holy Week. As a theological statement, the connecting of Passover with **the Son of Man** being **handed over to be crucified** portrays Jesus as the Passover lamb. Thus His death will have sacrificial significance and will provide for the redemption of God's new people, the Church.

Jesus had predicted in 16:21 that His death would be at the hands of the elders, chief priests and teachers of the law. Verse 3 describes the coming together of the **chief priests and elders of the people** to plot His death. Thus, from Matthew's perspective, Jesus set the process in motion by His statement about the Passover in verse 2, and then the very people Jesus had prophesied would kill Him began hatching the plot. One of Matthew's points is that Jesus' death did not just happen to Him. He deliberately set in motion the events that would lead to Calvary. The plotting parties met **in the palace of the high priest, whose name was Caiaphas.** He occupied the office of high priest from A.D. 18 to 36. His father-in-law, Annas, had preceded him as high priest and still appeared to be the power behind the scenes in the priestly circles. **Palace** gives the impression that **Caiaphas** was immensely wealthy and ran the office of the **high priest** like a king would. While both were true, one could translate that the parties met in the courtyard of the **high priest**. This implies a discussion behind the scenes lacking official status.

The first draft of the plot suggested that they **arrest Jesus and kill him** (26:4). This plot would need to be carried out **in some sly way** because they feared the reaction of the people. The Greek word translated **sly** literally means *by deceit*. Their deceitful plan must **not** take place **during the Feast** for fear of causing **a riot among the people** (26:5). Jesus will be killed by deceit, lack of integrity, and dishonesty. He will be betrayed. The element to notice is that the Jewish religious leaders decided not to carry out this plot during Passover because it was too dangerous. This conclusion contradicts what Jesus predicted in verse 2 that the plot against Him would unfold at Passover. Matthew's readers are left to ponder this contradiction while the scene changes.

Presumably the setting of verses 1–6 is the Mount of Olives, the last geographical location mentioned in 24:3. Matthew 26:6 places **Jesus in Bethany in the home of Simon the Leper**. Bethany was located on the eastern slope of the Mount of Olives, less than two miles from Jerusalem proper. According to 21:17, Jesus had been spending the night in Bethany. As a result, one might presume that the event at Simon's home took place in the late afternoon or evening two days before the Passover— Wednesday or possibly Thursday of Holy Week. Nothing is known of Simon the Leper beyond the information that can be derived from this account and its parallel in Mark 14:3–9. He could not have hosted the event described here unless he had been declared cleansed of his leprosy.

The comment that Jesus **was reclining at the table** (26:7) suggests that the event took place during the evening meal. There would have been three tables set up in a *U* formation with the center table looking out into the courtyard. The guests would have been leaning on their left sides, supported by their left elbows and eating with their right hands. Though there are some superficial similarities between this account and the story of the sinful woman washing Jesus' feet with her tears found in Luke 7:36–50, there is no reason to assume that this **woman** was morally suspect in the community. She brought **an alabaster jar of very expensive perfume** and **poured** it **on** Jesus' **head**. Matthew omits the details found in Mark 14:3 and 5 that the perfume was **nard** or spikenard and was worth 300 denarii, about a year's income. The fact that she poured it on Jesus' head suggests that her action was an anointing. The Messiah, literally the anointed one, is anointed for His suffering and death before He is betrayed.

MANNERS AND CUSTOMS

PERFUME FLASKS

The flasks in which perfume was kept in first-century Palestine were often made of alabaster, a translucent gypsum stone. Such flasks were usually carved with a long, thin neck that could be snapped off to pour out the perfume. Spikenard was an expensive, luxury perfume that was imported from India. While it was not unusual to anoint a guest's head with oil, the expense of the woman's perfume makes her actions an extravagant expression of devotion.

Despite the significance of this act, **the disciples were indignant** and described her expression of love as a **waste** (Matt. 26:8). They piously pointed out that the **perfume could have been sold and the money given to the poor** (26:9).

Jesus' response affirmed the woman's action by describing it as **a beautiful thing** done to Him (26:10). His subsequent comment that the **poor** are **always with you** is not a disparagement of the poor nor of ministry to them (26:11). Rather, it is almost a direct quotation from Deuteronomy 15:11, which commands openhanded, generous sharing with the poor. His point was that the poor are always present and money can always be given to them at any time. He, however, would not be with them much longer. In fact, the pouring of the precious perfume over His head was preparation of his **body for burial** (26:12). Though the chief priests and elders had put plans to kill Jesus on hold, the preparations instigated by God for this significant moment in time continued unabated. He then reaffirmed the importance of the woman's action by noting that **wherever this gospel is preached throughout the world,** her story of devotion **will be told** (26:13).

Matthew returns to the plot to kill Jesus in verses 14–16 with the simple account of Judas's agreement with the chief priests to betray his Master. With tragic simplicity Matthew tells the reader that **Judas Iscariot** was **one of the Twelve** (26:14). Judas had already been introduced in 10:4 as the one who would betray Jesus. The word **Iscariot** probably means *the man from Kerioth.* Kerioth is a village about twelve miles south of Hebron in the Judean desert. Judas was the only Judean among the Twelve, who, along with Jesus, were Galileans. Some have speculated that regional jealousy was his motive in the betrayal, but there is no support in the text for such a proposal.

Judas asked **what** the chief priests were **willing to give** him **if** he handed Jesus **over to** them (26:15). They offered and paid **him thirty silver coins.** Matthew does not state the denomination of the coins. If they were denarii, Judas would have taken thirty denarii to betray the Jesus the woman spent three hundred denarii to anoint. Some have suggested the coins were Tyrian shekels, which were worth about four denarii. This is still less than half the price of the perfume poured on

Jesus' head. Exodus 21:32 required thirty shekels of silver to be paid a neighbor whose slave was killed as a result of one's carelessness. Zechariah 11:12 mentions thirty pieces of silver as the price paid for the rejected shepherd. As tragic as was Judas's betrayal of Jesus, even more tragic is how little Jesus was worth to him or to the chief priests. But the price was paid, and **from then on Judas watched for an opportunity** to carry out the betrayal (Matt. 26:16).

2. JESUS' FINAL PASSOVER 26:17–35

The agreement with Judas reversed the delay the chief priests had accepted in their plan to arrest and kill Jesus (26:4–5). Once their plot was on again, Jesus' statement in 26:2 connecting the Passover with His death would need to be fulfilled. Matthew's account turns directly to the Passover in verse 17. Properly speaking, Passover came on the fourteenth day of the Jewish month Nisan. **The Feast of Unleavened Bread** ran from Nisan 15 through Nisan 21, but Passover was popularly called **the first day of** or the day of preparation for the Feast of Unleavened Bread. Leviticus 23:4–8; Numbers 28:16–25; and Deuteronomy 16:1–8 describe the Passover in relation to the Feast of Unleavened Bread.

The disciples asked Jesus where they should prepare for Him **to eat the Passover**. This phrase clearly means to eat the Passover meal commanded in Exodus 12:14 to be celebrated

Passover was a major Jewish festival in Jesus' time. Most scholars believe Josephus exaggerated in his claim that three million Jews gathered in Jerusalem each year for Passover. The city, nevertheless, was packed with visitors, and every room, nook, and cranny was pressed into use for families and groups celebrating the Passover. The lamb would be roasted in the courtyard, and the meal would include roast lamb, bitter herbs, unleavened bread, a nut and fruit mixture, a raw vegetable, and four cups of wine. Each of these items had symbolic meaning, which was explained as part of the Passover seder or order of service.

as a commemorative festival every year. Its purpose was to enable Israel to remember the first Passover, in which God delivered the people out of slavery in Egypt. The oldest known Passover seder (order of service) dates from the late second century A.D., but Jesus' final Passover meal described in the Gospels fits with the practices described in that seder.

Jesus' instructions to the disciples were to **go into the city to a certain man and tell him** that Jesus was going to **celebrate Passover at** his **house** (Matt. 26:18). Matthew gives no other indication of the identity of the man, though Mark 14:13 states that the disciples would meet a man carrying a water jar who would guide them to the house. Since carrying a water jar was woman's work in that society, some have speculated that the house owner must have been an Essene, since the Essenes were the only Jewish group of the time to forbid marriage. Matthew has no interest in the man's identity. Rather, his account shows the divine foreknowledge of Jesus, who was able to tell the disciples the exact course of events that would transpire to provide a place for them to eat the Passover. Further, all this would happen because Jesus' **appointed time** was **near**. In response **the disciples did** exactly **as Jesus had directed them and prepared the Passover** (Matt. 26:19).

Because Matthew could assume his Jewish readers understood the practices of the Passover meal, he provides very few details in his description of Jesus' final Passover. The expression in verse 20, **when evening came,** literally means when it was late. The Passover meal would have lasted several hours, and the preparation would have taken much time. Because the meal was a celebrative occasion, Jews felt no need to hurry through it. But Jesus dropped a bombshell into the joyful evening when He said, **I tell you the truth, one of you will betray me** (26:21). The solemn words, **I tell you the truth**, (literally, Amen, I tell you) affirmed that His shocking words were words from God. Jesus knew the plot that Judas thought a secret.

The disciples' response was shocked distress (26:22). The New International Version—**they were very sad**—fails to capture the sense of shock and grief implied by the Greek text. Their question, **Surely not I, Lord?** did not communicate uncertainty about their guilt. It is constructed to show that they expected the answer to be negative. We might phrase the question as an emphatic, "It isn't me, is it, Lord?" The title **Lord** on their lips as they answer the charge of betrayal is ironic. Jesus' response to them was ambiguous. The statement in verse 23, **The one**

who has dipped his hand into the bowl with me will betray me, probably said no more than verse 21. The disciples would have shared food out of a common bowl. Whether one or two bowls of each food would have been on the table is immaterial because all the bowls would have been passed to all the guests.

Jesus was aware that His impending death was part of God's revealed description of the coming salvation and declared, **The Son of Man will go just as it is written about him** (26:24). However, He pronounced a judgment lament upon the person whose choice would set the prophesied events into motion: **Woe to that man who betrays the Son of Man! It would have been better for him if he had not been born.** From the repeated protestations of the disciples, Matthew records that of Judas individually. His words in verse 25, **Surely not I,** were identical to those of the disciples recorded in verse 22. However, quite ironically, Judas can only address Jesus as **Rabbi,** not as **Lord.** Though Judas framed his question to show he expected a negative answer, Jesus spoke the truth: **Yes, it is you.**

Because Jesus' Last Supper became the foundation of the Christian Communion meal, the Lord's Supper, which in Church history was quickly reduced to a symbolic piece of bread and cup of wine, many readers forget the context was a full-course Passover meal. Matthew's phrase **while they were eating** (27:26) summarizes the roast lamb, the unleavened bread, the bitter herbs, the four cups of wine, and other elements of the meal. The process of giving **thanks** and breaking and distributing the bread to the group would have been the responsibility of the Passover host. As Passover was eaten, the father or host would interpret the symbolism of each part of the meal. In similar fashion **Jesus took bread** and explained its significance to the disciples: **This is my body.** As the loaf of bread was broken and given to each person present, Jesus' body will be broken and will become the bread of salvation for any who will receive such nourishment. Not only do Jesus' words squarely face His impending death, His command, **Take and eat,** called on the disciples to accept that death and to be willing to participate in its benefits.

In a similar fashion, **he took the cup, gave thanks and offered it to them** with words of interpretation (27:27). The Passover seder prescribed four cups of wine, each of which was introduced by a thanksgiving blessing. It is most likely that the cup described in verse 27 was the third cup. The cup would have been passed around with His command that **all of** them **drink from it**. The interpretation of the cup appears in verse 28: **This is my blood of the covenant, which is poured out for many for the forgiveness of sins.**

Jesus' description of the wine as the **blood of the covenant** would have called Exodus 24:8 to the disciples' minds. There on Mount Sinai, Moses sprinkled the blood of the fellowship offering on the people and called it **The blood of the covenant that the LORD has made with you.** Though the element of sacrifice was present, Jesus' words emphasized participation in the covenant relationship being offered through His death. The atoning effect of His blood would bring forgiveness of sins for many.

Jesus' further statement that He would **not drink of this fruit of the vine from now on until that day when I drink it anew with you in my Father's kingdom** (Matt. 26:29) apparently meant that He would not drink the fourth cup. At least by the second century, the fourth cup marked the end of the Passover meal. Was Jesus saying that He would not complete the Passover meal at that time and that it would remain unfinished until all believers are gathered into the coming Kingdom? Matthew passes over such questions and simply notes that after **they had sung a hymn, they went out to the Mount of Olives** (26:30). The second-century seder prescribes Psalms 116–118 as the closing hymn of the Passover meal.

As they left, **Jesus told** the disciples that they would **all fall away on account of** Him (27:31). In customary Matthean interpretation, this falling away was also prophesied in Zechariah 13:7: **I will strike the shepherd, and the sheep of the flock will be scattered.** But His coming death and the scattering of the disciples did not signal the end of either hope or planning for Jesus. He told the disciples, **After I have risen, I will go ahead of you into Galilee** (26:32). Jesus' plan is clear: He will die, the disciples will scatter; He will be raised, they are to rendezvous with Him in Galilee.

Peter had objected to Jesus' first prediction of His coming suffering, death, and resurrection in Matthew 16:21–22. Here he objects to the idea that he would be among the disciples who would **fall away** (26:33). The verb translated **fall away** here has been used eleven times in Matthew prior to verses 31 and 33. The New International Version has translated it **cause to sin** (5:29, 30; 18:6, 8, 9), **fall away** (11:6; 13:21; 26:31, 33), **take offense at** (13:57), **offend** (15:12; 17:27), and **turn away** (24:10). Peter was confident that **even if all** the others were caused to sin, he **never** would.

Sadly **Jesus answered** that Peter would **disown** Him **three times** on that **very night before the rooster** would crow announcing the next morning (26:34). The language of disowning Jesus had already been introduced in 10:33. Presumably, disowning Jesus was a worse failure than falling away. After Peter boasted that he would never fall away, Jesus told him that his failure would be even worse. **Peter** could not believe Jesus' words and **declared, "Even if I have to die with you, I will never disown you"** (26:35). Though **all the other disciples said the same**, none had any idea what the devastating events of the next few hours would do to them.

3. JESUS ARRESTED 26:36–56

The inability of the disciples to keep their promise will soon be evident. **Jesus went with his disciples to a place called Gethsemane,** apparently on the lower western slope of the Mount of Olives (26:36). Gethsemane is Hebrew for *olive press* and may have been a central oil press used by the many olive farmers who had olive groves on the Mount of Olives. Jesus instructed the disciples to remain there **while** He went further to **pray. He took Peter and the two sons of Zebedee**, James and John, **with him** (26:37). These three had been with Him on the Mount of Transfiguration (17:1–8), but they had also recently arrogantly declared their ability to endure whatever lay ahead for Jesus. James and John had made their claim when their mother had asked for the positions of honor at Jesus' right and left hands when He came in His kingdom (20:20–23), and Peter had just made his claim (26:33, 35).

Apparently because of the thought of His impending death, Jesus **began to be sorrowful and troubled.** He revealed the severity of His distress to the three disciples: **My soul is overwhelmed with sorrow to the point of death** (26:38). The words echo Psalms 42:6 and 43:5. Those words also raised the possibility that the emotional agony of what lay before Him might kill Him before the chief priests could carry out their plot (Matt. 26:3–4, 14–16). Jesus then asked the three to **stay and keep watch with** Him. The Greek word translated **keep watch** here simply meant to stay awake. If the three fell asleep, He would be left alone in the final moments of His struggle.

Jesus moved ahead **a little farther** and **fell with his face to the ground**, praying, **My Father, if it is possible, may this cup be taken from me** (26:39). The parallel passage in Mark 14:36 indicates that Jesus addressed the Father as *Abba*. This Aramaic term expressed the tenderly intimate relationship between Him and the Father, a relationship that would sustain Him in the dark hours ahead. The grammatical construction indicates that Jesus believed it was possible for God to remove the cup from Him. The Old Testament spoke of the **cup** as a person's lot in life. Though it could refer to a positive event, it more commonly referred to suffering and shameful treatment (Ps. 75:8; Isa. 51:17; Jer. 49:12; Ezek. 23:31–34). This suggests that Jesus' anxiety in Gethsemane was not over His fear of death, but because of His understanding that the **cup** would be the weight and punishment of sin that He would suffer.

The continued prayer, **Yet not as I will, but as you will**, made it clear that though Jesus knew God's power could grant Him relief from His suffering and death, He would choose God's plan instead. His commitment in prayer to the Father's **will** modeled what He taught in the so-called Lord's Prayer, where He instructed His disciples to pray that God's **will be done on earth as it is in heaven** (6:10).

When **he returned to** the three **disciples**, He **found**

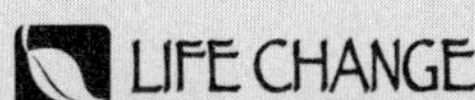

LIFE CHANGE

SELF DENIAL

At the most fearful juncture of Jesus' life, He prayed that God's will be done rather than His own will. Such denial of His own desires and fears models the instructions He gave His disciples in Matthew 16:24–25. Taking one's cross, denying oneself, and losing one's life to find it are exemplified by Jesus' prayer and His actions in Gethsemane. Had Jesus not been obedient in Gethsemane, the plan of salvation would have been lost. One wonders how much is lost when we refuse to deny ourselves and we pursue our own wills rather than the will of God.

them sleeping (26:40). They must have had no comprehension of what was happening or what was at stake that night to be able to fall asleep so quickly. Jesus reproached them for not even being able to stay awake with Him **for one hour**. It was critical for them to **watch and pray** lest they **fall into temptation** (26:41). His concern that they fall to temptation also calls to mind the petition of the Lord's Prayer that asks God to lead Jesus' followers away from temptation (6:13). Perhaps the temptation He wished them to avoid was the test that would come later that night, at which all of them would fall away (26:31).

Returning to His place of prayer, Jesus prayed **a second time** (27:42). This time He said, **If it is not possible for this cup to be taken away.** This indicates that Jesus recognized that God could not allow His power to override His love for the world. The slight change in wording represented the Savior's embracing more completely the way of the cross that lay before Him. Having achieved that deeper level of commitment, He went **back** to the disciples and **found them sleeping** (26:43). Apparently He was seeking their support in the loneliness of obedience, but He did not awaken them. Rather, He **went** back **and prayed the third time, saying the same thing** (26:44). The threefold repetition of His prayer expressed the completeness of Jesus' commitment to the Father's will.

After the third session of prayer, **he returned to the disciples** and this time He woke them up. His message to them was that **the hour is near** (26:45). The **hour** here has a meaning quite similar to its frequent use in John's gospel. It refers to the critical turning point in Jesus' life when the final events leading to His death will begin. Further, **the Son of Man is betrayed into the hands of sinners.** The present tense in both phrases indicates that, in fact, those final events were already underway. The exhortation, **Rise, let us go!** (26:46), called the sleeping disciples from their places of rest to the path where the **betrayer** was even then coming.

Matthew's words, **while he was still speaking** (26:47), show how quickly the transition from Jesus' prayer in Gethsemane to His arrest took place. He had hardly finished praying when **Judas, one of the Twelve, arrived.** The words **one of the Twelve** were not necessary for information; Matthew uses them for effect. One of history's supreme tragedies is that Jesus was betrayed by one of His own disciples. **A large crowd**

armed with swords and clubs accompanied Judas. If this large armed crowd was legitimately appointed, their presence implied fear that Jesus had armed rebels at His disposal. If this crowd was not legitimately appointed, they were outlaw vigilantes hunting down an innocent man. Matthew tells us that **the chief priests and elders of the people sent** this armed crowd. Clearly, the plot envisioned in the opening verses of chapter 26, and put into motion in the agreement with Judas (26:14–16), was about to come to fruition.

The prearranged **signal** Judas had designed was to **kiss the man** they should **arrest** (26:48). Jews rarely kissed in public, and the Gospels never describe a kiss between Jesus and a disciple other than this one. In Jesus' culture, a kiss signified respect and reconciliation. For Judas to kiss Jesus in order to betray Him was the greatest degree of hypocrisy possible. His salutation of Jesus, **Greetings, Rabbi!** (26:49), also exuded deceit. The Hebrew word used for **greetings** is *shalom*, usually translated *peace*. But Judas brought death, not peace. As he had in verse 25 when Jesus had foretold His betrayal, Judas addressed the Master as **Rabbi**. In contrast Jesus responded by calling Judas **friend** (26:50).

Once Judas's signal of kissing Jesus had been given, the mob **seized** Him **and arrested him . . . One of Jesus' companions drew out his sword** and attempted to defend the Master, **cutting off** the **ear** of a **servant of the high priest** (26:51). The gospel of John tells us that Peter was the sword-wielding disciple and Malchus was the victim. Luke's gospel states that Jesus restored Malchus's ear. Matthew omits these details to focus on Peter's violent response and Jesus' reprimand: **Put your sword back in its place** (Matt. 26:52). The proverb **all who draw the sword will die by the sword** provides the reason for the reprimand. Turning to such violence would not be necessary because Jesus could **call on** His **Father** and have **more than twelve legions of angels at** His **disposal** (26:53). A legion at full force consisted of six thousand Roman soldiers, though many legions operated in the field at less than full strength. Jesus' comment implied that He did not need the twelve disciples to defend Him because twelve legions of the angelic armies were available if He should call for them. However, if He called on the hosts of heaven to defend Him, **how would the Scriptures be fulfilled** (26:54) that spoke of Jesus' coming death?

Turning from Peter to the arresting **crowd, Jesus** pointed out the irony of their mob action against Him (26:55). Their **swords and clubs** would have been most appropriate if He had been **leading a rebellion**. But in fact, He had taught **in the temple** courtyard almost **every day** that week, and they had made no move **to arrest** Him. The irony is even greater because Jesus **sat** in the official position of teaching and thus had been respected as a rabbi. Surely no rabbi would be arrested in the middle of the night by a mob with swords and clubs. **But,** Jesus declared, **this has all taken place that the writings of the prophets might be fulfilled** (26:56). These words reflect a consistent theme in Matthew's gospel

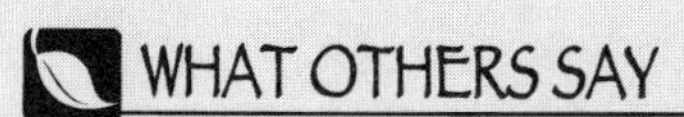

By these words he quenched their anger, appealing to holy Scripture. He prayed that the disciples might accept meekly whatever befell him when they had learned that this also is occurring according to God's will. His response is twofold: He is able to appeal to his Father, and he is able to resist the angry passions of his supposed defenders with these words, 'All who take the sword will perish by the sword.'

—John Chrysostom

that Jesus' ministry was the fulfillment of Old Testament Scripture. Matthew's next sentence is more ironic: **Then all the disciples deserted him and fled.** The prophets foretold the events of Jesus' death, but He— the greatest prophet—had predicted (26:31) that all the disciples would fall away. Their departure left Jesus alone in the hands of those who had plotted His death.

4. JESUS' JEWISH TRIAL AND PETER'S DENIAL 26:57–75

Following His arrest, the crowd **took Jesus to Caiaphas, the high priest, where the teachers of the law and the elders had** gathered (26:57). The procedures that followed are often called Jesus' *Jewish trial*, though the word *trial* is inaccurate. The frequent descriptions of this *trial* as illegal or contrary to Jewish law are only speculation. The legal codes available for comparison were written 150 years later in the *Mishnah*, so the correct procedures for a Jewish trial at Jesus' time are not known. A Jewish court could not order capital punishment under Roman rule.

Apparently the purpose of the session before Caiaphas was to determine the charges that would be taken to the Romans.

Prior to narrating the events before Caiaphas, Matthew positions **Peter** for the denial Jesus had foretold (26:34). In contrast to the other disciples (described as **all the disciples** in 26:56) who fled, Peter **followed** Jesus **at a distance, right up to the courtyard of the high priest** (26:58). That courtyard was an outdoor, enclosed area where the servants of the high priest would have gathered. Mark's gospel states that there was a fire there where the servants and passersby warmed themselves. Matthew simply observes that Peter **entered** the courtyard **and sat down with the guards** to await **the outcome.**

Though the legal purposes of the high priest may be unclear, Matthew's purpose in narrating these events is quite clear. He intends the so-called Jewish trial to provide the stage where Jesus can declare His messiahship to the official leaders of Israel. In addition to the **chief priests, the whole Sanhedrin** gathered to collect the **evidence** that would allow them to **put** Jesus **to death** (26:59). Matthew's language is quite compressed in verses 59–60. He states that the chief priests and Sanhedrin **were looking for false evidence against Jesus**. It is possible that the Jewish leaders were looking for false evidence. It is more likely, however, that they were looking for evidence that would allow them to put Jesus to death. Matthew knew any such evidence would be false. He then states in verse 60 that the Jewish leaders **did not find any, though many false witnesses came forward.**

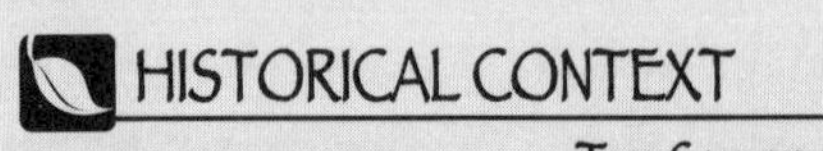

THE SANHEDRIN

The Sanhedrin consisted of priests, elders, and scribes and was recognized by Rome as the official local ruling body of Judea. The high priest presided over meetings of the Sanhedrin at Jesus' time. According to Josephus, the Sanhedrin normally met in the Temple courtyard. By the second-century *Mishnah*, it was composed of seventy-one members. Though exceptions occurred—such as Stephen in Acts 7—it is generally considered that the Sanhedrin did not have authority to decide capital cases.

If false witnesses came forward, all they found was false evidence. What Matthew meant was they found no evidence sufficient to execute Jesus.

Finally two came forward and delivered their witness. The fact that there were two such witnesses confirmed the truth of what they said according to the Old Testament principle that every legal matter had to be established by two or three witnesses (Deut. 17:6; 19:15). Thus Matthew regarded as true the accusation that Jesus had said, **I am able to destroy the temple of God and rebuild it in three days** (Matt. 26:61). Though nothing similar to this statement appears in Matthew's gospel, it is quite similar to Jesus' comment in John 2:19. The Johannine statement understood the Temple to refer to Jesus' own body and to, thus, foretell His resurrection. Jesus' statement, quoted in Matthew 26:61 did not threaten the Temple, but He had already predicted its destruction in 23:38 and 24:2. Because the Temple was so central to Jewish identity, and especially to the status and security of the priestly families, they perceived Jesus as a threat because of those predictions.

Once the accusation of destroying the Temple was on the table, **the high priest** demanded that Jesus **answer** the charge (26:62). Perhaps Caiaphas hoped Jesus would say something more incriminating than the charge that He had the power to destroy the Temple, **but Jesus remained silent** (26:63). His silence would have reminded the original readers of Isaiah 53:7, in which the suffering servant remained silent before those who oppressed and afflicted him. His silence also pushed **the high priest** to another question designed to elicit an answer that would justify the death penalty against Jesus. The high priest demonstrated his urgency, demanding, **I charge you under oath by the living God.** This is the only time in the New Testament the verb **to charge under oath** is used. Demanding that the oath be confirmed by the living God also raised the tension of the demand.

The high priest demanded that Jesus tell whether He was **the Christ, the Son of God.** To claim to be Christ was to claim to be the long-awaited Messiah, the one who would bring the consummation to God's plan to establish His kingdom on earth. Though Peter had confessed Jesus to be the Messiah in 16:16, the issue of messiahship had not been directly addressed with Jewish religious leaders. The claim to be Messiah might have been upsetting to the chief priests, but it certainly was no criminal offense. Whether Jesus was the Messiah had been a matter of public conversation. Whether the title **Son of God** had messianic overtones in first-century Judaism is uncertain. Certainly to understand the title as claiming deity would have been blasphemy.

Jesus' responded to Caiaphas' demand with a resounding **Yes, it is as you say** (26:64). Thus Matthew has arranged his account of the Jewish trial so that Jesus was able to declare His identity before the Jewish religious leaders. However, Jesus did not regard Caiaphas' formulation as adequate and declared that Caiaphas and all present would **see the Son of Man sitting at the right hand of the Mighty One and coming on the clouds of heaven.** These words are a close paraphrase of Daniel 7:13. Within the context of Daniel 7:13, the Son of Man was identified closely with God himself and as the one who would usher in God's glorious kingdom.

The high priest understood both the positive answer to whether Jesus was the Son of God and His claim that Daniel 7:13 applied to Him as **blasphemy** (Matt. 26:65). He **tore his clothes**, which was an Old Testament symbol of grief. By the second-century *Mishnah*, the tearing of clothes had become a symbol of blasphemy. If Jesus' words were sufficient evidence of blasphemy, there would have been no further need of **any more witnesses**. Caiaphas called for a verdict: **What do you think?** (26:66). The chief priests and Sanhedrin answered that Jesus was **worthy of death**. In response to both the charge of blasphemy and the sentence of death **they spit in his face and struck him with their fists** (26:67). As they beat Him they also mocked Him: **Prophesy to us, Christ. Who hit you?** (26:68).

The scene changes to **Peter sitting out in the courtyard** (26:69). **A servant girl** approached and commented, **You also were with Jesus of Galilee.** Given the fact that Jesus had just been condemned for the capital offense blasphemy, Peter, as one of His associates, was in danger also. A servant girl speaking these words was demeaning, if not threatening, to Peter, and **he denied** her statement **before them all** (26:70). There is no evidence at this point that Peter remembered Jesus' prediction that he would deny the Master three times that night (26:34). However, the reader cannot help but remember. Perhaps sensing the danger, Peter began to leave the courtyard. He had gotten **to the gateway** when **another girl** declared, **This fellow was with Jesus of Nazareth** (26:71). Since Nazareth was a village in Galilee, her comment communicated nothing beyond that of the servant girl. However, Peter felt the threat increasing, and this time **he denied** the girl's statement **with an oath** (26:72). Perhaps sadder, he denied even knowing Jesus.

The third charge came from men **standing there** who declared that Peter's **accent** gave him **away** as **one of them** (26:73). In that culture the fact that men made the accusation placed Peter in greater danger than the two previous comments made by girls. A Galilean accent was distinct from the Judean accent, and Judeans often mocked Galileans for their accent. Peter's response was more violent, and **he began to call down curses on himself and swore** that he did not **know the man** (26:74). Though the New International Version translates that Peter cursed himself, the Greek text allows the possibility of understanding him as cursing Jesus. Matthew punctuates the horror of these developments with the comment, **immediately a rooster crowed.** No reader could fail to realize that Jesus' prophecy of Peter's denial (26:34) had now been fulfilled.

The crowing of the rooster also brought those words of Jesus and Peter's confident affirmation that he would die before denying Jesus (26:35) to Peter' memory. The powerful effect of Matthew's comment lies in its directness and brevity. Peter **went outside and wept bitterly** (26:75). Though the other Gospels record Peter's restoration to the community, this is the final time Matthew mentions Peter.

27

JESUS' TRIAL BEFORE PILATE AND THE CRUCIFIXION

Matthew 27:1–66

Matthew's account of the final hours of Jesus' life that began in chapter 26 continues in chapter 27. The first ten verses of chapter 27 describe Judas's death. Verses 11–26 focus on the trial before Pilate and Jesus' condemnation to death. Verses 27–56 narrate Jesus' crucifixion, while 27:57–66 describes His burial. The journey to Jesus' death that began in 16:21 reaches its final, sad conclusion.

1. THE DEATH OF JUDAS 27:1–10

As Matthew has described the events of Jesus' final night, he has alternated points of view on the so-called Jewish trial of Jesus and his picture of Peter moving to deny his Master. After 26:68, he shifted from his description of Jewish leaders mocking Jesus to the story of Peter's denial in 26:69–75. In 27:1, Matthew returns to the Jewish trial **early in the morning**. It is possible that the Sanhedrin and the chief priests knew that bringing charges against Jesus in the middle of the night violated their law. Regardless of their motivation, **all the chief priests and the elders came to** an official **decision** once daylight had come.

Though they decided **to put Jesus to death**, the Sanhedrin did not have authority to execute a prisoner. As a result **they bound him, led him**

away and handed him over to Pilate, the Roman **governor** who did have authority in capital cases (27:2). Pilate normally resided in Caesarea, a port city on the Mediterranean coast, but during the major Jewish religious festivals like Passover, he often came to Jerusalem with a show of Roman military might. The Jewish religious leaders did not like Pilate, but because he had the ability to put Jesus to death they were willing to cooperate with him to accomplish that goal.

At this point Matthew shifts scenes one more time to record the death of Judas. **When Judas . . . saw that Jesus was condemned, he was seized with remorse** and tried to reverse his betrayal (27:3). This verse has given rise to theories suggesting that Judas **betrayed** Jesus in hopes of forcing His messianic hand. In the most common version of these theories, Judas believed that Jesus could indeed call twelve legions of angels to establish His kingdom and believed the threat to His life would motivate this action. While the theory fits with the evidence available in the New Testament, it is not necessary to explain Judas's actions. The Greek word translated **seized with remorse** is not the normal word for repentance but a weaker term indicating that Judas felt badly about the results of his actions.

HISTORICAL CONTEXT
PONTIUS PILATE

Pilate served as prefect in Judea from A.D. 26–36. A few years later the Romans began to call prefects *procurators*, as was the case with Felix and Festus in Acts 24–25. Jewish religious leaders hated Pilate because, early in his rule, he had placed in Jerusalem the army standards with images of the emperor, though previous governors had agreed not to do so. Later, trying to quell demonstrations in the Temple, his soldiers had killed a number of Jewish worshippers, perhaps referred to in Luke 13:1. The culmination of Pilate's public relations fiasco in Judea came in A.D. 36 when he ordered a vicious attack on a mob of religious fanatics near Samaria. As a result, he was relieved of his duties as prefect and recalled to Rome.

He **returned the thirty silver coins** and confessed that he had **sinned** by betraying **innocent blood** (27:4). The words **innocent blood** had often been used in the Old Testament to describe a wrongful death. According to the Greek translation of the Old Testament, the Septuagint, Deuteronomy 27:25 pronounced a curse on anyone taking a bribe to shed innocent blood. The **chief priests and the elders** brushed off Judas's confession and reminded him that his actions were his own **responsibility**. In response, **Judas threw the money into the temple and left** (Matt. 27:5). The Greek clearly indicates that Judas threw the money into the actual sanctuary of the Temple, not just somewhere in the Temple courtyard. This action suggests that when the priests refused to take the betrayal money, Judas decided to give it directly to God. **Then he went out and hanged himself.** In the Greco-Roman world, suicide was the only way one who had betrayed a teacher could restore his honor. However, it is not clear that Judas in particular, or the Jewish world in general, was familiar with this Greco-Roman understanding. Neither is it clear how Matthew's account of Judas's death should be reconciled with the description in Acts 1:18.

The chief priests retrieved **the coins** from the sanctuary but felt the moral inconsistency of putting such money **into the treasury** (Matt. 27:6) though they apparently had no problem taking it out of the treasury. The expression **blood money** paraphrases the Greek *price of blood*. The priests **decided . . . to buy . . . a burial place for foreigners** (27:7). Because non-Jews were not permitted to be buried with Jews, a cemetery for foreigners was an occasional need in Jerusalem. Thus the purchase of this cemetery was a charitable act accomplished through the price of the blood of Jesus. Matthew saw this use of blood money as the reason the burial place came to be **called the Field of Blood** (27:8) in his time.

Matthew also described the land purchased as **the potter's field**. This phrase would have connected the story of Judas once again to Zechariah 11:12–13. There the thirty pieces of silver were thrown to the potter. Jewish readers would have also heard echoes of Jeremiah 18–19 in Matthew's description of the burial field. Jewish interpreters of the Old Testament often combined passages where similar phrases occurred. Matthew only mentions **Jeremiah** as the **prophet** whose words were **fulfilled** (Matt. 27:9), but the quotation he provides includes phrases from both Jeremiah and Zechariah. Taking **the thirty silver coins, the price set on him** came from Zechariah 11:13. The purchase from the potter (Matt. 27:10) came from Jeremiah 19:1, and the command of **the Lord to buy** a **field** came from Jeremiah 32:8.

Though many modern interpreters are distressed by the odd mixture of phrases in Matthew 27:9–10 that the author presents as a quotation from Jeremiah, what Matthew did was a very common Jewish practice in quoting and interpreting Scripture. This is the final text for which Matthew uses the fulfillment formula that he has used so often in this Gospel. Matthew wants his community, which is concerned about the death of their Messiah, to understand that even the details of Judas's death were part of God's plan.

2. THE TRIAL BEFORE PILATE 27:11–26

Matthew's pattern of shifting back and forth between scenes is reflected in the use of **meanwhile** to introduce 27:11, though no transition word is present in the Greek text. Verse 11 returns to the description of Jesus before Pilate that began in 27:1–2 but was interrupted by the account of Judas's death in verses 3–10. **Jesus stood before** Pilate, who **asked him, "Are you the king of the Jews?"** The phrase **king of the Jews** appears only on Gentile lips in Matthew's gospel and would have been a Gentile equivalent to a Jewish claim of messiahship. Jesus' answer to Pilate, **Yes, it is as you say,** was identical—except for the tense of the Greek verb—to His reply in 26:64 to Caiaphas' question of whether He was the Messiah, the Son of God. Thus Jesus identified himself as Messiah in both the Jewish and the Roman trials.

Pilate's question may have come from his own curiosity about the rumors about Jesus, the prophet from Galilee. The trial proper began after the interchange recorded in verse 11 with accusations against Jesus by **the chief priests and elders** (27:12). **He gave no answer** to their charges, refusing to dignify them with a response. Pilate was not accustomed to Jewish defendants being quiet, and he puzzled at Jesus' silence. He asked, **Don't you hear the testimony they are bringing against you?** (27:13) in an attempt to get Jesus to defend himself. Roman legal precedent required that a defendant have three opportunities to respond before a guilty verdict could be handed down by default. Jesus' continued silence, refusing to respond **even to a single charge** brought **great amazement** to Pilate. However, it repeated the pattern

Jesus had established before Caiaphas in 26:62–63 and again called Isaiah 53:7 to mind.

Rather than allowing the charges to be presented three times without a response, Pilate shifted his tactics. He had established a **custom at the Feast** of releasing **a prisoner chosen by the crowd** (Matt. 27:15). The Gospels are the only documents of ancient history to mention this particular form of the custom. Roman rulers could release prisoners to gain favor with subjects, and on occasion such a prisoner release had been done by rulers in the area of Judea. It is likely that Pilate developed this amnesty for a few years to counter the strong hatred the Jews had for him. **At** the **time** of Jesus' trial, the Romans held **a notorious prisoner** by the name of **Barabbas** (27:16).

According to Mark 15:7 and Luke 23:19, Barabbas was in prison for murder committed as part of an insurrection. Presumably the insurrection was a local paramilitary action against Roman rule. This suggests both that Barabbas would have been a dangerous criminal and that he would have been a popular Jewish folk hero for his exploits in the insurrection. Speaking to **the crowd**, rather than the priests and elders who had brought the charges, **Pilate asked, "Which one do you want me to release to you: Barabbas, or Jesus who is called** the Messiah?" (Matt. 27:17). Part of the Jewish hatred of Pilate arose from a

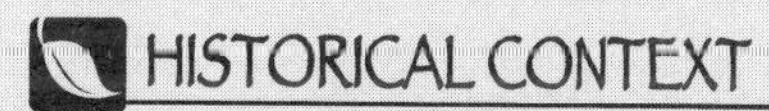

Verses 16 and 17 present a difficult problem in determining the correct reading of the text. Several Greek manuscripts and early translations of the New Testament read *Jesus Barabbas* as the name of the criminal Pilate offered in exchange for Jesus. Origen commented on the problem in the first half of the third century A.D. The best Greek manuscripts that are normally used to establish the correct text have only Barabbas. However, it is more likely ancient scribes would have deleted the name out of reverence for Jesus—as Origen suggested—rather than adding it when it was not present in the manuscripts being copied. The modern English translations demonstrate the challenge. Some, such as the NIV, omit the reference to Jesus as a name for Barabbas; others, such as the NRSV, include Jesus Barabbas in both verses 16 and 17; and most provide a footnote or marginal note of explanation.

perception that he treated Jews contemptuously. The offer to release Barabbas or Jesus may have been an expression of that contempt.

Matthew notes that Pilate **knew** the Jews **had handed Jesus over to him out of envy** (27:18).

In the middle of the trial, as **Pilate** sat **on the judge's seat**, he received a **message** from **his wife** (27:19). This brief account is found only in Matthew's gospel and reflects several Matthean themes. Pilate's wife warned him to have nothing **to do with that innocent man,** because she had **suffered a great deal in a dream** about **him.** Matthew had mentioned several Gentile women in the genealogy of Jesus in 1:2–17. Several warnings via dreams were given in the account of Jesus' birth (Matt. 1–2). Now as the Gospel moves toward a conclusion, a Gentile women brings a warning through a dream. Romans took dreams and omens very seriously, and this dream enabled Matthew to show that Pilate had been warned not to crucify Jesus and to give an authoritative— in that culture—statement of Jesus' innocence.

For all the reasons Pilate should have listened to his wife, there is no indication that he did. Matthew's narrative regarding the choice of Barabbas or Jesus continues. **The chief priests and the elders persuaded the crowd** to respond to Pilate's offer by asking **for Barabbas** to be released **and** for **Jesus** to be **executed** (27:20). The shift of **the crowd** from enthusiastic supporters of Jesus in 21:9 during the royal entry to calling for his death here should not be surprising. Their support of Jesus came from His ministry of miracles and messianic reputation. His arrest without resistance and His silence on trial would have changed their minds. Pilate's question, **Which of the two do you want me to release to you?** (27:21) puts him at risk. To release Barabbas, a murderous insurrectionist, could cause him trouble with his superiors. To release Jesus would cause him trouble with the Jewish leaders in Jerusalem.

When the crowd asked for **Barabbas, Pilate** then **asked, "What shall I do with Jesus who is called** the Messiah?" (27:22). One can only wonder at the governor who so abdicated his governing responsibility to a mob. Their call to **crucify** Jesus is mind-boggling. It is hard to imagine that a first-century Jewish crowd would ask for the Messiah to be crucified. Matthew clearly intended the reader to ponder the evil that had so twisted the Jewish leaders and the crowd that gathered.

Pilate's pitiful excuse for governance continued in his next question: **Why? What crime has he committed?** (27:23). If he knew Jesus had committed no crime, a competent governor would have released Him rather than offering the no-win question of releasing Barabbas. It is clear that any control Pilate had over the trial was gone when the crowd **shouted all the louder, "Crucify him!"** Any possibility that Jesus be punished with a sentence less than death disappeared because of Pilate's incompetent conversation with the crowd. The governor realized **that he was getting nowhere** and that **an uproar was** beginning (27:24). As a result he **washed his hands** of responsibility for Jesus' death, claiming to be **innocent of** Jesus' **blood**.

Verse 25 contains some of the most chilling words in human history. When Pilate pushed the responsibility for Jesus' death onto the Jewish crowd, they **all answered, "Let his blood be on us and on our children."** In the context of Jesus' trial before Pilate, these words simply accept Pilate's desire to transfer responsibility for Jesus' death from himself to the Jewish crowd. It is possible that by the time Matthew wrote his gospel, he thought of these words as contributing to God's judgment against Israel with the destruction of Jerusalem and the Temple in A.D. 70. There is no sense that these words should be taken as an eternal curse upon the Jewish people because of Jesus' crucifixion.

With this response from the crowd, Pilate **released Barabbas to them** (27:26). Nothing further is known of what became of Barabbas. The governor then **had Jesus flogged**. The Romans often had a prisoner flogged before execution, and not every prisoner survived the flogging. It was almost flaying the prisoner's flesh to the bone. When the flogging was completed, Jesus would be **handed over to be crucified**. The following verses describe these two horrible realities.

3. THE CRUCIFIXION OF JESUS 27:27–56

Matthew describes the crucifixion of Jesus in three stages. Verses 27–31 narrate the soldiers mocking Jesus in the Praetorium. Verses 32–44 focus on the initial events at Golgotha, including more mocking. The actual death of Jesus is then described in 27:45–56.

THE SOLDIERS MOCK JESUS IN THE PRAETORIUM

The Roman **soldiers** who would crucify Jesus, first **took** Him to **the Praetorium** (27:27). Scholars are uncertain whether the **Praetorium** was located in the old palace of Herod the Great in the western part of Jerusalem or in the Antonia Fortress on the north side of the Temple area. The statement that **the whole company of soldiers gathered around him** meant at least six hundred **soldiers** were involved. The technical term for a **company** was **cohort**, which was one-tenth of a legion. This large number suggests both the brutality of their treatment of Jesus and the importance of Jesus in Pilate's mind.

Such a large group of **soldiers** would not have felt they were in any danger from a single prisoner and so began to entertain themselves by mocking Him. After stripping His clothes from Him, they **put a scarlet robe on him** as if He really were a king (27:28). The fact that the robe was red suggests that it was borrowed from a soldier, since the soldiers' uniforms included a red tunic. Since a king should have a crown, they **twisted together a crown of thorns and set it on his head** (27:29). Though the **crown of thorns** was designed to mock Jesus as king, the thorns would have cut into His head and caused significant pain and some bleeding. Putting **a staff in his right hand** completed the process of costuming Jesus as a king, and so they **knelt in front of him** and laughingly proclaimed, **Hail, king of the Jews!** With these words Matthew both describes the mocking of Jesus and, ironically, the appropriate response to Jesus: to kneel before Him and proclaim Him messianic King.

As the mocking continued, the soldiers **spit on** Jesus, the same contemptuous action done by the Jewish religious leaders (26:67). Jerking the **staff** out of His hand, the company **struck him on the head again and again** (27:30). The description of Jesus being spit upon and beaten matches the description in Isaiah 50:6 of the servant who endured great abuse without losing faith that God would help him. When the soldiers had finished their cruel play, **they took off the robe and put his own clothes on him** (27:31) before leading **him away to crucify him.** The **robe** would have to be returned to the soldier who had contributed it to the mocking process. Historical evidence indicates that prisoners were often led naked to crucifixion. Perhaps the Romans realized that leading Jesus naked through the streets of Jerusalem might easily turn the fickle against them, and so they clothed Him on the way to the cross.

THE CRUCIFIXION OF JESUS

Matthew then states that **as they were going out, they met a man from Cyrene** (27:32). It is not clear whether the encounter occurred as they were going out of the Praetorium or out of the city. The man from Cyrene was **named Simon**, which indicates he was a Jew. Whether he was a visitor to Jerusalem for the Passover or had settled in Jerusalem is not stated. Acts 6:9 indicates that there was a synagogue in Jerusalem with a number of members from Cyrene, which was in North Africa. The mention of Simon's name as well as the names of two of his sons in Mark 15:21 may suggest that he and possibly his sons also became a part of the Christian community after the resurrection.

The soldiers **forced** Simon **to carry the cross** for Jesus. The word **forced** here is the same word used in Matthew 5:41 of forcing a traveler to accompany a soldier for a mile and carry his pack. The words used by Matthew do not allow us to answer the question of whether Simon was forced to carry the entire cross or just the crossbeam for Jesus. Some cities had permanent uprights in place and attached the victim to the crossbeam and hoisted him to the top of the upright piece. Other cities built the entire cross for each victim individually. How badly Jesus had been beaten by the soldiers may have led them to force Simon to carry the cross. It did not determine the question of whether he carried only the crossbeam or the entire cross.

The crucifixion would occur at **a place called Golgotha** (27:33). This word was an approximate spelling of the Aramaic word for skull, and thus Matthew notes that **Golgotha means The Place of the Skull**. The Latin word for skull is *calvaria*, from which the word *"Calvary"* has come. At the site of **Golgotha**, the soldiers **offered Jesus wine . . . , mixed with gall** (27:34). The reference to **gall** would have called Psalm 69:21 to mind. In some contexts, the word could also be translated *poison*. Presumably after the beatings and the beginning of the crucifixion, a victim would be dehydrated and ready to drink any liquid. Part of cruelty of the soldiers was to give them the bitter-tasting **gall**. However, once Jesus had tasted it, **he refused to drink it.** It is possible that the **gall**-mixed wine had some effect of drugging or deadening the pain of the victim. If this was the case, Jesus' refusal to drink the mixture indicated His commitment to experiencing the full pain of the cross.

The victim was usually crucified naked. Thus the phrase in verse 35 **when they had crucified him** probably means after they had hung Him up on the cross but before He died. As Jesus hung there, the soldiers **divided up his clothes by casting lots.** Given Matthew's interest in the fulfillment of Old Testament Scriptures, it is surprising that he does not draw attention to Psalm 22:18, which provides the very words for dividing the righteous sufferer's garments and **casting lots** for his clothing. Though so much of the crucifixion followed typical Roman practices, Matthew notes that the soldiers sat down and **kept watch over him there** (Matt. 27:36). These unusual words indicate that the soldiers recognized something unusual about Jesus, and so gave Him attention beyond the normal course of their duty.

HISTORICAL CONTEXT

GOLGOTHA

It has often been speculated that Golgotha was a skull-shaped hill, but it is equally possible that it was named because of the deaths that occurred there. The location of Golgotha has been debated for the past century and a half, but it was most likely located at the site of the present Church of the Holy Sepulcher. That location, though inside the present walls of Jerusalem, was outside the walls of the city at the time of Jesus. Wherever Golgotha was located, the Romans usually crucified people on a major road so passersby would see and be frightened into submission to Rome.

It was customary to hang a placard around the victim's neck with the crime for which he was being crucified. This was part of the Roman system of using crucifixion as a deterrent to rebellion. Though this placard normally was not fastened to the cross, it could be hung from the top of the upright rather than from the victim's neck. That is why **above Jesus' head** was **the written charge against him: This is Jesus, the King of the Jews** (27:37). The Romans would have seen this sign as warning passersby not to follow any rebels against the kingship of Caesar.

Matthew saw the sign as a true statement of Jesus' identity. Matthew also notes that **two robbers were crucified with him** (27:38), though he will give no other details about them until verse 44. The word **robber** does not indicate a petty thief but rather an insurrectionist who stole to support the guerilla warfare style of rebellion against Rome.

While still alive, and apparently still conscious on the cross, Jesus had to endure further mocking from the various audiences present. Matthew's words, **Those who passed by hurled insults at him, shaking their heads** (27:39), were drawn from Psalm 22:7. These passersby taunted Jesus with the challenge that He should **save** himself since He was the one **who** was **going to destroy the temple and build it in three days** (Matt. 27:40). These words echo the accusation that came at the beginning of Jesus' Jewish trial in 26:61. Then using the exact words of the devil in the temptation account (4:3, 6), **if you are the Son of God**, they dared Him to prove it by coming **down from the cross**. As in the temptation account, Jesus demonstrated that He was **Son of God**, not by avoiding the cross, but by obeying the will of His Father.

Then Matthew records the mocking of **the chief priests, the teachers of the law and the elders** (27:41). That it was **in the same way** suggests that the challenges of verse 40 were repeated in addition to the insults of verses 42–43. The statement from these hostile Jewish leaders that Jesus **saved others** was probably a reference to his healing ministry, since the Greek verb **saved** was often used for healing. The jeer that He could not **save himself** is ironic from Matthew's point of view. It was by refusing to save himself that Jesus saved others. Thus the statement that He could not save others was blatant unbelief on the part of these religious leaders. Their words **He's the King of Israel** were equally insincere. Given such unbelief, there was no reason to suppose their promise to **believe in him** if He would **come down from the cross** was true either.

The words of verse 43 draw from Psalm 22:8. **He trusts in God** is the first line of Psalm 22:8, and **let God rescue him** is the second line. But the mocking element comes with the question of whether God would even want Him, even though Jesus had claimed, **I am the Son of God.** In every imaginable way, the religious leaders taunted Him with the possibility of avoiding the cross. Even **the robbers who were crucified with**

him joined the chorus of mockers, heaping **insults on him** (Matt. 27:44). Though Matthew has tended to provide fewer details of the crucifixion than the other Gospel accounts, he is very detailed in the description of the mocking words of the passersby and the Jewish religious leaders. Perhaps similar challenges were still being raised by Jewish unbelievers at the time Matthew wrote his gospel.

THE DEATH OF JESUS

Matthew's account finally arrives at the events accompanying Jesus' actual death. He states that **from the sixth hour until the ninth hour darkness came over all the land** (27:45). The time is stated using the Roman system so that the sixth hour was noon and the ninth hour about three o'clock in the afternoon. To try to explain the darkness in natural terms like an eclipse or a dust storm misses the point completely. The darkness was a sign of God's judgment, as Amos 8:9 makes clear. It may have also indicated God's withdrawing of the first blessing He had created—light (Gen. 1:3).

As the **ninth hour** approached, **Jesus** suddenly **cried out . . . , "Eloi, Eloi, lama sabachthani?"** (Matt. 27:46). Matthew joins Mark in preserving the actual words of Jesus in Aramaic from Psalm 22:1, which reads, **My God, my God, why have you forsaken me?** Psalm 22 has been influential in the very wording of some of the scenes at the crucifixion. The psalm in its original context was a lament of a righteous sufferer. Though these opening words of dereliction described the agony Jesus experienced on the cross, they also introduce a psalm that concluded in hope and praise for God's salvation, a fact of which Jesus was not ignorant.

Matthew suggests that the bystanders misinterpreted Jesus' cry as a call for **Elijah** (Matt. 27:47). This is more understandable if Jesus' cry began, *Eli, Eli,* however, given His condition, clear articulation should not have been expected. Because Elijah was widely expected to return as the forerunner of the Messiah, a cry from Jesus to Elijah might well have been understood as a call to God for deliverance. **One** of the bystanders **immediately ran** and filled **a sponge with wine vinegar**, which he **offered to Jesus to drink** (27:48). The reference to **wine vinegar** again calls Psalm

69:21 to mind. Perhaps the bystander thought a drink might prolong Jesus' life long enough for Elijah to come. **The rest** of the crowd thought that drink was enough and said, **Now leave him alone. Let's see if Elijah comes to save him** (Matt. 27:49).

Apparently within a few moments, **Jesus cried out again in a loud voice** and **gave up his spirit** (27:50). Matthew's description of Jesus' death is simple and straightforward. He provides no agonizing details. The loud cry indicates that Jesus possessed sufficient strength to have survived for several more hours. As Matthew describes it, Jesus chose the moment of His death rather than finally dying when He could no longer survive. The moment Jesus had foretold in 16:21 had finally arrived. What He had not foretold was the series of events that followed His death.

KEY IDEAS

Eloi, Eloi or *Eli, Eli*

The NIV is the only English translation to read *Eloi, Eloi*, to introduce Jesus' cry of dereliction from the cross in Matthew 27:46. All other versions read, *Eli, Eli*. In the parallel passage in Mark 15:34, all English translations read, *Eloi, Eloi*, which exactly reproduces the letters of the words in the Greek text. Almost all Greek manuscripts read *Eli, Eli* in Matthew 27:46, and that has been the traditional English reading. But the two most respected fourth-century manuscripts discovered in the nineteenth century—Sinaiticus and Vaticanus—read, *Eloi, Eloi*, and the NIV follows those two manuscripts. It is often said that *Eloi, Eloi* reflects Aramaic, while *Eli, Eli* is the Hebrew text. While that is technically true, careful study of Jewish documents shows that such a distinction in the naming of God was not always observed.

At the **moment** of His death **the curtain of the temple was torn in two from top to bottom** (27:51). Though Matthew is not specific, it is most likely that the **curtain** referred to the second or inner curtain that divided the Temple into the Holy Place and the Holy of Holies. The passive voice—**was torn**—and the tearing **from top to bottom** suggest that this was an act of God. There are several possible meanings to this dramatic divine testimony to Jesus' death. It might symbolize God tearing His own garments as Jews of the time did as a sign of grief. It might point to God's departure from the Holy of Holies as judgment for the priests' putting Jesus to death. It might mean that through the death of Jesus access to the very presence and person of God—symbolized by the Holy of Holies—was no longer restricted to the priests and governed by the sacrificial system. Since Matthew gives no indication of the meaning of the tearing of the curtain, any or all of these interpretive possibilities are open to us.

Further, Matthew states that at Jesus' death, **the earth shook and the rocks split**. This is Old Testament apocalyptic language describing the judgment of God (see Isa. 24:19–20; 29:6; Jer. 10:10; Joel 3:16; Amos 8:8; Nah. 1:5–6). Thus the death of Jesus marked the end of the present evil age and opened the door to the age to come. Through that door Matthew offered a glimpse of the coming end time resurrection as he told of **tombs** breaking **open and the bodies of many holy people** being **raised to life** (Matt. 27:52). Verse 53 compresses a story of several days into a few words. These holy people who were raised at the moment of Jesus' death **came out of the tombs**, but it was not until **after Jesus' resurrection** that they entered Jerusalem and were seen by **many people.** It is clear that though Matthew had to separate the death and resurrection of Jesus in his narrative, the two events intertwined in his theology.

The centurion and those with him who were guarding Jesus provide the appropriate response to Jesus' death. Just as the Gentile Magi were the first to worship Him after His birth, the Gentile centurion and other Roman soldiers were the first to worship after His death, confessing, **Surely he was the Son of God!** Thus the titles **Son of God** and Messiah with which Matthew was most concerned in the opening chapters of his gospel are the titles confessed at the end of Jesus' life.

Matthew concludes his account of Jesus' death by noting the **many women** who witnessed this **from a distance** (27:55). These women **had followed Jesus from Galilee to care for his needs.** Luke 8:1–3 suggests that they provided financial support in addition to assistance with the necessary details of traveling. One might think their care of Jesus was now over, but Matthew had another purpose for mentioning these faithful witnesses here. He lists **Mary Magdalene, Mary the mother of James and Joses, and the mother of Zebedee's sons**, James and John (Matt. 27:56). This introduces the women, especially the two Marys, who will witness Jesus' burial (27:61) and his resurrection (28:1–10).

4. THE BURIAL OF JESUS 27:57–66

After the violence of the trials and crucifixion, Matthew's description of the burial of Jesus seems particularly subdued. The phrase **as evening approached** (27:57) reminded the readers that this was still Friday, and the sundown that would mark the beginning of the Sabbath had not arrived. **Joseph, a rich man from Arimathea, who** had been **a disciple of Jesus** came to care for his Master's burial. Nothing is known of **Arimathea**, though most scholars identify it with Ramathaim in Judea. Mark 15:43 and Luke 23:50 identify Joseph as a member of the Sanhedrin, which would mean that he would have known well the events leading to Jesus' death. John 19:38 identifies Joseph as a secret disciple for fear of the Jewish leaders. Only Matthew mentions that he was **rich**. Perhaps that detail is what gave him confidence to go **to Pilate** and ask **for Jesus' body** (Matt. 27:58). Probably Joseph's wealth motivated Pilate to grant the request.

The simple description continues: **Joseph took the body** and **wrapped it in a clean linen cloth**, which was the customary way of preparing a body for burial in that time (27:59). Matthew then reveals the special contribution of Joseph to the burial: He **placed** Jesus' body **in his own new tomb that he had cut out of the rock** (27:60). A tomb carved out of the rock would have been expensive and probably beyond the economic reach of most of Jesus' followers. The fact that it was a **new tomb** means that no one had yet been buried there. This meant there could be no confusion later regarding more than one body. Joseph then **rolled a big stone in front of the entrance to the tomb** and left. Many tombs cut from the rock had a track

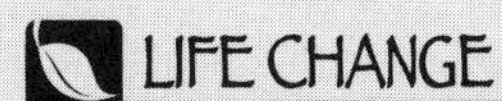

The gift of the tomb by Joseph of Arimathea and the faithful watching of the women are an important reminder of the diverse gifts disciples offer Jesus. We often think only of the leading disciples like Peter, James, and John, and think of discipleship in terms of leadership and responsibility. Actually, Matthew portrays the three leading disciples as often failing spiritually, while he holds forth Joseph and faithful women as examples for us to contribute what we have to the cause of the Kingdom.

in which a large round stone rolled to cover or open the tomb entrance. Joseph's generous care of Jesus' body was observed by **Mary Magdalene and the other Mary sitting there opposite the tomb** (27:61). This note made it clear they knew exactly in which tomb Jesus had been buried.

Only Matthew narrates the events found in 27:62–66. **The next day** would have been the Sabbath, a fact Matthew reinforces by calling it the day **after Preparation Day**, a common Jewish expression for Friday as the day when they prepared for the Sabbath. On Saturday **the chief priests and the Pharisees went to Pilate** (27:62) to petition for a guard at the tomb. The chief priests had been the engineers of Jesus' death, and the Pharisees were the primary Jewish opponents of Matthew's community when he wrote this gospel. That they went to Pilate and spoke with him on the Sabbath was mute testimony to their intense hatred of Jesus.

Their address to Pilate—**Sir**—is quite ironic (27:63). The Greek word is *kyrie*, which could also be translated *Lord*. That they would address the hated Roman governor as *kyrie* but would not so acknowledge Jesus was mind-boggling to Matthew. Their hostility is evident in the word they used to describe Jesus: **deceiver**. Their concern was His prediction **while he was still alive** that He would **rise again after three days**. The solution they proposed was for Pilate to **order the tomb to be made secure until the third day** (27:64). Without such a guard they were afraid **his disciples** might **come and steal the body** and claim He had **been raised from the dead.** In their minds the **deception** of a claim of resurrection would **be worse than** all the previous deceptions they were sure Jesus had perpetuated.

Pilate's response is not nearly as clear in the Greek text as the English translations suggest. The words **Take a guard** can also be translated, You have **a guard**. It is not clear whether Pilate granted them his soldiers to guard the tomb or demanded that they use their own Temple guard. In either case, he ordered them to **make the tomb as secure as** they knew **how** (27:65). As a result the chief priests and Pharisees **made the tomb secure by putting a seal on the stone and posting the guard** (27:66). With this account Matthew has evidence from the very actions of the

Jewish religious leaders to counter their claims later that Jesus' body had been stolen instead of resurrected. Those leaders had provided the security to make such a claim impossible.

28

THE RESURRECTION AND MISSIONARY COMMISSION OF JESUS

Matthew 28:1–20

The climax of Matthew's gospel comes in chapter 28 with two major divisions: Verses 1–15 give witness to the resurrection of Jesus; and verses 16–20 provide Jesus' final appearance and His giving of the Great Commission.

1. THE RESURRECTION OF JESUS 28:1–15

Matthew presents his resurrection account in two paragraphs. The witness of the women and Jesus' first appearance are narrated in verses 1–10. Verses 11–15 provide the guards' account of how the tomb came to be empty.

THE WITNESS OF THE WOMEN AND JESUS' FIRST RESURRECTION APPEARANCE

The New Testament never describes Jesus' resurrection. The evidence is always presented in one of two forms: (1) accounts of the empty tomb and (2) appearances by the risen Lord to His followers. Matthew gives both kinds of evidence of Jesus' resurrection in 28:1–10. Verse 1 provides the time (**After the Sabbath, at dawn on the first day of the week**), the witnesses (**Mary Magdalene and the other Mary**), and the location (**at the tomb**) of the first account of the empty tomb. With his opening phrase, **After the Sabbath**, Matthew has identified the third consecutive day in the series of events that began with Jesus' crucifixion.

The statement that it was **dawn** places this account in stark contrast to the darkness that came over the land just before Jesus' death (27:45). The renewed light and the reference to the first day of the week are part of the reasons the early church considered the resurrection the beginning of a new creation week. The presence of Mary Magdalene and the other Mary continues their role as faithful witnesses first mentioned in 27:56 and then in 27:61. These two **went to look at the tomb.**

There was a violent earthquake (28:2). The earth had shaken when Jesus died (27:51), and the resulting opened tombs had anticipated Jesus' resurrection (27:52–53). The **earthquake** was an apocalyptic sign of the end of the present, evil age and the beginning of the new age of the Messiah and of the Spirit. The more immediate reason for the **earthquake** was that **an angel of the Lord came down from heaven**, went **to the tomb, rolled back the stone** that had sealed the tomb shut, **and sat on** the stone. This is the first appearance of the angel of the Lord since chapters 1 and 2 of this Gospel. There the angel had interpreted the events of Jesus' birth. Here, the angel will interpret the events of Jesus' resurrection.

According to 28:3, the angel's **appearance was like lightning, and his clothes were white as snow.** This description of the angel borrows the language of Daniel 10:6 and 7:9, where these phrases describe God himself. It would also remind the reader of Matthew's gospel of the description of the transfigured Jesus given in Matthew 17:2, though the description of Jesus somewhat outshone the description of the angel. The effect of the angel's sudden and brilliant appearance is that **the guards were so afraid . . . that they shook and became like dead men** (28:4). These were the guards assigned to make the tomb secure (27:65–66). They had sealed the tomb and now were guarding it. Matthew's description is ironic: the guards who were to guard the dead one in the **tomb** are now as **dead men**, while the one who was dead in the **tomb** is now alive.

The guards were not the only ones frightened; the women were also terrified. The angel spoke to them—**Do not be afraid** (28:5)—with the common words of reassurance that accompany angelic appearances. One might wonder how the women could possibly obey this injunction given the terrifying circumstances in which they found themselves. The angel knew they were **looking for Jesus, who was crucified.** But the reason they were not to fear is that Jesus was **not** there; **he has risen, just as he said** (28:6). Though the angel had rolled the stone away, the women would not find Jesus' body in the tomb. But the reason was not tomb robbery; rather Christ had been raised. The Greek verb is passive, He has been raised, which indicates that God had intervened in a miraculous way to raise Jesus from the dead. Then the angel invited the women to inspect the empty tomb: **Come and see the place where he lay.**

Matthew does not say whether the women entered the empty tomb to see where Jesus had been laid. The message of the resurrection is not about proof; it is about sharing the good news, and so the angel instructed the women to **go quickly and tell his disciples** the marvelous news (28:7). That good news was that Jesus had been raised **from the dead and** that He was **going ahead of** them **into Galilee**, where the disciples would **see him**. The angel's instructions for the disciples to go to **Galilee** repeat the words of Jesus himself in 26:32. One might forgive the disciples for not remembering that instruction in light of the unbelievable events that had taken place since Jesus spoke it.

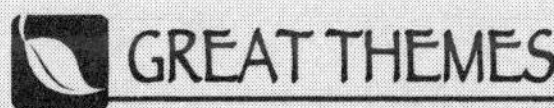

RESURRECTION

The resurrection of Jesus was more than simply a resuscitation of a dead body like that of Lazarus, Jairus's daughter, and the widow of Nain's son. They came back to life but eventually died—again. Jesus was raised to a new existence in which He would never die. His resurrection was in bodily form, but His resurrection body was not identical to His previous body of flesh. It was similar in that He was recognizable, He still had the marks of the nails and swords, and He ate, drank, and spoke with His disciples. It was different in that He could pass through doors and seemed to appear and disappear suddenly. The apostle Paul indicated in 1 Corinthians 15 that Jesus' resurrection marked the first step in a series of events that would culminate in the end of time and the gift of resurrection bodies to all who belong to Christ.

Obediently **the women hurried away from the tomb . . . and ran to tell** the **disciples** (28:8). Matthew makes the understated comment that they went **afraid yet filled with joy.** It is difficult now, in light of two thousand years of post-resurrection Christian faith, to imagine the conflicting thoughts and emotions that must have filled the women's hearts and minds. But before they could reach the gathered disciples, **suddenly Jesus met them** (28:9). His first word to them was **Greetings.** The Aramaic greeting would have been *shalom, Peace.* His appearing shocked them, but it made true peace possible for the first time ever. Their appropriate response was to bow before Him, clasp **his feet and** worship **him.** The detail that the women **clasped** Jesus' **feet** provided evidence of His bodily resurrection, but their worship is the true evidence of resurrection faith. Jesus then repeated the instruction of the angel to **not be afraid** but to **tell** His **brothers**, the disciples, **to go to Galilee** where **they will see** Him (28:10).

THE GUARDS' ACCOUNT OF THE EMPTY TOMB

The Christian evidence of Jesus' resurrection has been presented: The angel showed the women the empty tomb, and the risen Jesus appeared to the women. **While the women were** still **on their way** to find Jesus' disciples, Matthew provides another witness to the resurrection: **the guards** (28:11). **Some of the guards went into the city and reported to the chief priests everything that had happened.** With this comment, Matthew assures his readers that the Jewish religious leaders knew the truth of what happened at the tomb. However, that truth did not fit the purposes of the **chief priests** and **elders**, so they **devised a plan** to provide an alternative account of the empty tomb (28:12). The plan required them to give **the soldiers a large sum of money** in exchange for reporting that Jesus' **disciples came during the night and stole** His body **while** they **were asleep** (28:13).

Such a report by the guards was not without danger. To confess that they **were asleep** would mean that they had violated the conditions of their being posted as guards. In some cases soldiers who had fallen asleep on guard were executed. Further, the claim to having been asleep would raise the question of how they knew the disciples had come and stolen Jesus' body. And how did they manage to sleep through the breaking of the seal on the stone and its being rolled back? However, the **chief priests** and elders assured the guards that they would **satisfy the governor** if the word that the guards had been asleep ever got back to him. If the guards would but lie to save the chief priests' and elders' story, then those religious leaders would **keep** them **out of trouble** (28:14). By recording this story of the guards being bribed by the chief priests and elders, Matthew gave a counter explanation for the **story** that had **been widely circulated among the Jews** from the resurrection **to this very day** when Matthew wrote his gospel.

2. JESUS' COMMISSION TO HIS DISCIPLES 28:16–20

The meeting of Jesus and His disciples in Galilee that had been the subject of three sets of instructions (26:32; 28:7; 28:10) finally takes place. The account begins with what may be the most painful words of Matthew 28: **Then the eleven disciples**. This is the first time this expression occurs after the disciples had been described as the twelve throughout the Gospel. It is a painful reminder of the loss of Judas. Though Peter is not mentioned in this closing paragraph of Matthew, he was present. The eleven **went to Galilee, to the mountain where Jesus had told them to go** (28:16). The journey to Galilee was obviously taken in obedience to the instructions Jesus had given them. Matthew's gospel will reach its conclusion and climax in **Galilee** of the Gentiles with the command to embark on the Gentile mission. The mission of the disciples will begin where the mission of Jesus began (4:12–17).

When the disciples finally **saw** Jesus, their response was mixed. Some **worshiped him, but some doubted** (28:17). The women had worshipped the risen Jesus when they saw Him (28:9), and worship is the appropriate response to Jesus. What is the meaning of the phrase that **some doubted**? Matthew may simply be noting the strange mixture of faith and unbelief that necessarily accompanied the first appearances of the risen Christ. The women were **afraid** but **filled with joy** (28:8). It is also possible that in verse 17 Matthew observed the mixed nature of the

Church already, told by Jesus in the parable of the wheat and the weeds (13:24–30). Matthew seems more comfortable with the reality of doubt in the followers of Jesus than are many modern Christians.

Jesus' final words in this Gospel begin with the claim that **all authority in heaven and on earth has been given to** Him (28:18). Jesus demonstrated this authority through His teaching in the Sermon on the Mount in Matthew 5–7 (see 7:29) and through His healing ministry narrated especially in Matthew 8–9 (see 8:8–9; 9:8). It is then is no surprise for Jesus to claim **authority** on **earth**. The new truth, brought into being by the resurrection, is that all **authority in heaven** has also been given to Jesus.

The purpose of Jesus' statement about His authority was not so His followers would talk about His authority. The purpose of His authority was that His disciples would **make disciples of all nations** (28:19). Though almost all English translations render the word **go** as an imperative, it is a circumstantial participle in the Greek text. A most literal translation would be "When you go, make disciples." The commission of the Church is not simply to go; going is assumed. The mission of the Church is to **make disciples of all nations**. The process of **making disciples** that Jesus had modeled for three years was to be replicated with others from **all** the **nations** of the world.

Two specific tasks would be involved in making **disciples of all nations**. The first would be **baptizing them in the name of the Father and of the Son and of the Holy Spirit**. Clearly Jesus understood baptism to be the entry marker for these new disciples who would come to faith through the ministry of His disciples. This baptism is to be done in the name of the Triune God. This is the first and clearest reference to the Trinity in Matthew's gospel. It would be several centuries before the doctrine of the Trinity took clear shape in the Church, but the members of the Trinity have been at work in Matthew' gospel since its beginning.

The second task in making **disciples of all nations** would be **teaching them to obey everything** Jesus had **commanded** (28:20). Matthew, by his careful organization of his gospel into alternating blocks of narrative and teaching material, has prepared a document clearly designed to aid the Church in fulfilling this second aspect of the Great Commission. Teaching all nations the message of Jesus can be accomplished by working through the first Gospel.

The perspective of Jesus' final commission to His disciples is toward the future. He and Matthew envisioned a period of time when the present, evil age in which they lived would overlap the age of the Messiah, the kingdom of God, which had begun when Jesus began His ministry. In that overlap, the Church lives in confidence because of Jesus' final promise:

LIFE CHANGE

DISCIPLESHIP

In Matthew's gospel, the life of discipleship is always the journey of following Jesus. Even the final words of the Gospel, the Great Commission, are framed in terms of discipleship as the Christ-formed life. We do not need new techniques or marketing skills to be the followers Christ envisioned. If we will allow ourselves to be formed, informed, and transformed by Matthew's gospel, we will discover ourselves on a journey with Jesus into the heart of obedience to God the Father. God requires nothing more or less—of us.

surely I am with you always, to the very end of the age. Immanuel, whose name **means God with us** (1:23), does not disappear into heaven at the end of Matthew's gospel. Rather, He is always with His followers, guiding them on the way of discipleship.

SELECT BIBLIOGRAPHY

The student of Matthew's gospel has a large number of excellent commentaries and monographs available for his or her study. This bibliography is organized into the following categories: Technical Commentaries, Literary and Theological Commentaries, Application Commentaries, Other Commentaries, and Monographs and Collected Essays. The Technical Commentaries give attention to the Greek text and technical aspects of Matthean scholarship. The Literary and Theological Commentaries focus on the literary structures and the theological purposes of Matthew. The Application Commentaries are designed for pastors and lay Bible teachers. The commentaries listed under Other Commentaries are either general in nature or represent a specific approach (usually indicated in the title). Significant works on the Sermon on the Mount are also listed.

TECHNICAL COMMENTARIES

Betz, Hans Dieter. *The Sermon on the Mount: A Commentary on the Sermon on the Mount, including the Sermon on the Plain (Matthew 5:3–7:27 and Luke 6:20–49).* Hermeneia—A Critical and Historical Commentary on the Bible. Minneapolis: Fortress Press, 1995.

Davies, W. D. and Dale C. Allison. *A Critical and Exegetical Commentary on The Gospel According to Saint Matthew.* 3 vols. The International Critical Commentary. Edinburgh: T. & T. Clark, 1988, 1991, 1997.

Guelich, Robert A. *The Sermon on the Mount: A Foundation for Understanding.* Waco: Word, 1982.

Hagner, Donald A. *Matthew.* 2 vols. Word Biblical Commentary. Dallas: Word, 1993, 1995.

Luz, Ulrich. *Matthew 1–7: A Commentary.* trans. Wilhelm C. Linss. Continental Commentaries. Minneapolis: Augsburg Press, 1989.

————. *Matthew 8–20: A Commentary.* trans. James E. Crouch. Hermeneia—A Critical and Historical Commentary on the Bible. Minneapolis: Fortress Press, 2001.

————. *Matthew 21–28: A Commentary.* trans. James E. Crouch. Hermeneia—A Critical and Historical Commentary on the Bible. Minneapolis: Fortress Press, 2005.

Nolland, John. *The Gospel of Matthew: A Commentary on the Greek Text.* The New International Greek Testament Commentary. Grand Rapids, Mich.: Eerdmans, 2005.

Strecker, Georg. *The Sermon on the Mount: An Exegetical Commentary.* trans. O. C. Dean, Jr. Nashville: Abingdon Press, 1988.

LITERARY AND THEOLOGICAL COMMENTARIES

Allison, Dale C. *The Sermon on the Mount: Inspiring the Moral Imagination.* Companions to the New Testament. New York: Crossroad, 1999.

Boring, M. Eugene. "The Gospel of Matthew: Introduction, Commentary, and Reflections." *The New Interpreter's Bible.* Vol. VIII. Nashville: Abingdon Press, 1995.

Garland, David E. *Reading Matthew: A Literary and Theological Commentary on the First Gospel.* Reading the New Testament Series. New York: Crossroad, 1993.

Schnackenburg, Rudolf. *The Gospel of Matthew.* trans. Robert R. Barr. Grand Rapids, Mich.: Eerdmans, 2002.

Senior, Donald. *Matthew.* Abingdon New Testament Commentaries. Nashville: Abingdon Press, 1998.

Talbert, Charles H. *Reading the Sermon on the Mount: Character Formation and Ethical Decision Making in Matthew 5–7.* Grand Rapids, Mich.: Baker Academic, 2004.

APPLICATION COMMENTARIES

Blomberg, Craig. *Matthew.* The New American Commentary: An Exegetical and Theological Exposition of Holy Scripture. Nashville: Broadman Press, 1992.

Hare, Douglas R. A. *Matthew.* Interpretation: A Bible Commentary for Teaching and Preaching. Louisville: Westminster John Knox Press, 1993.

Keener, Craig S. *Matthew.* The IVP New Testament Commentary Series. Downers Grove, Ill.: InterVarsity Press, 1997.

Long, Thomas G. *Matthew.* Westminster Bible Companion. Louisville: Westminster John Knox Press, 1997.

Wilkins, Michael J. *Matthew.* The New International Version Application Commentary: From Biblical Text to Contemporary Life. Grand Rapids, Mich.: Zondervan, 2004.

Wright, Tom. *Matthew for Everyone.* 2 vols. Louisville: Westminster John Knox Press, 2002.

OTHER COMMENTARIES

Carter, Warren. *Matthew and the Margins: A Socio-Political and Religious Reading.* Journal for the Study of the New Testament Supplement Series 204. Sheffield: Sheffield Academic Press, Inc., 2000.

France, R. T. *The Gospel According to Matthew: An Introduction and Commentary.* Tyndale New Testament Commentaries. Grand Rapids, Mich.: Eerdmans, 1985.

Harrington, Daniel J. *The Gospel of Matthew.* Sacra Pagina Series, Vol. 1. Collegeville: The Liturgical Press, 1991.

Keener, Craig S. *A Commentary on the Gospel of Matthew.* Grand Rapids, Mich.: Eerdmans, 1999.

Neyrey, Jerome H. *Honor and Shame in the Gospel of Matthew.* Louisville: Westminster John Knox Press, 1998.

Overman, J. Andrew. *Church and Community in Crisis: The Gospel According to Matthew.* The New Testament in Context. Valley Forge, Penn.: Trinity Press International, 1996.

Patte, Daniel. *The Gospel According to Matthew: A Structural Commentary on Matthew's Faith.* Philadelphia: Fortress Press, 1986.

Simonetti, Manlio, ed. *Matthew.* 2 vols. Ancient Christian Commentary on Scripture: New Testament. Downers Grove, Ill.: InterVarsity Press, 2001.

MONOGRAPHS AND COLLECTED ESSAYS

Allison, Dale C. *Studies in Matthew: Interpretation Past and Present.* Grand Rapids, Mich.: Baker Academic, 2005.

Aune, David E., ed. *The Gospel of Matthew in Current Study: Studies in Memory of William G. Thompson, S.J.* Grand Rapids, Mich.: Eerdmans, 2001.

Luz, Ulrich. *Studies in Matthew.* trans. Rosemary Selle. Grand Rapids, Mich.: Eerdmans, 2005.

————. *The Theology of the Gospel of Matthew.* New Testament Theology. Cambridge: Cambridge University Press, 1995.

Minear, Paul S. *Matthew: The Teacher's Gospel.* New York: Pilgrim Press, 1982.

Powell, Mark Allan. *God With Us: A Pastoral Theology of Matthew's Gospel.* Minneapolis: Fortress Press, 1995.

Senior, Donald. *The Passion of Jesus in the Gospel of Matthew.* The Passion Series. Collegeville: The Liturgical Press, 1985.

Stanton, Graham N. *A Gospel for a New People: Studies in Matthew.* Louisville: Westminster John Knox Press, 1993.

Vaught, Carl G. *The Sermon on the Mount: A Theological Investigation.* rev. ed. Waco: Baylor University Press, 2001.

Westerholm, Stephen. *Understanding Matthew: The Early Christian Worldview of the First Gospel.* Grand Rapids, Mich.: Baker Academic, 2006.